How People Judge Policing

D1610232

How People Judge Policing

P.A.J. Waddington
Professor Emeritus, University of Wolverhampton
Visiting Professor, London School of Economics

Kate Williams
Senior Lecturer in Criminology, University
of Wolverhampton

Martin Wright
Visiting Senior Research Fellow, Canterbury Centre
for Policing Research, Canterbury Christ Church
University

Tim Newburn
Professor of Social Policy, London School of Economics

OXFORD
UNIVERSITY PRESS

OXFORD
UNIVERSITY PRESS

Great Clarendon Street, Oxford, OX2 6DP,
United Kingdom

Oxford University Press is a department of the University of Oxford.
It furthers the University's objective of excellence in research, scholarship,
and education by publishing worldwide. Oxford is a registered trade mark of
Oxford University Press in the UK and in certain other countries

© Oxford University Press 2017

The moral rights of the authors have been asserted

First Edition published in 2017
Impression: 1

Crown copyright material is reproduced under Class Licence
Number C01P0000148 with the permission of OPSI
and the Queen's Printer for Scotland

Published in the United States of America by Oxford University Press
198 Madison Avenue, New York, NY 10016, United States of America

British Library Cataloguing in Publication Data
Data available

Library of Congress Control Number: 2017930521

ISBN 978–0–19–871888–8

Printed and bound by
CPI Group (UK) Ltd, Croydon, CR0 4YY

To Paramjit Singh
without whom this research would never have been accomplished

Acknowledgements

This research rests on foundations laid by many hands who have toiled to understand how the public appraise the police, and whilst we may criticise the details of this previous research, we want to acknowledge here the debt we owe to generations of researchers throughout the developed world. We must also acknowledge the British Library of Political and Economic Science at the London School of Economics and Political Science, for without access to their electronic resources, the content of much of the previous research literature would have remained a mystery.

We are also deeply indebted to 'Pram' Singh, of the Central Institute for the Study of Public Protection, the University of Wolverhampton, who administered our research and also enabled us to access his dense web of contacts throughout the Black Country region of the West Midlands. Without him, many of the groups we were able to talk to would have remained beyond reach.

'Pram' administered the funding we received from the Economic and Social Research Council under grant RES–000–22–3571 for which we are immensely grateful. We note with regret that the 'Small Grant Scheme' under which we acquired funding has been withdrawn. Not all social science research requires funding on the scale of 'big science' in order to expand knowledge and be useful to others. We hope that the decision to withdraw the Small Grant Scheme will be reviewed and hopefully this vital source of funding for relatively inexpensive research will be restored.

Our greatest thanks go to the circa 350 people who attended our focus groups and participated with such enthusiasm in the tasks that we gave them. We hope that, if they read this book, they will consider that our analysis does them justice.

It should go without saying that we are all immensely grateful to our families for their forbearance. Fieldwork is often disruptive of family life, but in this case it was even more so, given the trials and tribulations to which our families were exposed.

Contents

Contents

How *Does* the Public Judge the Police? What We Know and Why It Isn't Enough?

Introduction

Public attitudes to the police have been the focus of attention that has produced a mountain of research data during recent decades. Why do we seek to add to it? In this chapter we sketch a map of that 'mountain' and attempt to show areas that remain unexplored and other areas where we believe errors have crept in. In the following chapter we describe and justify how we conducted this exploration. In the remaining chapters we discuss and analyse what we discovered, before concluding with some discussion of wider issues arising from our own and others' research.

'The Police'

Many liberal democratic countries indulge in official fretting about the esteem in which the public hold the police. Britain has been no exception: Sir Henry Willink's Royal Commission on the police commissioned the first such research in the early 1960s (Shaw and Williamson 1972) and, since its launch in 1982, repeated British Crime Surveys (now the Crime Survey for England and Wales (CSEW)) have been devoted to how the public generally and victims of crime in particular appraise the police (Allen 2006; Aye Maung 1995; Bucke 1997; Chivite-Matthews and Maggs 2002; Clancy et al. 2001; Flatley et al. 2010; Hough and Mayhew 1983; Nicholas et al. 2008; Mayhew et al. 1989; Myhill and Allen 2002; Moxon and Jones 1984; Scribbins et al. 2010; Skogan 1990a; Pease

1988; Kershaw et al. 2008; Walker et al. 2009; Southgate with the assistance Paul Ekblom 1984; Skogan 1994; Jansson 2006a; 2006b; Mayhew et al. 1993). There is now also a substantial body of academic research relating to various aspects of police–public relations; some inquire about specific topics like victim satisfaction or police–race relations. This appetite shows no signs of abating.

Police officers attired in their distinctive uniform are symbolic public figures in many jurisdictions; a national icon that adorns souvenir shops and populates television screens. 'The police' is also something of which people readily express opinions. Generally speaking, the British public is favourably disposed to them (Belson 1975; Allen et al. 2006; Nicholas et al. 2008; Scribbins et al. 2010; Painter et al. 1988; IPCC 2016). The British police also compare favourably with the police of other countries (Alvazzi del Frate and Van Kesteren 2004; van Dijk et al. 1990). They also compare favourably with other criminal justice agencies in Britain (Bradford et al. 2008; Hough and Roberts 2004; Page et al. 2004; Smith 2010; Allen et al. 2006). All this needs to be said, because often the impression may be gained that the police are desperately unpopular, when actually they enjoy levels of support that others might envy. However, neither can it be said that the police enjoy unalloyed praise. They fare less well when compared to non-criminal justice state agencies like medical staff, teachers, firefighters and social workers (FitzGerald et al. 2002). Perhaps even more worrying for the police is the long-term trend in public opinion, which has seen a steady reduction in public confidence and a 'levelling down' so that groups who once rated the police comparatively highly no longer do so and have converged with those who have consistently shown a significant measure of disfavour (Bradford 2011); this is a trend that suggests a general social process of homogenisation similar to what Reiner (1995) regards as a loss of the 'sacred' status that the police once enjoyed (see also Loader and Mulcahy 2003 who found that some people believed that the police had become yet another flawed public service). More striking has been changing assessments of residents in major cities. In London, FitzGerald et al. (2002) found that an increasing minority regard the police as 'less responsive, less visible, less accessible, more interested in their policing tactics and less engaged with the community than they would like' (p 105).

It seems that the safest conclusion to draw is that the police in Britain, as in many comparable jurisdictions, remain very popular, but in Britain they are less popular than they once were.

Diversity

It is also true that the police are not, and probably never have been, *universally* popular. 'The public' is diverse and it has long been recognised that such diversity is reflected in divergent attitudes towards the police (Shaw and Williamson 1972; Bayley and Mendelsohn 1969; Belson 1975; Smith 1983; Decker 1981; IPCC 2016). Let us consider the principal axes of that diversity.

Race and Ethnicity

Since the 1970s the issue of police–race relations has figured prominently on the policy agenda. This has been reflected in research publications, both official and academic, which echo similar concerns in other countries, most notably the United States, whose history of race relations is even more tortured than those in Britain. Looking further afield, what does seem common to many countries is that race and/or ethnicity forms a major social cleavage that impacts markedly on policing. The result is that sizeable minority populations are more critical of the police than the majority population.

Black and white

Needless to say, it is America that has hosted most research on this topic (see Huebner et al. 2004 for a detailed review of this literature). It has long been true (see the pioneering research by Bayley and Mendelsohn 1969) that there are considerable deep and persistent differences in support expressed for the police by white and African Americans respectively(Weitzer and Tuch 2005a: 288; see also Weitzer and Tuch 1999; 2005b). In Britain too, successive British Crime Surveys show that '[t]he difference between black respondents and others is striking' (FitzGerald et al. 2002: 88).

Weitzer and Tuch (2004a) attribute these differences to the extent to which the police are regarded by African Americans as serving the sectional interests of dominant ethnic groups. Whites emphasise crime control and worry less about equality of treatment, whilst African Americans also want crime control but not at the expense of equal treatment. However, this view is not limited to the police, for African Americans tend to regard the criminal justice system per se as biased, in contrast to white Americans who believe it delivers 'equal treatment before the law' (Henderson et al. 1997; see also Wortley and Hagan 1997; Walker et al. 1972). In Britain too, the taint of racism extends beyond the confines of the criminal justice arena to infect other institutions in the policing environment. Non-white people showed less confidence in the impartiality of the Independent Police Complaints Commission than did their white counterparts (Inglis and Shepherd 2007) and the courts have introduced special measures to expunge accusations of racism that surrounded them (Hood and Cordovil 1992; Shute et al. 2005).

Explanations for such racial and ethnic disparities tend often to extend no further than the 'institutional racism' of police officers (see also Macpherson of Cluny et al. 1999; Holdaway 1996). Sometimes the entire social structure is implicated, racial and ethnic affinity eclipsing class and status differences. The extent and nature of this society-wide racist disposition is illustrated by the experience of racial *profiling*. This is often associated with exclusively *police* practices, but Gabbidon et al. (2009) shows that African Americans also experience profiling in airports and retail outlets (Gabbidon and Higgins 2009) and, no doubt, elsewhere.

Experience and belief

'Unfair' treatment is not restricted to 'profiling' and one-third of all those inter-viewed by Jones et al. believed that unfairness was common (Jones et al. 1986; see also Painter et al. 1988; and Smith and Gray 1983). However, this raises a problem that forms the central problematic in this research: this data (like almost all such data) relies on what people *believe*. If the research problem is limited to what people believe and with what consequences, then it is perfectly appropriate to point out that young people (or any other group) *believe* some-thing to be true and are inclined to act on that belief. On the other hand, if one wishes to go further and declare that such beliefs are *true*, then reported per-ceptions are not enough, because there are many occasions when people voice with certainty claims that are palpably *untrue*, such as the widespread belief that crime was increasing, even though it was actually declining.

How might we assess whether claims of unfair treatment by police and others are true or not? One way is to observe how the police behave and assess whether they act unfairly. Monumental research focused on the London Metropolitan Police by the Policy Studies Institute (1983) found that in matters like stop and search there was abundant observational and interview evidence that officers were, at the very least, not fulfilling their duties correctly and probably were creating unfairness, especially towards young black men. So, the claim that contemporary police officers are continuing to act unfairly enjoys some cred-ibility, despite the enormous changes there have been in law and practice since the early 1980s. On the other hand, ethnic and racial minorities have been shown to believe that police officers habitually treat them unfairly, even when they did not. Higgins et al. (2008) commented that their research showed that 'Black individuals ... may be hypersensitive ... and thus perceive [racial profil-ing] as being widespread' (2008: 1538; see also Lasley 1994). In other words, the belief may act as a 'frame' imposed upon experience to give meaning to experiences and feelings that arise from them. This is consistent with Jackson and Bradford's view that 'just as the police represent for many [people] order, stability and cohesion, to people from [low socio-economic] groups they ... may represent the unfair priorities of the dominant social order, an interfer-ing state, or even oppression' (Jackson and Bradford 2009: 499; see also Engel 2005; Scaglion and Condon 1980; Webb and Marshall 1995; Waddington and Braddock 1991). Such beliefs may be authoritatively reinforced by scandals and subsequent inquiries, such as the murder of Stephen Lawrence, which 'have left these groups willing to accept that the police habitually discriminate against young black men' (FitzGerald et al. 2002). This is something to which we will return.

Racial 'diversity'

Often, discussions about race and ethnicity are conducted under the banner of 'diversity'. However, in the literature on public attitudes to the police there

is a failure to acknowledge the breadth of actual racial diversity. It is domi-
nated instead by a crude 'black/white' dichotomy. In America and, to a lesser
extent, Britain the principle social rift *is* between white Europeans and those of
African dissent. However, this is not the case in other countries: in France, the
Iberian Peninsula and the northern Mediterranean rim it is North Africans and
'Arabs' that constitute the principal fault line. In Australasia, South America
and to a lesser extent Canada it is native populations who suffer social exclusion and coercive policing (Dixon and Maher 2002; Queensland Crime and
Misconduct Commission 2006; see also Redner-Vera and Galeste 2015). In
Japan it is Koreans who are regarded as the troublesome ethnic minority (Ames
1981; Bayley 1976). However, this hardly does justice to the variegated pattern of ethnicities found in America, and even in many European countries. In
America there is tremendous diversity amongst the 'white' population, whose
heritage stretches back to waves of migration from Ireland, Italy, Scandinavia,
Germany, Poland and many more. Amongst 'minorities' there are Hispanic/
Latinos, Native Americans, Chinese and other Southeast Asian populations;
people from Africa and those from the Indian subcontinent (who themselves
represent a rich mix of ethnicities and religious affiliations). If race truly determines attitudes to the police, then we would expect distinctions to surface
amongst these various minorities whose cultures vary enormously, but research
has remained largely silent on this issue, principally because it serves a policy
agenda that is selective about which racial/ethnic groups are of concern to policy. The only recognition *diversity* receives is conceptual recourse to the notion
of 'racial hierarchy', with white people at the top and African Americans at the
bottom, and other minorities located between them. Reflecting this hierarchy,
attitudes to the police are most positive amongst white people, least positive
amongst African Americans, with Hispanics/Latinos in between these extremes,
acting as a proxy for all the diverse groups that are omitted (Weitzer and Tuch
2005a: 289).

American authors tend to attribute the 'black'/'white' divide to the history
of slavery. African Americans are largely composed of descendants of slaves,
whereas other groups arrived in America as immigrants (Wortley and Hagan
1997: 664–5). Even after slavery was abolished, African Americans suffered
the depredations and indignities of racial segregation in the southern states of
the USA—a system enforced by *white* police officers. Hispanics, on the other
hand, willingly migrated to the USA, often doing so as 'undocumented ille-
gals'. Hence, white people have tended to support the police as guardians of
their privileged status; African Americans have opposed them as oppressors;
and Hispanics/Latinos have equivocal attitudes reflecting their own equivocal
status. If true, this is a historically and culturally very specific theory about
America. Nevertheless, it is implicitly taken as a template for police–race relations elsewhere, but are the similarities only skin deep? Britain has no history
of slavery, but its colonies in the Caribbean most certainly did, and it was overwhelmingly from those colonies that, until recently, black people migrated to

the UK. We might, therefore, concede that there are surface similarities between people of African descent in Britain and the USA. On the other hand, people from the Indian subcontinent, did not descend from slaves, but migrated to Britain. Like Hispanics/Latinos they migrated from different countries: India, Pakistan, Bangladesh and Sri Lanka, and in one case of forced migration arrived in Britain from Uganda. Does this put them in a similar position to Hispanic/Latino migrants in the USA? Hardly, for the countries from which they migrated had been *colonised* by the British, a relationship of domination, but falling short of slavery. They spoke diverse languages, rather than all speaking Spanish/Portuguese; they were religiously diverse (defining distinctive ethnicities like Sikhs) and India is home to the distinctive caste system. There are also enmities between different nations on the subcontinent: Pakistan and India have fought four wars and conflict continues to rumble in Kashmir; Sri Lanka hosted a civil war between the Ceylonese and Tamils that prompted the assassination of Rajiv Gandhi allegedly by the Tamil Tigers. Conflict between Sikhs and the Indian state concluded with a military assault on the Golden Temple in 1984, followed by the assassination of the prime minister of India, Indira Gandhi, and retaliatory riots claiming the lives of some 10,000 Sikhs. Religion is also diverse, with Hindus, Muslims, Sikhs and Buddhists. Their migration histories were also diverse: most migrated directly from the Indian subcontinent, but a substantial minority were expelled from East Africa where an 'Asian' diaspora had long been established. Also, unlike their black predecessors, many migrants from the subcontinent arrived in Britain with little or no grasp of the English language, whereas the first language of 'black' people in America and Britain was that of their hosts. Putting all this diversity into a single 'Asian' category seems questionable at the least. If we attempt to apply the same template to police–race relations in Australasia, we would find still further differences.

We should also remind ourselves that the 'host society' is not ethnically homogeneous either: in Britain, there is a significant migrant, largely Catholic, population whose forebears migrated from, what is now, the Republic of Ireland. They would be included as 'white' and yet might have a distinctive experience of policing and attitudes towards the police. For instance, they appear—at least in North London—to have been one of the population groups most disproportionately stopped and searched by the police (Young 1994). More recently there has been considerable migration from Eastern Europe, and these immigrants, like the Irish, are 'white Europeans' and many are Catholic. Can we assume that their attitudes will be indistinguishable from those of their Irish predecessors? Finally, whilst we have concentrated on diversity amongst the settled population, there is throughout Europe nomadic populations, variously described as 'gypsies', 'tinkers', 'travellers' and 'Roma', with very distinctive cultures and a history of abrasive relationships with the police, but who remain 'hidden minorities' (Chakraborti et al. 2004). Although the influence of race and ethnicity on contemporary attitudes to the police cannot be doubted, their causal antecedents are far from clear. As Weitzer and Tuch (2005a) remark: 'Much has been written about Black–White differences in views of the police, but most of this literature does little to explain why these differences exist' (p 279. See also Carter 1985; Vogel 2011; Weitzer and Tuch 2004a).

A second issue to arise from the notion of a 'racial hierarchy' is the assumption that whatever the scale of racial diversity, the 'white'/'non-white' distinction represents the principal racial cleavage in modern societies. FitzGerald et al. (2002) found, to the contrary, that in London there were many interracial rivalries and conflicts amongst groups that did not fit neatly into the white/non-white dichotomy.

Class, Age and Gender

Race is often regarded as an important influence, but it is not always the dominant influence and neither does it explain many of the differences between people's attitudes to the police. There are a number of additional influences that need to be taken into consideration in order to enhance understanding. The principal candidates for inclusion in any explanation have been social class or status, gender and age. Let us consider these in turn.

Class

We have already seen above that class tends to reinforce race and ethnicity, since in most societies racial minorities tend to occupy the lower rungs on the social status hierarchy. Class has been recognised as having a profound influence since the earliest pioneering research on public attitudes to the police (Bayley and Mendelsohn 1969; Belson 1975; Brown and Benedict 2002; Schuck et al. 2008; Weitzer and Tuch 1999; 2002; 2005a; Taylor et al. 2010; Frank et al. 2005; Wu et al. 2009). This, it was assumed, was to be expected, since criminality and disorder was also associated with deprivation, which was linked closely with social class. People in higher social classes had much less to gain and much more to lose by engaging in crime and disorder and hence regarded the police more favourably as a bulwark against victimisation. However, the interplay between race and class can produce surprises. For instance, Wortley and Hagan (1997) found that more middle class African Americans believed that discrimination was rife in the police, more than did their working class counterparts or middle class white people.

Age

Criminality and disorderliness have long been associated with the young. The archetypal image of the 'hooligan' is that of a lower class *youth* (Pearson 1983). Youth crime has a panoply of criminal justice procedures, arrangements and institutions, devoted to scrutinising, controlling, penalising and rehabilitating youthful offenders. It is no wonder that age, in combination with race, has repeatedly been found to be strongly associated with attitudes towards the police (Decker 1981; Bridenball and Jesilow 2008; Cox and Falkenberg 1987; Gabbidon et al. 2009; Reisig and Parks 2002; Ren et al. 2005). Reviewing the American literature, Brown and Benedict observe: 'The vast majority of studies which included age as a variable indicate that younger persons view the police less favorably than older persons' (Brown and Benedict 2002: 554). In Britain, researchers have found a similar pattern: 'criticism of police conduct decreases sharply with age' (Smith 1983: 253; Painter et al. 1988; see also FitzGerald et al. 2002; Inglis and Shepherd 2007). This *does not* mean that the young generally are positively *hostile*; they are not! They are simply less enamoured of the police than their older counterparts (Chow 2010: 504; see also Vogel 2011). There are, however, dissenting voices: Stewart et al. (2014) insists to the contrary, that the predominant tendency amongst youth is consistency: attitudes remain high if they start high, low if they start low. Home Office researchers found that the age profile was sensitive to the question that was asked. If the question asked about 'the way crime is being dealt with, both in the local area and nationally', then it 'is *highest for those aged 16–34 and lowest for those aged 55 or over*' (Page et al. 2004, italics added).

It is with people at the other end of the age span that youth is often contrasted and the older people become the more they positively incline towards the police and the criminal justice system as a whole (see, for example, Jones et al. 1986; Chivite-Matthews and Maggs 2002; Smith 1983). The division between age groups can be overstated, for Stoutland (2001) found that in a crime-ridden, deprived area in Boston, older people sympathised with the young, who they feared were not being treated with sufficient respect, even though the police crackdown in the area was credited with reducing crime.

By contrast, relatively little attention has been paid to the views of younger children. The oft-published public relations photographs showing a smiling and kindly community constable comforting, talking to or just posing for the camera with a young child hardly does justice to Australian research, which found that:

> ... children emphasise the punitive role of police; very few children identified with non-punitive roles. This punitive theme was evident irrespective of the children's experiences, age, and whether they could recall television shows involving police (Powell et al. 2008: abstract).

Gender

Just as crime and disorder is disproportionately associated with youth, so it is also very largely seen as the preserve of men and, therefore, as a group men might be expected (and are often found to be) less favourably disposed to the police than women. However, in reality the role of gender is not as simple as this picture suggests (Brown and Benedict 2002), for whilst women are more supportive of the police than are men, the statistical significance of gender differences is unclear. Many researchers qualify their conclusions, whilst several studies simply fail to find gender differences (Reisig and Parks 2002; Merry et al. 2012; Decker 1981) and women are not always found to be more positive towards the police than men; occasionally they are less so (Correia et al. 1996). The influence of gender tends to make itself felt when combined with age, race and 'community context' (Cao et al. 1996) so that the least favourably disposed to the police are young black *men* living in disadvantaged conditions whilst the most favourably disposed are older white middle class *women* (Kershaw et al. 2008; Lasley 1994; Merry et al. 2012; Painter et al. 1988; Walker et al. 1972; Weitzer et al. 2008).

There are also competing theoretical explanations for the gender differences that are observed. Most researchers rely implicitly or explicitly on the gender imbalance in criminality and disorderliness to explain differences, but occasionally researchers venture into how the female social role brings a different perspective to bear on the police and policing. Applegate et al. (2002) refer to the social expectation that women should be more caring towards others to explain gender differences. They suggest that 'women, more so than men, seem to hold a general view that the government should not simply be an instrument of punishment and accountability but also should provide assistance to people with needs' (Applegate et al. 2002: 98). Crawford et al. (1990) agree that women have a distinct agenda, which emphasises police action to protect women from domestic violence and safeguard children from abuse.

Neighbourhood

Race, age and class are important influences upon attitudes because they are 'brute facts' of social differentiation that impact on individuals. In most societies age groups are treated differently: the young are protected from the rigours of adult life and the aged are venerated. Gender differences are equally universal. Social class reflects life chances and the capacity to control resources, which overlaps with racial differentiation. However, quite why a young black working class man's attitudes to the police differ from those of a middle aged white woman is not entirely apparent. This atheoretical correlation of 'brute facts' with attitudes to the police surely requires some understanding of why differently situated people apprehend the police differently (Schafer et al. 2003). One attempt to do so lies in the influence of 'neighbourhood culture', especially in areas of 'concentrated disadvantage'—an argument reminiscent of the 'Chicago School' of urban sociology (Shaw and McKay 1942; Park et al. 1925). Following in this tradition, the 'social disorganisation theory' explains how:

> Neighborhoods characterized by high levels of poverty, racial heterogeneity, and residential mobility would breed aggregated dissatisfaction with police because in these areas, there is an imbalance between formal control and informal control. Informal control decreases as neighbors are unable to agree upon and work toward common goals, as predicted by the theory of social disorganization. When informal social control is weak, formal social control

increases, producing an increased likelihood of conflicts between neighbor-hood residents and police officers. Socially disadvantaged neighborhoods also have the weakest ability to '... influence political and economic decision-making and to acquire externally based goods and services that may increase its ability to control crime in the area' (Wu et al. 2009; see also Crank and Giacomazzi 2007; Ren et al. 2005; Skogan 1990b; Bridenball and Jesilow 2008; Kershaw et al. 2008; Peak et al. 1992; Schafer et al. 2003).

This tends to create a lack of 'community cohesion': people leading unhappy lives, feeling themselves alienated from neighbours and likely to refer neighbourhood disputes to the police. In London, Policy Studies Institute researchers found that these neighbourhoods were also disproportionately pop-ulated by those leading 'unconventional, disorganised lives' (Smith and Gray 1983: 259) and were home to a disproportionate number of ethnic minorities (Vogel 2011; Lambert 1970).

Crank and Giacomazzi (2007) ask rhetorically: 'if the community is not cohe-sive, what can the police do?' (p 124). Well, we know *what they actually do*!

> Some high-crime neighborhoods experience saturation patrolling, but even the more routine police practices in high-crime and disorderly areas may amplify friction between officers and residents ... the street crime typical of some of these communities offers far more opportunities for police corruption and other abuses of power—namely, robbing drug dealers, planting evidence, and otherwise mistreating residents ... police typify certain neighborhoods as being troublesome ... [officers] stereotype residents as uncooperative, hostile, or crime prone, approach residents with greater suspicion, ... behave more aggressively, and ... act more punitively ... police officers' verbal and physical abuse, unjustified street stops, and corruption are more prevalent in disadvan-taged and high-crime areas ... residents typically lack the capacity to constrain such behavior and hold officers accountable (Weitzer et al. 2008: 401–2; see also Schuck et al. 2008).

No wonder that, as Parker et al. (1995: 403) put it: 'High crime areas fostered attitudes that saw the police as "corrupt, dumb, unfriendly, and cruel"' (see also Smith and Gray 1983 for a British example; Schafer et al. 2003 and Reisig and Parks 2000 supply further American evidence). Also, those residing in these areas are likely to regard the police as responsible for allowing them to become crime-ridden. This is, after all—they might reason—the prime responsibility of the police (Schafer et al. 2003). These areas are also prone to suffering 'incivili-ties' that act as 'signal crimes' (Innes 2004a; 2004b) communicating disturbing information about the local area—a vandalised bus shelter may communicate to some residents that the neighbourhood is sliding into lawlessness (Scaglion and Condon 1980; Wilson and Kelling 1982; Kelling and Coles 1996; Skogan 1990b; Sampson and Raudenbush 1999). On the other hand, where there is a coherent culture favourable to the police, people feel less isolated and vulner-able. This, according to Reisig and Parks (2002) was the 'biggest factor' influenc-ing residents' 'sense of safety' that eclipsed individual characteristics like race and age (see Schafer et al. 2003; but see also Sindall et al. 2012 for an alternative view). Indeed, so strong are neighbourhood influences on attitudes towards the police, that some researchers estimate that it reduces considerably the importance of race and ethnicity. In other words, the influence of race and ethnicity arises because certain neighbourhoods suffer deprivation and decay, and are also—more or less exclusively—home to distinct ethnic and racial groups (see Engel 2005; see also Schuck et al. 2008; Sampson and Jeglum-Bartusch 1998; Taylor et al. 2010; Inglis and Shepherd 2007; Reisig and Parks 2002). Weitzer compared middle and working class areas and found that the influence of *individual* class position on attitudes towards the police was not nearly as profound as that of the class or status of the neighbourhood amongst whom they resided (Weitzer 1999). Recent research in London concluded that neighbourhood influences were paramount in generating levels of trust and confidence in the police (Jackson et al. 2012a). However, it ought to be noted that other research contrasted London boroughs according to the prevalence of stop and searches and whether they were conducted on the basis of 'reasonable suspicion' (under section 1 of the Police and Criminal Evidence Act 1984) or section 60 of the Criminal Justice and Public Order Act 1994, which requires no suspicion. This found that borough effects were very modest indeed, which somewhat goes against the trend. The authors of this research acknowledge that their results may have resulted from using borough-wide data, rather than smaller data from neighbourhoods (Miller and D'Souza 2015).

The significance of 'neighbourhood culture' is that it breaks the deterministic linkage between material circumstances and attitudes. It does not necessarily follow that race, class, age and gender *determine* opinions and beliefs, but these 'brute facts' of existence are filtered through a neighbourhood experience and culture. This allows some limited scope in which the police might seek to influence attitudes by amending how they are culturally perceived. However, those attempts to exert cultural influence can themselves be resisted culturally. For instance, it has been found that a 'deep cynicism' is often felt by many minority groups towards police reforms and dooms attempted 'outreach'. Millings (2013) describes how the 'Prevent' strand of the British antiterrorism strategy, designed to divert vulnerable young people from the lure of 'radicalisation', is defeated by 'a broader attack on the integrity and credibility' of the police (2013: 1087). In the United States attempts to ameliorate black hostility to the police by 'community policing' interventions seem to have enjoyed little success (Cheurprakobkit 2000: 334). Not even attempts at improving police–minority relations by increasing the proportion of non-white officers seems to have made much impact on ethnic and race relations in the USA (Brown and Benedict 2002). Whilst this must be intensely frustrating for policymakers, it also raises the more fundamental conceptual issue that once cynicism becomes so deep, is it limited to attitudes about reform? Such cynicism is likely to form a 'lens' through which policing generally is viewed. Such 'deep cynicism' is unlikely to be limited to the passive interpretation of actions and events. It is likely that it would contribute to how those 'cynical' minorities would act and react to police interventions. Mazerolle et al. (2013a) suggests that such a shared 'tradition' might include non-compliance with those in authority that would make reform difficult to implement and the execution of police duties fraught.

Media

So far we have concentrated on enduring features of individuals, groups and the wider society that might sway attitudes, but the mass media is quite a different type of influence. Few would doubt that the police enjoy an almost unequalled media profile. Television programmes featuring police officers, both fictional and factual, litter the air waves, bookshelves and the internet. So what impact does this rich media diet have on the audiences who consume them? Answering this question requires us to distinguish between the background hum of regular appearances of police officers in the media and the more occasional intensive treatment of exceptional events, *causes celebre*, scandals and the like.

Let us turn first to the long-term routine treatment of the police. There can be little doubt that the press and broadcast media are a prominent source of information about the police for most people (FitzGerald et al. 2002). Moreover, those interviewed regarded what they read, heard and saw about policing as being *accurate*, despite a plentiful academic literature suggesting that the media image of crime and policing is not only misleading, but may even be the opposite of the truth (Surette 1998; Yim and Schafer 2009; Gallagher et al. 2001). The inaccuracy of fictional representations of policing works very much in their favour, generally being found to overestimate or exaggerate police effectiveness in crime control (Reiner 2003).

For their part, the police have long cultivated the media, whose coverage they tend to regard as negative and unhelpful (IPCC 2016):

> Policing, especially in Britain, has always been a matter of symbolism as much as substance ... Most sophisticated police leaders have realised this. From the architects of modern British policing in the early nineteenth century, such as Sir Robert Peel, up to today's chief officers, there has been a continuing concern with constructing and maintaining a favourable image of policing as a benign, honourable and helpful service (Reiner 2003: 259).

Providing briefings for journalists and acting as consultants on police procedures for fictional programmes (Chibnall 1979; 1975a; 1975b; Ericson 1989; Jenkins 2009; Mawby 2003; 2002) have been just some of the channels through which the police influenced the press and broadcasters. In the late 1980s the Metropolitan Police were so concerned about their public image that they commissioned the public relations consultancy, Wolff Olins (1988), to advise them how to improve it and which led directly to the 'Plus Programme' (Fleming and McLaughlin 2012; see also Lee and McGovern 2013). So close has been the relationship between the police and, at least some, journalists that it has aroused anxieties amongst parliamentarians (Home Affairs Committee 2009; Leveson 2012). With the growth of electronic communication many police forces worldwide have developed websites and participate in social media that address directly the audiences they wish to reach, without intermediaries, like journalists, imposing their 'news values' (Rosenbaum et al. 2011). These various efforts have (despite their inconsistencies and contradictions) apparently been successful, because observers conclude consistently that the image of the police conveyed by the media is overwhelmingly positive (Skogan 1990a; Reiner 2003; Reiner et al. 2003). Moreover, the worst that seems to happen is that readers, viewers and listeners find their pre-existing attitudes confirmed (Jackson et al. 2012a; Dirikx and van den Bulck 2014; Dowler and Zawilski 2007).

It is into this otherwise benign media environment that extraordinary events occasionally intrude. As McLaughlin (2006) points out, news stories—especially those that can amount to 'trials by media'—are driven by the intense competition between newspapers chasing an ever-shrinking readership. This invigorates the long-established appetite that all media outlets have shown for 'moral panics' (Cohen 1972) so as to include formerly sacrosanct institutions such as the NHS and the police (Bayley 1996; Reiner 1995). Depictions of police officers using what appears to be 'excessive force' against suspects are the quintessential extraordinary events and the widespread use of mobile recording devices and the capacity to readily upload video onto websites like 'You Tube' mean that such episodes have become increasingly commonplace (Smith 1983: 266; see Brown and Benedict 2002 for a general review). The increasingly common scenes of officers hitting suspects and sometimes hapless individuals caught in the midst of a riot (the fate that befell Ian Tomlinson during the 'G20' riots in London in 2009) add weight to public demands for 'heads to roll'. As Hough observes: 'there are heavy pressures on politicians to provide simple solutions to complex problems: they operate increasingly in a populist environment where the consequence of offering complex solutions is electoral defeat' (Hough 2007: 207; see also Jenkins 2009).

Perhaps the archetypal public scandal was the beating of Rodney King in 1991, captured by George Holliday's video recording and widely broadcast on American television (see <https://www.youtube.com/watch?v=sb1WywIpUtY> to watch the full video and Lawrence 2000 for an analysis of the affair). Allegations of similarly excessive use of force were common enough before the Rodney King incident, but the latter showed, for the first time, the full horror of the beating inflicted, resulting in numerous injuries, including broken bones. It was the viciousness of the attack on King that prompted outrage, not only in Los Angeles and throughout America, but also internationally. The eventual acquittal of four officers on charges of assault prompted the Los Angeles riots lasting seven days, in which fifty-three people were killed and property damage estimated at $1 billion was caused. A special commission was established (Webster and Williams 1992) and the long-serving Chief of Police, Daryl Gates, was forced to resign and the LAPD was required to make reforms. What effect did this have on attitudes to the police? Fortunately, Lasley (1994) was conducting a 'multi-wave' series of surveys focusing on 'inner-city' neighbourhoods in Los Angeles, including South Central. Two of the 'waves' had been completed and whilst the questions asked could not anticipate the onset of the riots, they still allowed an unprecedented picture of how riots affected public attitudes to the police generally. This showed that its impact was felt unevenly by different ethnic/racial groups and tended to wane quickly.

However, there is no consensus about the longer term impact that such events have. Reiner (1995) attributes the progressive loss of the 'sacred' status of the police in Britain to a succession of scandals that began to befall it from the end of the 1960s onwards. Bradford (2011) agrees, attributing the selective decline in approval amongst those sections of the population that had previously given the police strong endorsement to the continuing succession of scandals (see also Semukhina and Reynolds 2014). Loader (2006) tends to agree that for many middle class people, the police have joined the ranks of yet another failing public service. However, Sindall et al. (2012) maintain that the public seem to have a 'short memory' when it comes to assessing the performance of the police as the public are fairly forgiving and will respond quickly to any improvements that the police make in delivering their service. By the same token, however, long-term strategies implemented with the aim of increasing public confidence are likely to count for little if high-profile events exert a 'short-sharp shock' to confidence (Sindall et al. 2012: 759; see also Tuch and Weitzer 1997). Anecdotally, this seems to have occurred after the mistaken fatal shooting by English counterterrorism police officers of a wholly innocent migrant in 2005 (Jean Charles de Menezes) erroneously suspected of being a 'suicide bomber'. Following the initial shock public confidence in the police seems not only to have recovered, but improved slightly.

On the other hand, repeated exposure to media allegations of misconduct tends to cultivate distrust in the police, both at the level of the neighbourhood and city wide (Weitzer and Tuch 2004b; 2004a). Kaminski and Jefferis (1998) examined a highly publicised aggressive arrest in Cincinnati and found that it had greater impact on the specific question of police use of force, but did not affect attitudes to the police as a whole. Excessive use of force is not alone in prompting public outrage, so too are episodes played out before the camera of what appears to be gross incompetence. One of the most seminal moments in the recent history of English policing was the interviewing by two experienced detectives of a woman complaining that she had been raped, which was broadcast in 1981 in a much publicised first ever series of documentaries on policing under the direction of Roger Graef. The outrage that followed prompted greater attention being paid to crimes against women and how they were treated by the police (Jones et al. 1994). Equally, sometimes the police stand accused of wilfully refusing to do their duty, such as appearing to stand aside whilst riotous looters ransacked retail premises in various cities throughout England in the summer of 2011. However, Hohl et al.'s use of regular repeat surveys found that these events tended to reinforce pre-existing attitudes, rather than create new ones (Hohl et al. 2013). Similarly, Weitzer and Tuch (2005a) found that African Americans, amongst whom attitudes to the police have long been unfavourable, tended to be selectively sensitive to incidents of apparent police misconduct.

We should also be aware that it is not an undiluted stream of misery for the police; sometimes extraordinary events can rally support from the public, especially in conditions of conflict. The press and mass media in Israel during the Second Intifada (1998–2007) were eager to appeal to patriotic sentiments and emphasised the scale of the terrorist threat, succeeding in depicting the police as a heroic bulwark against terrorism (Sela-Shayovitz 2015). On a much smaller scale, when four young black men invaded a 'swanky' restaurant in Toronto, killing a young woman in the process, the following media storm increased support for the criminal justice system as a whole (Wortley and Hagan 1997). Even when the police are criticised for their slow response to an emergency like the mass 'spree' killing of young political activists by Anders Behring Breivik in Norway in 2011, public assessment of the police appeared to have been quite resilient (Thomassen 2014). Whilst such events may be located in a particular police organisation and involve particular officers the ramifications may be much more widespread. When the Metropolitan Police were excoriated for their incompetence and 'institutional racism' displayed in their investigation of the murder of Stephen Lawrence (Macpherson of Cluny et al. 1999), the force of that criticism was felt not only by the officers directly involved, or the administrative unit in which they worked, or even the Metropolitan Police, but had an impact on the police nationwide (Foster et al. 2005).

Equally, when officers perform their duties heroically, or pursue policies that meet with public approval, such as 'community policing', then this is intended to create a warm glow around the police per se. As Manning (1997) reminds us, police funerals are carefully choreographed rituals suffused with symbolic significance designed to reinforce in the eyes of the public the image of the police as selfless protectors of the public, not threats to liberty. This is important in influencing the context within which real police officers encounter members of the public (Dean 1980; Scaglion and Condon 1980; Brandl et al. 1994). However, what officers then do in those encounters has a more specific and profound impact on the attitudes of those members of the public and it is to that that we now turn.

'Diffuse' and 'Specific' Attitudes

So far we have been focusing on the police and policing generally, and how impersonal social forces can impact upon them. Not all research focuses on this level of analysis. Some researchers focus specifically on the interpersonal level: how did a person feel about how they were treated by an officer they encountered. This highlights the difference between 'specific' and 'diffuse' attitudes. White and Menke (1982) describe 'diffuse' attitudes:

> ... there exists a reservoir of support and goodwill for the police as a part of the criminal justice institution ... Values such as order, justice, fairness in procedure, protection under the law, duly constituted authority, and so on, are at the heart of this ideology (White and Menke 1982: 226; see also Brown and Benedict 2002; Loader and Mulcahy 2003).

If 'diffuse' and 'specific' attitudes were the same, then it would hardly be worth drawing the distinction between them. However, they are not the same: it has been found consistently (and in different jurisdictions) that specific approval of the actions of police officers is lower than diffuse attitudes towards the police institution as a whole (Walker et al. 1972). However, conceptual confusion remains: some surveys ask not about 'the police', but attempt to specify to whom in the police they are referring. Frequently, they refer to the 'local police' as distinct from police nationwide (see, for example, Kershaw et al. 2008; Page et al. 2004; Scribbins et al. 2010; Sims 2003), but how 'local' is 'local'? Does it refer to the officers responsible for a specific neighbourhood? Or, perhaps, all those working from the same local police station? Or does it refer to the police organisation of which they form a part? In England this might refer to several hundred personnel in small rural forces and thousands in the large urban centres. Furthermore, is it any less 'diffuse' to say that the 'local police' are 'doing a good job', when the referent of 'doing a good job' is so all embracing? (For an American example, see Reisig and Correia 1997.)

Contact

An alternative approach to examining 'specific' attitudes focuses on the reactions of those who have had recent contact with specific police officers. Just how often do members of the public have direct, face-to-face, contact with police officers? Official Home Office and, in the USA, Department of Justice estimates are that, depending on the type of contact and who exactly it was with, approximately half the civil population have some kind of contact annually with the police (Allen et al. 2006; Scribbins et al. 2010; Durose and Langton 2013). The police are very much part of the social landscape of modern developed societies.

This familiarity comes at a cost to the favour with which the police are regarded, for the orthodox conclusion has been that contact, of whatever kind, breeds lower levels of approval and satisfaction, compared to those who remain blissfully untouched. The more extensive a person's experience of the police, the lower their estimation of them (Allen et al. 2006; Harris Research Centre 1987; Aye Maung 1995; Scribbins et al. 2010; IPCC 2016). This, it should be acknowledged, is not a peculiar reflection upon the police in Britain, but appears to be widespread (see, for example, Hwang et al. 2005; Huebner et al. 2004; Brown and Benedict 2002; Walker et al. 1972; Bridenball and Jesilow 2008; Frank et al.

2005). This suggests that public attitudes reflect common, cross-jurisdictional features of policing per se. Whatever they are, it means that (in Britain, at least) the police are quite unlike other public services—such as the National Health Service—of which those who have little or no direct experience tend to be disparaging, but once they have direct experience, are inclined to revise their estimation in a favourable direction (Bradford et al. 2008). Not every researcher agrees with this picture, however (see: Hinds and Murphy 2007; Bolton 1972; Bayley and Mendelsohn 1969; Hawdon and Ryan 2003; Kautt 2011; Wortley and Hagan 1997; Nicholas et al. 2008), but theirs is a dissident voice compared to the chorus of opinion that contact does the police few favours.

Puzzlingly, it is also widely found that contact with the police leaves most members of the public with a *favourable* impression (Walker et al. 1972; Smith 1983; Hough and Mayhew 1983; Hurst and Frank 2000; Frank et al. 2005; Scribbins et al. 2010; Eith and Durose 2011; Vogel 2011; Merry et al. 2012; Durose and Langton 2013; Flatley et al. 2010). How can this be? The answer is that estimations of the police made by people without recent experience of the realities of policing are remarkably, even stratospherically, high. When they acquire direct experience, their evaluation of the police diminishes to levels that are not quite as elevated as before, but remain high nevertheless. Why is this not more widely recognised? For policy reasons, leaving people satisfied with the service they have received is to accomplish no more than fulfilment of the obligations of public service. It is also important to improve service delivery, hence policy-related research is predisposed to look for areas of weakness; which is particularly so in policing. On the other hand, it is difficult for real-life officers to live up to the glamorised media images of police superheroes![1]

Not only is mundane reality likely to fall short of exaggerated expectations, dissatisfaction with direct contact seems to weigh more heavily on the judgements people make than does satisfaction with the service provided—what has become known as 'negativity bias' (Skogan 2006; 2012; Hohl et al. 2010; Myhill and Quinton 2010; Myhill and Bradford 2012; Merry et al. 2012; Decker 1981; but see also Cheurprakobkit 2000). This 'bias' is particularly important, because when weighed against other possible influences, contact has proven a more powerful explanatory variable than 'race, religion, income, marital status, or education' (Scaglion and Condon 1980; see also Brandl et al. 1994; Schafer et al. 2003). To some extent, such a bias is to be expected: since people value the police so highly, there is simply more opportunity to disappoint. If officers performed their duties impeccably, what more can someone who already rates them most positively say? Whereas, if officers delivered only a mediocre service, a reduced rating reflecting that would amount to a reduction of several points on the scale. More worrying for the police, perhaps, is that unsatisfactory contacts are not evenly spread throughout the population, but are concentrated on

---

[1] This is also witnessed in allied fields, such as forensic science, where programmes like *CSI* lead juries to have exaggerated expectations of what forensic analysis can produce.

17

those sections of the population who regard them with least affection—young ethnic minority men from deprived neighbourhoods (Walker et al. 1972; Chow 2010; Scaglion and Condon 1980; Cheurprakobkit 2000; Engel 2005; Bradford et al. 2009b; Hawdon and Ryan 2003; Skogan 1994: 15; Quinton et al. 2000; Smith 1983; Miller et al. 2000a; FitzGerald et al. 2002; Taylor 2003; Huebner et al. 2004; Allen et al. 2006; Ivkovic 2008; Dean 1980; Bridenball and Jesilow 2008; Campbell and Schuman 1971 cited in Decker 1981; Sivasubramaniam and Goodman-Delahunty 2008; Eith and Durose 2011; Harris Research Centre 1987; Meredyth et al. 2010; Scribbins et al. 2010).[2] The reason for this concentration of dissatisfaction lies mainly in how members of the public believe they have been treated. For instance, it has been repeatedly found that satisfaction with how well officers dealt with members of the public relies crucially upon whether contact was 'initiated' by the person or by the police officer(s) who approach them. Broadly speaking, when the public approach the police for service they are much more likely to be satisfied with the encounter than when the police approach them unbidden, as in a stop and search (which typifies police-initiated contact). According to official figures,[3] there are around one million stop and searches each year in England, only 12 per cent of which result in arrest. Stop and search can be accomplished more or less professionally, but however it is done, it remains a grossly intrusive and humiliating experience for the person stopped. It is little wonder, then, that having been stopped and searched is closely associated with expressing dissatisfaction with the police (Bradford et al. 2009a; see also Skogan 1994; 2005; Crawford et al. 1990; Cheurprakobkit 2000; FitzGerald et al. 2002; Havis and Best 2004; Jackson et al. 2012a; Smith 1983; Skogan 1990a; Gibson et al. 2010; Weitzer and Tuch 2002; Miller et al. 2000a; Murphy 2009; Correia et al. 1996). As Skogan observes:

> ... the largest reservoir of dissatisfaction with police-initiated encounters was concentrated in those who have been stopped on foot ... The events that transpired during these stops, and the manner in which officers conducted themselves, almost totally account for the link between public assessments of the quality of the police service and social and economic divisions in the population ... (Skogan 1994: 31).

What is surprising is that so many people who are stopped and searched express *satisfaction* with how the officers conduct the encounter (Nicholas et al. 2008; Jackson et al. 2012a; see also Eith and Durose 2011; Reisig and Correia 1997; Bradford et al. 2009a; Smith 1983; Mayhew et al. 1989). This seems to extend internationally (van Dijk et al. 1990; see also Flatley et al. 2010).

---

[2] There is an intriguing exception to this rule and one that recurs, at least, in the USA in a slightly different guise. This is the propensity of middle class people to express dissatisfaction with the police. In the *Policing for London* report it is attributed to a clash of expectations, that 'may reflect greater expectations of police deference' (FitzGerald et al. 2002: 74). In the USA it is found in the lower satisfaction levels found amongst middle class African Americans.

[3] College of Policing, <https://data.police.uk/data/stop-and-search/.>

Making a complaint of criminal victimisation typifies public-initiated contact and whilst satisfaction levels are higher than those for stop and search, there is still a sizeable minority who are dissatisfied with the police. Why? The same refrain is heard repeatedly, not only in British victimisation surveys, but also internationally.

> The main reasons for dissatisfaction were that the police 'didn't do enough' ... were 'not interested' ... 'didn't find the offender' ... 'didn't recover my property' ... 'didn't keep me properly informed' ... or 'didn't treat me correctly' (van Dijk et al. 1990: 70).

Let us consider complaints as they arise in the normal sequence of police response to victimisation.

Before the police can become involved in a situation, it is necessary that they become aware of it. This is normally because the victim or some other concerned member of the public takes the trouble to *report* the incident to them. However, the majority of even quite serious crimes are never reported to the police (see numerous British Crime Surveys). Some might worry that this is a 'vote of no confidence' in the police, but very commonly it is because the offence is regarded as too trivial to justify police involvement, or could, in the eyes of the victim, better be handled through alternative means (Mayhew et al. 1993). There are incentives to report certain types of crime, for example, the procedures for insurance claims require it. However, Shapland and Vagg (1988) conclude that reporting serious crime to the police is also regarded by many as a civic duty and is not done for any instrumental purpose. When Policy Studies Institute researchers posed a series of hypothetical situations to the survey respondents, the reply was that they would report approximately two-thirds of them (Smith 1983). Very few expressed reluctance to involve the police. The exception to this was that black people, especially the young and unemployed, were more reluctant to do so because of a general antipathy to the police. It was only those scenarios of the gravest nature that overcame this reluctance and elicited willingness to report from members of this group. However, the authors stress that differences are small (Smith 1983).

Whilst there are complaints about non- or tardy attendance at the scene of the incident, this is not a major source of criticism. Most attention focuses on how police officers conducted themselves when they arrived at the scene of the alleged offence. A common refrain amongst those left dissatisfied was that the police seemed to 'lack interest' in the victim's plight and failed to 'do enough' (Skogan 1990a; 1994; Mayhew et al. 1993; Bradford et al. 2009a). One reason for this is that often there is little the police can do (Southgate and Ekblom 1986; Mayhew et al. 1989). A great deal of what appears to be investigative activity is little more than performing the 'rituals' of investigation—interviewing neighbours, 'dusting for fingerprints' and so forth. It is very unlikely that any of this will make a difference to the outcome of the case, but these 'rituals' placate and reassure victims, because it is official acknowledgement that something untoward had occurred and the victim was justified in feeling aggrieved (Mayhew

19

et al. 1993: 107; Maguire 1982). If these 'rituals' are not observed then dissatisfaction is likely to result. What is not a ritual is that victims are not kept sufficiently well informed as they should be about the progress of the case, aspects of the trial and the sentence (including the eventual release). Whilst this is a broad complaint about the criminal justice system, it tends to be the police who the public hold responsible.

However, perhaps even more important is that the police *do not* provide a 'service' to those who present themselves as a 'victim', for whilst in retail 'the customer is always right', when it comes to policing the 'customer'/victim needs to establish their 'victimhood' to the satisfaction of the officer and they may find that they become the object of suspicion themselves (contra Ekblom and Heal 1982; Reisig and Parks 2002).[4] This is often the case with sexual offences, where the defence frequently rests on the assertion that no offence was committed because the accuser *consented* to what occurred. Sometimes drunken drivers try to hide their culpability for traffic collisions by absconding from the scene and reporting that their vehicle has been 'stolen'. Brawlers often mutually accuse each other of initiating violence. House owners may occasionally allege thefts and burglaries in order to make false claims on insurance. Moreover, since the person accused of a crime is, in law, presumed innocent, then it is incumbent upon the police to test, as thoroughly as possible, whether sufficient grounds exist to merit prosecution and that entails testing the credibility of the putative victim. In an adversary system credibility does not simply reside in *what* is alleged, but also the credibility of *who* alleges it. This tends to act to the detriment of marginal sections of the population. Policy Studies Institute researchers found that in London those who became 'victims', often had previously been 'offenders' or 'suspects'. It is little wonder that victims belonging to marginal groups are also those who tend to be least satisfied with the police.

Shapland and Vagg (1988) found that victims often felt a sense of 'ownership' over their victimisation and tended to resent being marginalised by the investigation and prosecution process. What this highlights is a fundamental—yet common—misunderstanding of the criminal justice process (Angle et al. 2003; Kershaw et al. 2008; Whitehead 2001). Charges are brought, not in the name of the 'victim', but that of the Crown. This, as Nils Christie (1977) pointed out, makes victims serial losers in the criminal justice system, being 'denied rights to full participation in what might [be] one of the more important ritual encounters in life'. Until very recently 'victims' were not recognised as having any special position in the trial process. They were merely 'witnesses' with evidence to provide, where necessary. In law and procedure the crucial relationship is not between the police and the victim, but between the police and the person accused. The *Police and Criminal Evidence Act* (1984), and its Codes of Practice,

---

[4] Indeed, one might suggest that the entire literature on public attitudes to the police is misconceived, since it implies that members of the public should be satisfied with what the police do.

that regulates the exercise of police powers, contains page after page itemising in detail how the police should treat suspects. Almost no attention is paid to what 'victims' are entitled to expect. This illustrates an even more profound issue: power inequalities suffuse *any* police–public encounter. As Sykes and Brent (1983) meticulously document, on arrival at an incident it is the police who ask questions and members of the public who answer them. Anyone breaking this, so-called, 'adjacency pairing'—*Officer*: 'What's going on?' *Citizen*: 'Who wants to know?'—is likely to experience coercive treatment.

This imposed subordination is nowhere more visible than when the police use force against those they feel it necessary to subdue. 'Force' includes a wide range of physical coercion. It is rarely experienced, or even witnessed, with equanimity and is frequently an occasion for complaints of excessive use (Eith and Durose 2011; Smith 1983; Weitzer 1999; Painter et al. 1988; IPCC 2016). Occasionally, issues of use of force—usually of the most extreme form—erupt into the public sphere (such as the arrest of Rodney King, to which attention has already been drawn). What was most striking about those events was how it divided opinion along racial lines (Cullen et al. 1996; see also Jefferis et al. 1997; Kaminski and Jefferis 1998; Johnson and Kuhns 2009). 'White opinion' was much less outraged than attitudes expressed by African Americans. In India, Belur detected a widespread culture of denial, particularly prevalent amongst high status sections of the population, surrounding the apparently high proportion of 'encounters' between members of criminal gangs and the police in which the former invariably met their deaths (Belur 2009; 2010a; 2010b; 2010c). These were dismissed as mere 'encounters' and even celebrated in the news media, but rarely questioned. In Anglo-Saxon common law jurisdictions public opinion seems to be more sceptical. In England and Wales there has been controversy about police shootings, deaths in custody and public order tactics like 'kettling'. On the other hand, such controversy appears to be very short-lived (Tuch and Weitzer 1997). This suggests a profound ambivalence amongst the general population about recourse to violence by the police. Bittner (1970; 1985) recognised this ambivalence, for despite *defining* the police as 'monopolists of force in civil society', he also referred to the 'taint' that the association with violence inflicts on police officers and that 'taint' can, perhaps, be seen in how the police are viewed by the public, a significant minority of whom believe that the police frequently use excessive force (Jones et al. 1986; Smith 1983). Strikingly, Thompson and Lee (2004) found that it was middle class whites in America who were amongst the most sceptical about police use of force, especially when used against non-whites, and concluded that it provoked quite fundamental ideological beliefs.

The Rodney King incident highlights an issue mentioned previously, namely: what is 'contact'? (See Van de Walle 2009.) Contact is normally regarded as a direct, 'face-to-face' encounter between members of the public and police officers. However, almost no one who viewed the online video showing PC Harwood striking Ian Tomlinson with a baton and pushing him to the ground during disorders connected to the G20 meeting in London in 2009, was present at the scene. Nevertheless, public outrage insisted that the officer be tried in a court of law, but when a jury heard all the evidence and returned a verdict of 'not guilty' to manslaughter, this did not placate public opinion, but inflamed it. Harwood was dismissed from the Metropolitan Police for 'discreditable conduct', but the outrage lingered. (See also the Rodney King incident, above.) This raises the wider issue of *vicarious* experience, for this appears to influence opinions and reinforce stereotypes as significantly as direct experience itself (Rosenbaum et al. 2005; Hurst and Frank 2000). Thus, vicarious experience is likely to spread amongst and influence not only individuals, but also 'the socio-economic or racial group of which he is a part' (Walker et al. 1972: 68) and would now include online social networks to which the person belongs. This 'contagion' is facilitated in neighbourhoods and communities in which there has been a history of institutional oppression and corruption, where the public view the police generally in a poor light (Reynolds et al. 2008; Hwang et al. 2005; Eschholz et al. 2002; Brunson and Weitzer 2009; Smith and Gray 1983; Tuch and Weitzer 1997; Weitzer and Tuch 2004b; Myhill and Quinton 2010). Weitzer and Tuch (2004a) suggest that the mass media exert their influence not only directly on the reader or viewer, but also via the cultural 'resonance' media images have on different sections of the population, especially if it chimes with their own direct experience (see also Eschholz et al. 2002).

Thus, what appears at first glance to be a simple causal connection between contact and attitudes is actually a more subtle complex of influences that act upon individuals.

Procedural Justice

Concentrating on contact between police officers and members of the public focuses attention on the most proximal and specific influences on public attitudes to the police. The evidence is that those who gave lower approval ratings were simply reflecting their dissatisfaction with the contact they had with the police (Reisig and Parks 2000: 621). Demographic characteristics made themselves felt because police did not treat everyone alike, but instead treated people differently on the basis of age, class, ethnicity/race, gender and so forth, thus completing the chain of causality. This lent credence to complaints that had long been made about police discrimination and misconduct against groups like ethnic minorities, which gave impetus for reform. It also connected the notions of 'specific' and 'diffuse' attitudes, because what occurred *specifically* produced attitude changes *diffusely*. Such a model is consistent with theories of attitude dissonance (Festinger 1962), in which specific experimental manipulation conflicting with prior attitudes produces general attitude change (for instance, Darley and Batson 1984). On the other hand, there was no coherent explanation of what precisely were the drivers of dissatisfaction at the interactional level. What was it, exactly, that made for unsatisfactory contact? The distinction between 'police-initiated' and 'public-initiated' contact is crude and could not explain why so many of those stopped and searched seemed to have *no* complaint with how officers conducted themselves. What was required was a theoretical framework that brought conceptual order to the kaleidoscope of experience contained in a 'contact' (see Van de Walle 2009 for a comparable discussion).

This void was filled by the notion of 'procedural justice'. This is founded on the general principle that 'justice' lies mainly in *how* decisions are made, rather than their outcome. It also explicitly acknowledges that officers are figures of *authority* who are expected to act justly. What convinces members of the public that justice has been done during 'a contact' can be stated simply: any authority figure should treat others with *respect* and *fairness*, encouraging (or at least allowing) participation of interested parties in decision-making, and cultivating trustworthiness through explaining and justifying their own decisions and actions (Bluder and Tyler 2003; Mazerolle et al. 2013b; 2012). Following these precepts will be rewarded by *compliance* and long-term *rule following*, even in the absence of the authority figure, and *cooperation* even with decisions that are not to the liking or advantage of those following them. This theory has been applied and confirmed in a range of laboratory experiments and field studies (Taylor and Lawton 2012; Tyler 1990; 2004; 2011a; 2011b; Tyler and Fagan 2006; Tyler and Huo 2002; Tyler and Wakslak 2004; well summarised by Hough et al. 2010; Tyler and Hollander-Blumoff 2011; Engel 2005; McCluskey 2003; McCluskey et al. 1999; Murphy 2009; Hinds and Murphy 2007; Murphy 2004; Murphy 2013; Mastrofski et al. 1996; Reisig and Correia 1997).

This approach also has obvious theoretical synergies: the willingness to comply with procedurally just authority figures conforms to the near-universal 'norm of reciprocity' (Gouldner 1960): when people are treated respectfully and fairly, they are likely to feel that the authority figure *deserves* a respectful and fair response; on the other hand, when people are treated disrespectfully and unfairly, their response is likely to be one of *defiance* (Sherman 1993). Psychologically, to refuse compliance to a procedurally just authority figure would be not only cognitively dissonant (Festinger 1962), it would militate against one's sense of 'self' (Mead and Morris 1934).[5] Most people want others to think well of them and defying instructions reasonably made is not a recipe for being so regarded. When compared to demographic and other external considerations, procedural justice is more influential in promoting positive attitudes to the police (Tyler 2005). It even blunts the inevitably demeaning experience of being stopped and searched (Tyler 2004).

Theorising has not stopped still, but continues to develop. There has been a growth in the number of dependent variables that procedural justice has been found to influence. For instance, it encourages not only approval but also 'trust

---

[5] Note also that treating 'all persons with respect' is the first obligation under the Oath of Office, the attesting of which is the defining act of becoming a 'constable'.

and confidence' (Tyler 2004; 2011a; Jackson et al. 2012a); enhances feelings of identity with social institutions and groups (Tyler 2009); empowers discretionary decision-making (Tyler and Mitchell 1994); improves police–minority relations (Murphy 2013; Murphy and Cherney 2012); fosters support for anti-terrorism policies amongst American Muslims (Tyler et al. 2010); helps with crowd management (Stott et al. 2012); encourages the rehabilitation of offenders (Tyler et al. 2007); explains why officers comply readily with policies devised by superiors (Haas et al. 2015); and enhances the management of police officers (Roberts and Herrington 2013), including those involved in major investigations (Wheatcroft et al. 2012). It has also been recognised that the impact of any specific encounter not only has these immediate benefits, but also influences future contact. When an authority figure acts in a procedurally just manner, those affected by decisions that are made tend to infer that the authority figure has honourable intentions. This creates 'motive-based trust' which facilitates future contact and thereby increases the prospect that future contacts will conclude amicably. If errors are made by the authority figure then they tend to be 'given the benefit of the doubt'. Hence, a virtuous circle emerges as all parties invest 'motive-based trust' in each other (Tyler 2011b). This is more than a social science theory; it also 'holds out the promise of a criminal justice system predicated on a more cooperative and the exclusive relationship between the police and public than often seems to be the case' (Stanko et al. 2012: 320–1).

This is not to say that evidence universally supports the procedural justice theory or that it is without critics. For instance, Salvatore et al. (2013) found that the impact of procedural justice could be more complex than allowed by the theory. In a process reminiscent of Skogan's concept of 'negativity bias' (Skogan 2006; 2012) it was found that people expect procedural justice as a matter of course, but when denied it they are deeply affronted. Procedural justice theory also emphasises the impact of 'process', rather than 'outcomes', but Murphy (2009) found that both were more or less equally influential on those who had initiated contact with the police. This is hardly surprising, since the point of invoking police assistance is often to achieve some goal. The balance of influence shifted towards process elements when contact was *police*-initiated, which also is hardly surprising since being approached by the police is usually unwelcome in itself and one expects officers to behave properly (see also Murphy et al. 2014).

Procedural justice does not seem to be equally influential on everyone. Murphy (2015) found that it was more influential on the attitudes of younger people than it was in the case of adults. Research in 'developing' countries has found that people have other priorities: in Jamaica, whilst procedural justice improved attitudes towards the police amongst young people, they remained reluctant to say that they would *assist* the police (Reisig and Lloyd 2009). In Ghana, Tankebe (2009; 2011) found that people supported vigilantism, not because of procedural injustices by the police, but because of their ineffectual crime-fighting. He also found (Tankebe 2010) that Ghanaians preferred a modest level of police corruption rather than the impersonal approach mandated by Western notions of procedural justice. This, of course, raises the issue of how migrants from 'developing' countries adjust to different cultural expectations in the host society. Sargeant et al. (2013) found Vietnamese and Indian immigrants to Australia to be less concerned about procedural justice than they were about police performance. There may also be ethnic and racial differences amongst long settled populations: Sunshine and Tyler (2003) found that performance weighed as heavily on the attitudes of non-migrant African Americans to the police as did procedural justice. Acquired personal characteristics can also be important: Reisig et al. found that mental impairment—due to illness, drugs or alcohol—'attenuated rational decision-making' and thus discouraged deference to the police, whose attempts at persuasion had little impact (Reisig et al. 2004: 256). On the other hand, hard-bitten gang members inadvertently subscribe to the procedural justice principles in justifying their 'hating the cops' on the grounds that they are treated without respect or fairness by officers (Carr et al. 2007).

In addition to these empirical qualifications of procedural justice theory, there are also theoretical issues that arise from its precepts. How does a commitment to 'respect' and 'fairness' translate into actions? Let us consider an example:

> A favourite comment of police officers is that they try to talk to each member of the public in his/her 'own language'. They do not mean by this that they literally speak in people's 'own language'; what they do is to adjust their speech and behaviour according to whom they are dealing with. This may or may not work as intended and it will only do so if the person accepts the role into which the officer seems to have cast him (Southgate and Ekblom 1986: 27).

This approach is probably well meant—avoiding superiority—but is it respectful? If nothing else, to 'cast' someone into a role and presume to talk to them accordingly is an assertion of power: it is the officer who *casts* the person, not the person who casts themselves. Rarely is the assent of the other person sought. If police officers are 'public servants', does that not imply that their role is subservient to citizens? Yet, this is absurd, because officers are endowed with *coercive 'powers'*, which influences not only abrasive encounters, but also more positive contact. As Punch observed:

> A benign and experienced constable, polished at handling 'domestics', still brings to the situation a uniform, weaponry and a battery of resource charges which can be called upon if he fails to negotiate a satisfactory outcome (Punch 1979: 147).

It is also a common feature of policing that officers expect and often demand the respect of members of the public. Failure to show respect can lead to arrest on a variety of charges that amount to 'contempt of cop' (Hepburn 1978; Sykes and Clark 1975). It can even prompt officers to use force (Westley 1953). This is more than simply an unfortunate habit of officers; it reflects the underlying power imbalance that is present in *all* police–public encounters (Viki et al. 2006). That power imbalance means that *any* encounter is conducted on terms allowed or dictated by the officer, however subtly. This comes to the fore in the way that police officers routinely exercise their powers on the basis of suspicion that something is awry, usually that a criminal offence has been, or is being, or will be committed.[6] FitzGerald et al. (2002) found that Londoners 'took exception to being stopped and questioned when, in their view, they were simply going about their lawful business' (FitzGerald et al. 2002: 45; especially when no adequate reason for suspicion is given Smith 1983; see also Shapland and Vagg 1987). However, perfectly innocent behaviour could arouse suspicion, such as staff working on Sunday to fulfil a task incompatible with normal opening hours. This raises a further issue for procedural justice: fairness. If an officer erroneously, but honestly, forms a suspicion that an innocent person is engaged in wrongdoing, can the encounter be conducted fairly? This is a particularly acute problem when inevitably it is the officer *in situ* who must act as the sole arbiter of proof. Apart from the speed with which such a judgement may need to be formed, it is also the case that it is very likely to be formed in conditions of ambiguity, confusion and contestation. Apart from the likelihood that a person will resist the officer—orally or (less often) physically—if suspicion dissolves, then how do officers manage the closure of an encounter? The answer seems to be 'not well'.

> Officers seemed to find it very threatening either to be wrong in any way or to be accused of behaving unjustly. Apologies for mistakes were often not offered when they might reasonably have been expected. Apologies are difficult for a person whose job is, in a sense, to be right, and who is very concerned not to lose face with people he deals with in case they no longer respect him. (Southgate and Ekblom 1986: 39; see also Holdaway 1983).

Not much had changed twenty years later, when unpublished research by Waddington, Stenson and Don (an unpublished component of research published as Waddington et al. 2004) found inter alia that officers appeared to conduct 'stop and search' as a means of 'closing' otherwise inconsequential encounters with the public, creating an official record of the encounter lest there was any 'comeback'. Of course, the use of force by police merely exacerbates all these issues.

Needless to say, dealing with such circumstances makes heavy demands on the professionalism of officers. This has now been magnified by the

---

[6] The power to intervene to *prevent* an offence being committed relies inevitably on a counterfactual, ie the officer must imagine that if no intervention is made, then an offence will be committed at some future time and that intervention will forestall this happening. For instance, officers might divert opposing groups of soccer supporters to keep opponents apart and thereby unable to abuse or fight each other. By intervening, officers are unable to validate that their intervention was justified because they may 'prevent' an offence that would not have taken place in any case. However, to abstain from intervening in these circumstances would be a neglect of duty and place the officers in jeopardy.

ubiquitous presence of video recording devices with the capacity to elevate any brief encounter to public prominence through the internet (Brown and Benedict 2002; Goldsmith 2010; Brown 2016). One response has been the growth of complaints machinery, voluminous internal disciplinary codes and organisational policies and devices like 'body-worn cameras'. However, a persistent obstacle to public confidence is that such internal mechanisms appear to be the 'police investigating themselves' (Brown 1987; Russell 1976; 1978; 1986; Goldsmith 1991; 1996). Yet, those who avail themselves of institutional complaints mechanisms are surprisingly satisfied by them; what is unsurprising is that members of groups that have common experience of abrasive contact with the police simply do not avail themselves of these formal channels at all (Inglis and Shepherd 2007; Flood-Page and Taylor 2003; Sims 2003; Smith 1983).

'Legitimacy'

A recent addition to the conceptual armoury of research has been the impact of procedural justice on 'legitimacy'. For all practical purposes this has been equated with whether or not it encourages a felt obligation to obey (Jackson et al. 2012a; 2012b; 2012c). Since we will be exploring the implication of this research for the concept of legitimacy in the final chapter we will defer an in-depth discussion of it until then.

Perception

We now turn to an issue that has ran unacknowledged throughout the discussion above: it is the curiously behaviourist depiction of police–public contact that dominates the research literature. The police are implicitly regarded as *stimuli* to which members of the public *react*. This was implicit in the search for demographic correlates of variation in satisfaction, in which people with particular configurations of demographic characteristics *reacted differently* in terms of expressing satisfaction or approval. The debate was between those who attributed divergent reactions to the life circumstances of different demographic groups and those who regard it as a reaction to discriminatory policing—but in either case, causation lay in external variables. In these studies, 'explanation' was typically equated with discovering those configurations of such external characteristics that most efficiently explained statistically different reactions.

Procedural justice represents a break with this behaviourist approach, because it is founded explicitly in broader psychological theories regarding how authoritative decisions are *understood* by those whose lives are affected by them. From this, more humanistic perspective, people are deemed to *construct* trustworthiness and to *interpret* the actions of others through active processes of inference and attribution. First, 'justice' is not simply a reflection of who 'wins' and 'loses', but also involves comparing particular circumstances with universal standards of due process: decisions should be taken *fairly* after all interested parties have had an opportunity to 'have their say'. Those standards are not simply a checklist, but the active application of an *abstraction* to the empirical particularities of a specific situation. This alone is no simple or unproblematic task. Secondly, not only is an officer required to weigh evidence of whether wrongdoing has been done or is afoot, but also other participants are regarded as having the ability to infer the subjectivity of the officer and assess whether he or she has properly applied those precepts. Thirdly, officers are duty-bound not only to address what has happened and is happening, but also prevent future wrongdoing. This involves the officer imagining potential future scenarios and how to forestall those that are unwanted; but it also credits others with the ability to peer into the officer's imagination and arrive at a judgement about whether any scenario needs to be forestalled. Even when an officer gives a reason for making a decision, other interested parties will infer whether the reasoning is genuine, or whether it disguises bias. The fact that people habitually accomplish this complex task with such alacrity should not obscure its inherent complexity.

This dense subjective web is embedded in assessments of whether an officer's demeanour was 'rude', 'arrogant', 'unfriendly', 'over-casual' (Aye Maung 1995; Sims 2003) or was 'polite', 'respectful', 'courteous', 'approachable', 'friendly', 'professional', 'fair' and 'helpful' (Murphy 2009). It is also embedded in assessments that implicitly rely on notions of proportionality such as 'used *undue* force' and 'didn't do *enough*' (Skogan 1994: Table 3.8, p 33, italics added). It is also reflected in the word 'perception' (and its derivatives) that litters the literature. Methodological rigour dictates that researchers must not claim more for their data than it can properly support. Survey studies properly stop short of asserting that procedural justice was or was not *actually* a feature of the encounter, but that it was *perceived* by interviewees to have been present or absent. Perception is, of course, important in its own right, but also allows for the possibility that perceptions of the same scene by different participants may come to varying conclusions. Perceptions may be false, distorted and even contradictory (FitzGerald et al. 2002; Rosenbaum et al. 2005; Mayhew et al. 1993; Lasley 1994; Viki et al. 2006; Henderson et al. 1997; Higgins et al. 2008). It is impossible to know whether police *actually* failed to adhere to the standards of 'procedural justice' or whether those who concluded that the encounter had proven unsatisfactory were more inclined to interpret events in a way consistent with how they subsequently felt about it (Murphy 2009: 175; see also Schafer et al. 2003).

> Was a stop, or at least the reasons given for it, justified? Was the officer polite? Did it appear that the police took their complaint seriously? The way in which behaviours by the police that are associated with these questions are interpreted could easily be collared by the metal frame imposed upon the encounter from the outset (Skogan 2012: 276; see also Brandl et al. 1994; Weitzer 1999; Rosenbaum et al. 2005; Myhill and Quinton 2010; Stewart et al. 2014; Kleinig 2009; Lasley 1994).

This 'mental frame' is incorporated into concepts like 'motive–based trust' that suggests that prior experience and inferences influence the perceptions that are made at a later time (Tyler 2011b; see also Hurst and Frank 2000; Hwang et al. 2005; Reisig and Chandek 2001). These expectations of future conduct are rarely value-free predictions, but rather entail notions of *entitlement*, and if these are not met, then the person can feel affronted (Burrows 1986; Lowe and Innes 2012). Judgements of another's future conduct may be individual perceptions independently arrived at, or shared cultural understandings relying on vicarious experiences (Decker 1981; Karstedt 2009; Reisig and Parks 2000; Rosenbaum et al. 2005; Lloyd and Foster 2009; Sivasubramaniam and Goodman-Delahunty 2008; Eschholz et al. 2002; Bradley 1998; Leiber et al. 1998). It is also not clear whether specific experiences influence diffuse attitudes, rather than the reverse (Brandl et al. 1994; Wu et al. 2009). We also need to keep in mind what is sometimes overlooked in the literature: that police–public encounters are *inter*actions between people who are actively constructing meanings about themselves, each other, their circumstances and the context. What applies to members of the public, applies equally to the police. They too rely on perceptions and understandings that might be erroneous, prejudicial and biased (Amendola 1996; Parker et al. 1995).

Neither is this process of subjective inference without its practical and policy consequences: Bradford et al. (2014) describe longitudinal research confirming that procedural justice can prompt a virtuous cycle in which relationships between police officers and local people become progressively positive. This is consistent with the benign image of 'community policing' (Ren et al. 2005); the National Police Reassurance Programme rested on the observation that a community-based policing policy 'could serve to reduce both actual and *perceived* levels of crime and disorder, as well as to improve the public's *perceptions* of the police' (Carole Willis's forward to Tuffin et al. 2006, italics added).[7] Do the police concentrate on reforming their actual behaviour, or on public perceptions of it? It would be naïve to suppose that if the police change their behaviour, this would be recognised and appreciated in the way that they intended (Brogden 1983).

Yet, despite the central importance of perception in any explanation of public attitudes to the police and notwithstanding its frequent explicit acknowledgement, it largely goes without the attention it rightly deserves.

Conclusions

The literature on public attitudes to the police is voluminous. It is worth reiterating that the police receive high levels of specific and diffuse support, but some

---

[7] Note that the distinction between 'actual and perceived' is tacit recognition that perceptions may be erroneous.

minorities are less enthusiastic in giving praise than others. What seems to be crucial (not surprisingly) is how the police deal with the public and especially whether they adhere or not to standards of procedural justice. However, the police role is ambiguous, for they are 'public servants' and yet exercise powers *over* those they notionally serve. How, for instance, does an officer use force whilst treating people respectfully? Our research was designed to address these issues directly by examining how people perceived actual examples of specific, more or less routine, encounters between officers and members of the public. In the following chapter we will explain and justify how we did this.

How We Did the Research

Introduction

Two of the principal issues to emerge from the previous discussion will be the focus of this volume: 'specificity' and 'perception'. To address these issues this research relied on two methodologies that will be considered in this chapter: the use of video clips as a medium for delivering vignettes or scenarios; and focus groups as a forum for research participants to discuss their evaluations of the officers depicted in those video clips. Let us consider each in turn.

Video Clips

In the previous chapter, we saw that researchers have progressively shifted the explanatory emphasis away from broad generalities about 'the police' towards how they were treated by police officers during recent contact. We also recognised that this amounted to each individual describing and/or evaluating a unique event, which defied objective verification. The fact that a person who found their most recent contact unsatisfactory also believes that the officer(s) had been disrespectful, did not equate with the officer having *actually* been disrespectful. It was at least as likely that because the person was dissatisfied with the officers, they would recall the episode as one in which they were treated disrespectfully. This is not a unique problem: in psychological research, perceptual bias is often studied using ambiguous images that are displayed to subjects who are asked what they see and thereby reveal their perceptual biases. In this research we adopted a similar approach, selecting standardised images of police–public encounters and inviting people to assess the behaviour of officers.

A readily available supply of such images is provided by the BBC, from which copies of programmes (including extracts) can be purchased on licence. 'Reality' programmes, like *Traffic Cops*, show episodes of police–public contact that could be shown to research participants and to which they would be invited to

give their appraisal. Waddington had amassed a significant library of such videos for his own use. These programmes contained a total of 292 separate incidents. Various factors were taken into consideration when selecting a shortlist.
Clips were excluded when: first, the time and date of broadcast was unknown;
secondly, when the clip displayed straightforward arrests of people unproblem-
atically found committing offences, such as disqualified drivers found driving
vehicles; thirdly, where contact with members of the public was non-existent
or very peripheral, such as raids on premises for drugs where suspects were
glimpsed being bundled into 'prisoner transport' vehicles; and, finally, if the
camera arrived at an incident at which other officers were already in attendance
and the role of the featured crew was merely supportive, such as major traffic
collisions where casualties were surrounded by paramedics and firefighters, and
police were left to sweep debris from the carriageway. A further consideration
was that the video clip should raise issues of wider and enduring criminological
interest, such as racism, use of force, 'contempt of cop', criminal investigation,
vulnerable victims and so forth. Various video clips were considered for inclusion before, eventually, ten clips were selected as representing a range of sufficiently problematic encounters to arouse interest. These were then piloted by
showing them to a sample of volunteers from the notably diverse student body
at the University of Wolverhampton who were asked to rate each clip on a brief
questionnaire according to how positively or negatively they evaluated the conduct of officers depicted therein. The questionnaire also included space for the
respondents to insert any comments and many did so. The final selection of
five video clips (lasting in total just over twenty-five minutes) was selected by
taking the most and least favoured clips, and three of those from the remainder
about which there was most disagreement amongst this pilot sample. The final
sample of five video clips all featured officers who appeared to be very experienced in policing. Three video clips featured 'roads policing' officers, but only
one of these involved a specifically 'roads policing' issue. Even that one—concerning a suspected stolen car being driven on a motorway—was not a 'traffic
offence', but instead a suspicion of criminal wrongdoing. The other incidents
dealt with by 'traffic' officers were a home invasion and robbery of an elderly
man and the drowning of a reveller who appeared to have fallen into a disused
dock around which several 'night-time economy' venues were located.[1] One
of the remaining two video clips involved a plain-clothes officer apparently
stationed within a large shopping mall, who was alerted by security staff that
three young men were breaking into a car in the car park. The final video clip
featured a group of officers deployed as a mobile 'public order' unit who made
a forceful arrest of an 'aggressive man' outside an entertainment venue in the
early hours of the morning. Thus, this selection of video clips depicts policing
that is rather different from the policing that typically occurs 'on the streets',
because all four of the video clips to be discussed here involve officers dealing

---

[1] This video clip is not featured in this book for reasons of space.

with criminal matters—talking to victims and suspects, and, in three of them, using powers of arrest—with a focus on 'crime-fighting' that might be assumed to favour the police. The video clips also depicted a flattering image of policing because the police were actively engaged in discrete tasks, reflecting the inevitable bias of broadcasters to show action-packed incidents, rather than the more mundane realities of policing. On the other hand, there was nothing that was egregious in the conduct of the officers; after all, the video clips had been broadcast to viewers. Of course, the officers featured in the video clips, those whom they directly encountered and bystanders would all have been aware of the presence of a bulky video camera, which perhaps encouraged featured officers to behave in accordance with good practice.[2] Hence, the inevitable bias in our data favours the police. However, this detracted from our research aims hardly at all, because, crucially, it remained the case that our focus group participants would all be evaluating exactly the same police–public encounter. Moreover, we sought to examine why more or less routine encounters aroused negative assessments of police conduct, rather than the impact of egregious wrongdoing.

Vignettes, Scenarios and Context

Our approach represents a departure from the 'stimulus–response' model that dominates the literature on attitudes to the police. The stimulus–response model aspires to find a question or statement that evokes the very particular attitude that is the focus of attention. If done thoroughly, attitude scales emerge from the meticulous sifting and editing of questions or statements to ensure that they truly measure what they purport to measure, and nothing else. It is essentially a process of distillation, trying to find the 'key' that unlocks each person's attitude about a given subject. Apart from being time-consuming, arduous and expensive, this is an approach that rests on questionable *a priori* assumptions, for it assumes that specific features of the world around us stimulate equally specific dispositions. However, people do not experience the world as a disaggregated jumble of stimuli, but as a coherent whole. Our video clips were just such a collection of coherent whole episodes. What they represent, we maintain, is an example of a fundamentally different approach to the elicitation of attitudes. However, we do not claim any proprietorship over the method since it has emerged largely unheralded over almost a century of social science inquiry in the guise of 'vignettes' or 'scenarios'.

In the 1930s Piaget (1932; see also Kohlberg 1968) pioneered vignettes in his research into the moral development of young children. He posed moral dilemmas to children of different ages and recorded the growing sophistication of their reasoning. In criminology, Stanton Wheeler (1968) posed moral dilemmas to prisoners at different stages of their incarceration. More recently, Waddington

---

[2] Although in the judgement of Martin Wright, a retired member of the West Midlands Police, there were plentiful examples of poor practice displayed in these video clips.

et al. (2009) presented officers in six countries with a fictitious, complex unfolding scenario in which police characters escalated their use of force to apprehend two suspects. Roberts and Hough (2011) described the facts of criminal cases and invited interviewees to impose an appropriate sentence and discovered that people were more lenient than the courts had been in the actual cases, debunking the idea that the public has a more punitive appetite than the courts. Cullen et al. (1996) also used the circumstances about a court case—the famous 1985 Supreme Court case of *Tennessee v Garner*—to explore the public's views on police use of force. Haas et al. (2014) posed fictitious vignettes that were subtly manipulated to test whether people would or would not support vigilantism under slightly different circumstances.

In all these examples, and many more, the aim is to contextualise the 'stimulus' in much the same way that it would be encountered in the real world. For instance, Klockars et al. (2004) presented interviewees with vignettes of police wrongdoing and asked respondents to rate the seriousness of the infraction, what action would be taken in respect of it in their organisation and so forth. One such vignette was:

> At 2 am, a police officer, who is on duty, is driving a patrol car on a deserted road. She sees a vehicle that has been driven off the road and is stuck in a ditch. She approaches the vehicle and observes that the driver is not hurt but is obviously intoxicated. She also finds that the driver is an off–duty police officer. Instead of reporting this accident and offence, she transports the driver to his home.

By placing wrongdoing in context, the aim of the authors was to pose the kind of moral dilemma that might be encountered in actual circumstances, for example, the driver was drunk but the road was deserted and no harm was done to a third party, and he was a fellow officer. However, herein are exposed the limits of the *textual* vignette methodology, for the amount of detail conveyed by a written vignette can vary from meagre and selective accounts to rich and exhaustive detail. The vignette above tells us very little about the participants in the story. Neither the degree of the driver's intoxication nor the severity of the accident is clear. Real-life factors that might have made a difference to the respondents' assessment of seriousness are left to conjecture. On the other hand, why draw attention to the gender of the on-duty officer? Is this designed to alert the interviewee to gender issues in policing? If the vignette is intended to be realistic, then much more information would be required about the situation. But to do so in a written vignette would consume so much time that it would test interviewees' patience and limit the number of vignettes that could be employed.

Verisimilitude and Technology

Technological advances offer a ready solution to this problem: video clips provide significantly more information at a glance than is possible with a written vignette. Interviewees can witness simultaneously the demeanour, speech and actions of all the participants as it actually occurred. They might pay attention to any of a host of cues without any of them being explicitly drawn to their attention. If researchers are interested in the effects of gender on police–public contact, the videos could contain a mixture of incidents in which officers are either male or female, or belong to a mixed crew. In other words, it affords greater verisimilitude compared to other modes of delivery.

At the same time, the video clip retains the standardisation of written vignettes. If different sections of the population respond differently to exactly the same video clip, then the explanation for those differences lies not in the behaviour portrayed, but in the subjective judgements applied to it. On the other hand, if everyone agrees that some aspect of the officers' behaviour is noteworthy, then this may suggest a common cultural disposition.

Waddington (1993) has exploited technology to produce real-life scenarios to present to interviewees. When people call the police for assistance, the police telephone system automatically records the conversation and thus provides a supply of audio vignettes containing all the information available to the call handler at the time of the original call. These recordings can later be replayed to interviewees who are asked to say how they would have dealt with the call. This can elicit distinctive patterns of response from interviewees. One caller, concerned about her missing fourteen-year-old son gave her address as a notorious street in a dilapidated area of the town. Once this was disclosed by the caller, a group of officers to whom the recording was replayed spontaneously erupted into gleeful mirth, amid derogatory remarks about the caller, the missing boy and the circumstances in which he had disappeared. This amply illustrated the unseemly side of police culture. In this case, those completing the questionnaire had only audible information to go on, but they shared that handicap with actual call handlers and at least everyone could hear the woman's voice and gauge her distress, none of which needed to be specially highlighted.

Acquiring Suitable Video Clips

The issue is how to source suitable material. Police forces have videos that are used for training purposes, in which trainers act out various parts. Unfortunately, these are, predictably, amateurish and the plots suitably simplistic to highlight the training purpose. Secondly, there are dramatic portrayals of policing which have the advantage of sometimes posing acute ethical dilemmas; the film *Dirty Harry* has given its name to a fundamental issue in policing—the use of illegitimate means to achieve legitimate ends (Klockars 1985). However, the demands of drama often overwhelm the mundane qualities of much police work and detract from verisimilitude. Thirdly, there are 'fly-on-the-wall' documentaries that have become common on television, representing a vast, but hitherto unused, store of video clips that could be used as vignettes for research purposes. There are distinct advantages to using this source: (a) these series collectively contain a considerable number of distinct episodes of police–citizen encounters covering a wide array of circumstances; (b) whilst there is an obvious tendency to focus on scenes of some kind of action, many of the episodes depict mundane reality; and (c) verisimilitude is maintained.

The fact that television documentaries are not produced for the purpose of academic research, and the behaviour depicted in them may not be representative, does not reduce their utility for research. The purpose of vignettes is to stimulate and provoke judgements by interviewees, not necessarily to reflect 'reality' in all its complexity. Newspaper articles that make no pretensions to objectivity have been successfully employed (Sasson 1995; Gamson 1992; Dixon and Gadd 2006). On the other hand, research that aims to study public appraisals of *routine* police–public encounters would seek to avoid episodes that were unduly sensational or otherwise inappropriate. 'Reality' television programmes, like those from which our video clips were taken, have a reputation for presenting a favourable image of the police and policing; for example, they tend to show officers as more active than they are in reality. However, previous research has found that audiences respond in ways that reflect patterns of opinion expressed through surveys, most notably that African Americans respond to such videos less favourably than other ethnic groups (Eschholz et al. 2002).

There are limitations to the use of video clips as vignettes: first, they are edited for broadcast from the 'rushes' recorded at the scene. Hence, incidents which may have taken several hours to resolve may be depicted in just a few minutes, and what is discarded 'on the cutting room floor' may provide information that, if known to focus groups, might have affected their opinions. By the same token, the attention of focus groups could and should not be needlessly taxed by lengthy displays of videos containing no important information. It is also likely that many police–public encounters are brief or the view of third parties is fragmentary and of short duration. In 'real life', focus group participants would be unlikely to see the whole incident, but a snippet from it. Secondly, the view of the camera may be partial; for instance, it is recorded from a police point of view. The camera accompanies officers to the scene of the incident and is privy to any information provided en route, which would be hidden from other members of the public. Thirdly, once at the scene the camera is effectively an 'onlooker' or 'bystander', rather than a 'victim' or 'suspect'. The perceptions of parties to the encounter are likely to differ markedly from those of a disinterested 'onlooker' and we do not suggest otherwise. However, we will see in the final chapter that this is perhaps a blessing in disguise, since the perspective of the disinterested 'bystander' may be more important to the process of legitimation than the views of 'victims', 'suspects' and even 'witnesses'. Finally, the presence of the camera is unlikely to go unnoticed and may have influenced how incidents developed. What we *do* maintain is that the video clips displayed to our focus groups were of high verisimilitude compared to alternative means of representing what occurred in a particular situation and, most importantly, they were exactly the same from one group to the next.

Hitherto, there was a major obstacle to the use of video clips as research vignettes—copyright. According to the Education Recording Agency,[3] whilst off-air video recordings can be used *within* educational establishments, this does not extend to conducting academic research beyond the academy. Broadcasters have showed little interest in making available copies of videos for this purpose. However, this has recently changed with the creation of the *BBC Motion Gallery* and the comparable archives of other broadcasters. Not only has this opened up to wider use the vast archive of broadcast material stored by the BBC, but also makes available clips from individual programmes that are exactly suited for use as vignettes in research. Being restricted (at the time) to only BBC output was a limitation, but not a fatal one, since the BBC archive was extensive. *Motion Gallery* supplied material with a one-year licence for public display and using this archive thus avoided copyright problems. By carefully specifying the location and duration of each clip, or portion thereof, it was possible to effectively excise 'to-camera' interviews that often accompany video recorded at the scene and in which officers often justified their actions, which might have influenced our focus groups. We were also able to mute voice-over commentaries that tend to give a distinctive slant on what the camera was recording. What could not be removed was the pervasive background music, which tended to add an air of drama to incidents and moments within them.

Focus Groups

The use of video clips is unconnected with how the responses of research participants are recorded. There is no reason why participants could not have been asked to complete a questionnaire or attitude scale to rate whether officers depicted in the video clip had treated others with 'respect', or had been 'polite', or not. We decided against doing so, not least because the literature showed no settled way in which to express attitudes. What the British Crime Survey demonstrated, moreover, was the remarkable sensitivity of respondents to the precise terms in which attitudes were elicited. Between the 2002/03 and 2003/04 surveys, the phrasing of the 'response categories' that survey respondents used to rate their local police was altered, with a marked impact upon the results obtained (Scribbins et al. 2010).

We reasoned that since there was no form of words that could be relied upon to produce a valid picture, it was safer to allow respondents to respond in whatever way they chose. The only limitation was that once each video clip was viewed, our participants were asked to complete a short version of the crude questionnaire used to elicit the views of pilot groups. They were invited to express on an eleven-point scale ('+5' to '–5') how positively or negatively they assessed the officers depicted in the video. They were also invited to write in a text box

---

[3] See <http://www.era.org.uk.>

anything they wanted to say in their own words. It was reasoned that this would focus their attention on the police officers (rather than others depicted in the video, such as suspects and victims). This data plays no part in this analysis.

Focus Group Discussion

Focus group participants were invited to express their opinions and almost invariably this provoked vibrant and animated discussion, which was recorded in digital audio format.[4] We eschewed transcription of the discussion of each focus group on the grounds that it would amount to a severe loss of qualitative non-verbal information. Transcription for the purposes of publication was left until the manuscript of this book was produced, so that all decisions about the handling of the data would be based upon full audio recordings of discussions.[5] However, we did code the discussions using NVivo8 software, in which portions of the soundtrack of each discussion were identified by a mixture of 'deductive' and 'inductive' coding categories.

Deductively, we were influenced by Fielding's research on community policing (Fielding 1995), which follows the temporal sequence of an encounter. The temporal dimension was less relevant for our focus group discussions, but an equivalent framework suggested itself: Who? Where? When? What? How? Focus group discussions were coded according to their referents in the video clip: *who* were the 'characters' in the video clip to which our focus group were referring? This often involved empathetically appreciating what participants meant when they used identifiers, such as 'he, they, him'. Since the number of characters appearing in any clip tended to be limited, it was not difficult to identify whether it was a police officer, suspect, bystander, victim or some other person. In making this judgement we relied heavily on the context in which the attributed actions took place. If a participant observed that 'He pulled over straight away', it was evident from the context that this referred to the *only* vehicle that the police had stopped! Other cues were contained in the complex of the framework. *Where* had limited utility, since most of the encounter was limited to the same place, even where that 'place' was a motorway stretching over several miles. *When* referred to the stage of the encounter referred to. Thus, if a participant remarked, 'When he went to the door ...', then it was clear that the participant was referring to the officer who knocked the door of an elderly man's bungalow where a robbery had allegedly taken place. If someone said, 'When he was taking the statement ...', it was clear that this referred to the officer's crewmate who was filmed writing a statement made by the elderly

---

[4] Anonymised copies of which are now available from the Economic and Social Data Archive.

[5] It is worth mentioning that no attempt has been made to reproduce the various accents used by our participants. 'Black country' English alone is varied and difficult to express in text—'he woe' could mean 'he didn't or couldn't'. Since, as Pinker (1995) reminds us, language is used to convey meaning and so extracts have been transcribed to remain as faithful to the original utterances as possible without sacrificing their meaning.

man. *What* was it about the police officer(s)' behaviour that drew comment? *How* did they describe police officers as behaving?

Whilst the 'who', 'where', 'when', 'what', 'how' classification applied to all video clips, it is equally clear that the specifics of each situation demanded detailed coding according to the circumstances. For instance, in one video clip police personnel at the scene included two Scenes of Crime Officers and our focus groups usually distinguished them from the two uniformed officers. Hence, within the 'Who?' category for *this* video clip there was a code for 'police' and another for 'SOCOs' ('Scenes of Crime Officers'). These codings were, of necessity, specific to each video clip. 'What?' and 'How?' were not only specific, but attempted to interpret the quality of what was said by focus group partici-pants as they discussed the officers' handling of the various encounters. In this sense, the codings aimed to grasp the meanings of participants inductively.

Finally, each portion of the sound track was assessed for whether the content and tone of the discussion was 'very positive', 'positive', 'negative', or 'very negative' towards the police officers depicted in the video clip. On some occa-sions discussion was such that both positive and negative opinions jostled for attention and so these passages were coded simultaneously as both positive and negative. Five focus groups were selected at random and coded indepen-dently by two researchers. Their respective codings agreed on more than 75 per cent of occasions and the variation was largely attributable to the start and end points of the portion of audio recording to which the codes were applied. There were no cases in which gross disparities arose, and consequently we were confident that a high level of inter-coder reliability was achieved.

In the interests of transparency, Tables 2.1–2.4 present the coding frameworks for each of the video clips together with the cross-tabulated evaluative frame-work. The cells contain NVivo's aggregation of the total time devoted to each combination in minutes and seconds. However, it is important to note that this coding exercise was used merely as a tool to guide analytical attention. It was through listening to the focus group discussions and interpreting the meaning that was given to the video clips that we arrived at our analytical conclusions. Hence, whilst the figures given here reflect the strict co-occurrence of codings, for interpretative purposes we extended listening beyond the strict boundaries of the codes in order to preserve context.

Focus Group Selection

We strove to select focus groups from diverse neighbourhoods through-out the 'Black Country' of the West Midlands comprising Wolverhampton, Dudley, Walsall and Sandwell. The West Midlands is ethnically diverse and suffers high levels of deprivation; features that are concentrated in the 'Black Country' region, with Sandwell being counted amongst the twenty most deprived areas in the country and all four 'Black Country' authorities figur-ing in the most deprived half of authorities throughout the West Midlands

Table 2.1 Robbery of Elderly Man in His Home

Deductive	Inductive	Assessment of police			
		Very positive	Positive	Negative	Very negative
Who	Police	40:55.1	51:17.4	1:03:37.1	14:01.2
	• First officer to enter home	34:22.0	52:35.3	1:03:04.1	27:16.4
	• Crewmate	31:01.3	37:05.8	41:19.0	22:23.3
	• SOCOs	13:52.1	14:48.7	10:08.7	2:04.7
	• CID	8:03.5	12:02.5	8:11.2	1:56.6
	• Officers searching for robber	0:00.0	0:00.0	0:57.5	0:38.6
	• Police generically	0:01.4	2:54.5	3:41.1	2:03.8
	Not police	12:58.1	24:56.3	45:12.0	30:42.6
	• Elderly man	8:43.9	13:19.0	29:25.1	12:31.8
	• Chantelle	5:35.1	15:41.2	33:17.6	33:27.5
Where	Inside home	31:41.5	35:26.6	51:45.9	28:27.1
	Outside home	8:12.5	13:37.2	10:45.1	7:29.6
When	Arrival and first contact with Chantelle	7:52.8	12:35.4	17:12.9	11:30.7
	Entering the sitting room and talking to elderly man & Chantelle	17:22.5	23:02.9	41:05.6	21:59.4
	Taking statements	13:50.5	17:21.2	21:39.1	11:54.4
	Forensic examination	8:44.6	6:25.4	3:30.4	1:13.5
	Leaving	1:52.0	3:11.6	8:35.1	4:26.6
	Throughout incident	15:24.2	18:09.7	22:38.2	14:44.3
What	Attendance	8:44.9	12:39.5	9:44.9	6:49.1
	Relationship between elderly man and Chantelle	0:34.2	5:02.2	12:29.6	7:18.6
	Investigation	37:46.2	41:49.0	48:05.0	22:56.3
	Knife marks	1:16.6	2:45.3	2:13.7	5:47.4
	Psychological condition of both victims	0:00.0	1:00.7	1:45.3	3:09.2
	Medical attention	3:46.8	12:01.8	22:41.2	12:08.3
	Aftercare	1:55.6	4:29.7	9:41.0	7:36.9
	Looking at watch	0:19.6	0:47.0	1:27.2	0:01.3
How	Routine	0:50.8	5:49.1	9:07.7	6:44.9
	Friendly & informal	7:27.1	2:55.7	5:22.6	3:27.4

Deductive	Inductive	Assessment of police			
		Very positive	Positive	Negative	Very negative
	Urgency/Seriousness	14:33.8	19:33.0	26:03.4	7:27.4
	Sensitive/Considerate	13:13.5	15:42.9	27:10.7	20:39.2
	Competent/Thorough	28:01.4	44:55.2	49:44.3	22:09.7
	Suspicion	8:53.0	26:13.9	30:25.5	14:20.9
	Calm/agitated	7:01.2	3:40.9	0:54.9	0:05.0
	Polite/impolite	1:23.8	0:58.7	0:43.8	0:59.3
Other	Authenticity of crime	7:50.8	20:53.0	30:48.6	33:35.4
	Relating to other events	1:21.1	6:49.3	3:52.7	3:51.4
	Camera	0:26.5	1:39.0	3:01.8	0:28.1
	Partner agencies	0:03.1	1:20.1	0:00.0	3:11.7
	Perceptions of the public	02:17.1	06:23.9	04:09.6	04:57.1

Table 2.2 Stopping Suspected Stolen Car on the Motorway

Deductive	Inductive	Assessment of police			
		Very positive	Positive	Negative	Very negative
Who	Car occupants				
	• Car passenger	0:00.0	0:08.7	0:00.0	0:42.3
	• Driver of car	12:34.5	27:27.7	26:13.4	32:22.1
	Others				
	• Dealers	0:02.4	1:31.8	2:00.0	2:14.1
	• Filling station	1:18.9	0:17.0	3:35.8	1:19.5
	Police	31:53.4	43:40.1	36:09.3	2:09:10.6
	• Officers arriving later	0:09.9	0:00.0	0:44.7	0:49.6
	• Patrol car crew	28:06.0	38:25.0	30:27.0	2:03:56.5
	o Driver	23:48.7	32:53.7	39:10.5	1:44:57.7
	o Passenger	26:40.0	36:29.3	30:16.6	1:36:12.7
	o VDRS officers	5:42.5	7:07.5	9:21.6	6:30.3
Where	Motorway carriageway	16:07.7	16:59.7	12:58.2	23:55.6
	Hard shoulder	19:02.5	28:29.6	20:32.1	1:12:25.0
	Inside patrol car	13:35.4	18:34.7	29:50.7	1:20:54.9
When	Following	13:27.6	13:22.8	13:37.1	18:46.2
	Stopping	12:48.3	11:22.3	8:51.1	19:35.5

(*continued*)

Table 2.2 (Continued)

Deductive	Inductive	Assessment of police			
		Very positive	Positive	Negative	Very negative
	Arrest of driver	20:56.9	29:35.9	25:30.1	1:20:06.5
	Explaining reasons for arrest	0:51.6	0:14.9	0:11.0	4:30.7
	Investigation of plates	0:31.9	2:26.2	3:31.7	1:46.7
	Conversation with driver	13:54.1	18:03.4	30:34.6	1:22:25.7
What	Suspicion re car	9:24.1	24:28.6	26:44.5	28:48.9
	Mobilising assistance	6:45.3	4:19.0	3:46.2	3:56.7
	Car pulling over	6:12.0	6:01.4	5:04.9	9:26.5
	Struggle on hard shoulder	17:29.4	20:37.8	19:20.9	1:10:44.3
	Discussing VDRS	8:13.4	14:08.9	23:24.2	1:01:05.6
	Fine	5:54.0	5:55.7	7:44.6	31:35.7
	Allowing driver to drive away	0:00.0	0:03.1	0:02.5	4:17.6
	Referring to driver's age	0:04.9	0:49.0	0:16.4	8:35.2
	S.5 re swearing	1:36.7	0:20.5	4:43.8	14:43.0
	Absence of VDRS record	0:02.3	0:48.1	5:05.0	1:40.0
	No apology	1:07.5	3:44.4	2:11.0	6:26.3
	14 days	7:38.2	13:49.7	18:26.2	14:44.3
	Remaining on hard shoulder	0:03.1	0:00.0	0:45.1	0:51.5
	Not handcuffing driver in the police car	0:03.1	0:00.0	0:51.1	0:55.3
How	Action	0:00.0	0:35.4	4:17.9	3:49.2
	Calm	0:00.0	0:32.0	0:25.8	1:48.4
	Credibility	0:00.0	0:56.6	2:28.9	0:00.0
	Legality	0:00.0	0:33.8	2:28.9	0:16.9
	Tension high	0:00.0	0:00.0	0:00.0	2:45.2
	Aggression	15:03.4	20:42.6	16:42.4	1:18:23.1
	Sarcasm— condescension— patronising	2:18.7	8:42.5	11:06.5	44:55.7
	Belittlement— demeaning	0:26.9	1:26.7	2:20.5	23:47.7
	Malice	5:22.0	1:46.6	5:35.8	29:39.3
	Prejudice	2:26.4	3:06.9	6:12.7	17:40.5
	Reference to age	0:18.1	0:52.5	1:32.8	9:35.7
	Danger	6:40.0	8:24.5	9:56.7	22:28.5

| Deductive | Inductive | Assessment of police | | | |
		Very positive	Positive	Negative	Very negative
	Necessity	24:50.4	27:37.2	30:15.1	1:39:08.8
	Competence	32:05.4	35:51.0	41:25.9	1:22:17.5
	Cooperation	11:09.1	11:42.2	12:29.3	23:06.9
	Annoyance	1:31.6	5:55.3	10:49.2	6:30.5
	Arrogance	0:01.5	2:48.2	3:22.2	8:35.2
Other	Camera	0:00.0	3:52.8	0:50.6	3:16.6
	Immediate reaction	0:30.0	1:22.1	1:25.1	7:32.3
	Perception of the public	0:10.8	1:16.0	5:05.1	1:14.6
	Related to other experiences	4:09.5	9:38.4	9:48.4	32:35.8

Table 2.3 Suspected Car Theft in Superstore Car Park

| Deductive | Inductive | Assessment of Police | | | |
		Very positive	Positive	Negative	Very negative
Who	Police	30:07.0	49:13.9	54:49.4	28:50.1
	• Police officer	37:43.6	53:21.4	57:57.8	44:27.4
	• Police generic	0:40.4	6:06.2	7:37.6	6:59.7
	Suspect(s)	5:36.9	5:31.2	20:19.2	23:10.4
	• Arrested	2:54.4	0:51.1	1:25.6	3:40.9
	• De-arrested	0:30.8	0:16.1	0:56.0	0:22.6
	Others				
	• Security staff	0:21.2	0:18.1	1:19.7	0:54.6
	• Victim(s)	0:29.1	1:31.8	1:24.6	3:32.5
	• Witnesses, bystanders et al.	0:28.8	0:55.5	2:41.1	3:39.5
Where	Car park				
When	Arrival	8:39.9	21:53.3	35:34.8	28:33.4
	Kicking off	24:26.0	33:07.0	43:19.8	46:54.1
	Entry	22:01.8	43:24.1	1:04:54.0	46:00.5
	Encounter	2:15.2	1:02.7	7:41.8	3:05.9
	Exit	10:04.1	7:03.7	5:18.0	5:20.6
What	Age	0:00.0	0:34.8	2:36.8	0:19.5

(continued)

Table 2.3 (Continued)

Deductive	Inductive	Assessment of Police			
		Very positive	Positive	Negative	Very negative
	Apology	0:00.7	0:00.0	1:26.7	0:30.0
	Appearance	2:08.5	10:03.9	22:56.8	16:12.6
	Arrest	26:05.3	40:49.3	50:09.7	47:41.3
	Capacity	0:09.5	0:36.9	0:59.6	0:39.5
	Communication	2:51.4	1:14.8	3:10.9	7:41.4
	Control	12:48.9	20:55.3	24:23.6	13:47.3
	Dangerous	4:47.1	11:27.1	2:54.4	0:24.2
	Ethnicity	9:44.8	4:53.8	3:42.2	6:55.6
	Gender	0:00.0	0:00.0	0:00.0	0:31.3
	Innocence	7:03.4	13:00.3	25:17.8	26:24.6
	Investigation	10:06.9	13:16.4	16:57.6	22:48.3
	Number of officers	4:57.9	9:32.8	8:30.2	8:20.7
	Public space	0:17.8	0:00.0	0:00.0	0:00.0
	Responsibility for outcome	5:38.2	3:26.9	27:36.2	39:21.6
	Teamwork	0:13.8	0:19.6	1:11.6	0:00.0
How	Action	3:54.4	2:49.4	6:35.3	5:11.3
	Aggressive (force)	7:22.3	16:36.7	20:25.8	15:41.4
	Aggressive (verbal)	9:46.3	10:25.6	17:48.7	19:56.2
	Calm	7:56.8	5:56.5	12:56.1	15:44.6
	Compassionate	0:00.7	0:47.6	1:19.8	0:01.4
	Competent	14:39.7	17:04.0	19:44.0	23:05.0
	Compliant, helpful	1:22.9	1:43.4	6:49.2	7:09.3
	Credibility	5:04.1	4:26.9	14:57.4	14:51.4
	Discrimination	9:11.3	5:01.0	5:29.0	4:52.2
	Fair	14:31.4	16:26.3	22:05.0	25:09.8
	Formality	2:28.4	9:17.5	14:36.9	13:25.9
	Legality	5:29.6	8:17.4	9:01.1	11:40.2
	Malign	0:02.1	0:00.0	0:06.6	3:07.0
	Proportionate	13:51.3	19:20.1	20:42.3	21:23.4
	Respectful	0:04.4	3:53.8	4:26.8	6:10.8
	Spite	0:00.0	0:50.2	0:00.7	2:31.4

Deductive	Inductive	Assessment of Police			
		Very positive	Positive	Negative	Very negative
Other	Camera	0:20.1	1:01.0	1:12.8	0:46.7
	Public perception	1:25.5	1:35.5	3:14.9	3:25.5
	Specific to the police force concerned	0:19.4	1:09.0	0:42.1	0:19.7

Table 2.4 Violent Arrest Outside Nightclub

Deductive	Inductive	Assessment of police			
		Very positive	Positive	Negative	Very negative
Who	Police	12:31.6	56:48.5	57:07.0	14:22.1
	Arrested man	0:15.2	0:02.3	0:34.5	2:42.0
	Bystanders	0:00.0	0:31.3	0:04.6	0:00.0
Where	In police van	0:00.0	0:52.9	0:37.1	0:03.5
	Outdoors	12:31.6	53:44.5	56:44.5	16:54.7
When	Forcing man to ground	9:07.1	34:19.7	39:10.2	19:53.6
	Whilst man on ground	8:30.4	26:02.9	32:07.1	9:49.1
	Putting man in van	2:43.4	3:57.1	3:34.4	2:01.5
	Throughout incident	11:05.9	39:43.9	44:58.6	14:50.3
What	Grappling	2:44.1	17:07.9	21:57.7	6:13.1
	• Holding face/head	1:36.7	1:18.7	1:06.4	2:45.1
	• Into gutter	1:12.7	0:00.0	0:00.0	1:35.3
	• Man hitting head on ground	0:00.0	3:43.0	6:38.8	1:37.1
	• Police dragging man across ground	2:44.1	14:39.4	17:28.9	6:29.1
	Resort to force	0:17.3	4:46.8	7:45.1	4:35.5
	• Build-up to incident	0:00.0	0:46.5	0:57.6	1:27.8
	• Officer trying to fight with man	0:17.3	2:14.7	2:59.0	2:26.4
	• Police not negotiating with man	0:17.3	2:07.7	3:39.9	1:13.0
	• Police swearing at man	0:00.0	0:00.0	1:01.2	1:37.1
	Focus on man				

(*continued*)

Table 2.4 (Continued)

Deductive	Inductive	Assessment of police			
		Very positive	Positive	Negative	Very negative
	• Lack of attention to bystanders	0:27.5	1:49.3	1:56.1	0:01.9
	• Lack of attention to casualty of CS gas	0:06.4	0:54.9	2:48.0	1:55.3
	Communicating	0:27.5	2:06.4	4:28.4	2:10.5
	• 'Mind your head' putting in van	0:00.8	0:33.0	0:11.1	0:00.0
	Number of police officers involved	3:57.2	29:06.1	32:28.2	9:50.5
	Speed	3:50.4	4:22.8	3:22.7	0:02.0
	Violence of man	4:56.8	19:31.6	13:49.0	4:00.3
How	Forceful	3:13.0	29:28.4	33:58.0	11:30.3
	• Aggressively	4:02.6	25:40.0	24:55.9	17:00.4
	• Not aggressively enough	0:00.0	1:09.6	1:09.6	0:00.0
	Violently	0:22.1	5:51.0	7:00.5	8:29.0
	• Proportionality	9:58.5	44:34.3	30:19.0	8:49.0
	o Necessary	9:08.9	43:27.9	29:42.4	9:26.5
	o Disproportionate	2:05.0	35:18.1	49:07.1	14:37.3
	o Abuse of police power	0:00.0	1:03.5	1:03.5	0:43.7
	o Brutally	0:00.0	0:14.6	0:25.4	0:54.4
	o Excessively	0:59.9	27:24.7	38:01.5	10:03.1
	o Potentially harmfully	0:26.7	13:23.4	18:57.6	8:30.5
	o Unnecessarily	2:00.4	6:34.4	11:34.8	10:28.3
	o Violently	0:22.1	5:51.0	7:00.5	8:29.0
	• Excusable	0:00.0	3:45.3	1:57.5	1:53.2
	o Red mist	0:00.0	0:46.0	1:17.9	0:57.3
	o Understandable	0:00.0	3:45.3	1:52.3	1:02.5
	• Competence				
	o Competently	11:20.3	35:14.7	27:59.2	12:20.2
	•Competent	9:34.2	13:28.7	13:27.2	5:42.2
	•Preventing possible further violence in crowd	4:59.9	17:46.6	11:49.0	0:24.2
	•Quickly	3:15.9	4:43.0	2:58.6	0:09.1
	•Routinely	0:00.0	5:06.4	3:35.4	0:00.0
	•Safely	5:45.0	7:12.7	3:31.3	2:16.2

Deductive	Inductive	Assessment of police			
		Very positive	Positive	Negative	Very negative
	o Incompetently	0:00.0	2:43.9	10:49.5	3:16.9
	•Police exacerbated situation	0:00.0	2:34.7	9:22.6	1:39.8
	•Too slowly	0:00.0	0:09.2	2:12.8	0:00.0
	•Unprofessionally	0:00.0	0:00.0	0:44.4	3:00.7
	o Alternative means of restraint	0:46.9	5:05.8	8:40.6	0:44.7
	•Other methods of restraint should have been used	0:46.9	1:07.0	4:14.1	0:37.6
	•Should have used CS or Taser instead	0:44.0	5:05.8	5:44.8	0:11.9
Other	Camera	0:00.0	1:08.2	2:18.7	0:02.3
	Public perception	0:59.6	9:00.8	11:11.1	10:37.6
	Unpleasant aggressive police action	0:01.6	8:26.2	3:30.5	1:09.1

(Department for Communities and Local Government 2012; Medland 2012). Like other conurbations, the West Midlands also suffers higher levels of crime than most other police areas in England and Wales.[6] A total of thirty-four groups was selected to represent diverse interests, including resident groups in housing areas of varying affluence; faith groups (including Sikhs—conducted in Punjabi); groups dedicated to older and younger age groups; various marginal groups (including a hostel for homeless people, young offenders serving community sentences); groups with a special interest in community safety, cohesion and crime prevention were included, as were those focused on race equality issues and volunteering.[7] Perhaps the only voice that was not represented adequately was that of mid-career professionals with young families.[8] Access was denied to only one group—elderly users of a local authority run community centre—and we decided against including one group whose grasp of English was so problematic that moderators

[6] Her Majesty's Inspectorate of Constabulary (HMIC) crime comparator <http://www.hmic.gov.uk/crime-and-policing-comparator/?force=west-midlands&crime=all-crime> (accessed 22 February 2013).

[7] These 'activist' groups attracted a small number of retired police officers, who naturally drew upon their police experience in discussing the video clips.

[8] An unplanned advantage of using groups that were already in existence (rather than formed specially for the purpose of being a focus group) was that they were likely to share a common culture. Since neighbourhood influences seem to be strongly cultural, pre-existing groups might also exhibit similar influences, even more so perhaps because of their self-selectivity.

found it necessary to 'lead' them. None of the groups that we approached refused to cooperate; many were positively eager to do so. Focus groups varied considerably in size from four to seventeen participants (mean 10.4) and discussions lasted approximately seventy-eight minutes on average, but ranged from fifty-three minutes to two hours. Participants were rewarded with vouchers to the sum of £15 redeemable at major 'High Street' chain stores.

Conclusions

This research, like much before it, seeks to explore how attitudes towards police behaviour are articulated. In using innovative methods, however, an attempt was made to overcome some of the potential shortcomings of traditional research in this area that has tended to rely upon standard survey techniques. Building on a long tradition of research using scenarios—though relatively infrequently used in policing research—this study used video clips drawn from factual television programmes, thus enhancing the verisimilitude of the police actions being assessed. An identical series of video clips was shown to a great many of the major demographic groupings, as well as a range of diverse interests located throughout the 'Black Country' region of the West Midlands. After each video clip was viewed, members of each of the focus groups was asked to record how 'favourably' they viewed the police officers depicted in the clip on an eleven-point scale and write any remarks that occurred to them. Thereupon, focus groups were invited to discuss their views of each video clip in whatever terms they chose. It is these assessments and these open-ended discussions that form the basis for what follows.

3

Consensus and Dissension

Introduction

The issue at the heart of this research can be stated simply: how do members of the public evaluate the *actual behaviour* of police officers dealing with real-life incidents? This chapter examines the most prominent feature to emerge from our fieldwork: the *dissension* between and within focus groups whose members viewed and then discussed video clips of police–public encounters. Often focus groups erupted into vibrant exchanges, sometimes before the video clip concluded. It continues the discussion in Chapter 2 and suggests that instead of trying to discern the 'signal' and ignore the 'noise' in the data, researchers should focus on 'noisiness', because that is the most prominent feature of our data. Focus groups disagreed within and between each other, and often did so fundamentally. About what did they disagree so strongly?

To facilitate analysis, this chapter will concentrate on just two of the video clips; these video clips (the second and third shown to the groups) were respectively the most positively (video clip 2) and most negatively (video clip 3) rated by our focus groups on our crude ratings of approval, which corresponded with our intuition as moderators. They were also at the extremes in another respect: there was a strong consensus that the video clip showing officers dealing with a report of an elderly man robbed in his own home at knifepoint was the most positive video clip, but the video clip showing how a motorway patrol stopped a suspected stolen car polarised opinion. There were also strikingly different interpretations of what had occurred and why. In the following analysis, we will consider each in turn.

Robbery in an Elderly Man's Home

Two officers were dispatched to an urgent call alleging that an elderly man had been robbed at knifepoint in his retirement bungalow on a public housing estate. When the police arrived the officer was greeted by a young woman who said that she was visiting the elderly occupier and had, just a short while earlier, answered the door to a hooded man who asked for another woman by name who also visits the premises. The hooded man then pushed passed this young woman and entered the sitting room where he had threatened both the woman and the elderly man with a knife, cut the telephone wires and stolen the elderly man's pension. The officers began by separately taking statements from the man and the woman; meanwhile (unseen by viewers) CID officers attended and began interviewing neighbours. Two Scenes of Crime Officers (a man and a woman) arrived and began 'dusting' for fingerprints and photographing the scene. There was some good natured banter between the elderly man and the woman SOCO as she photographed the telephone. Cans of lager and the empty wrapper in which the pension money was kept were found outside the bungalow, photographed by the SOCO and seized as evidence. Eventually, the officers bade farewell to the elderly man and the young woman, asking as they left if the elderly man was going to remain alone that evening and he cheerily replied he would and he would be 'alright'. The officer (who has heard the elderly man's 'war stories') remarked that no doubt the man had coped with worse situations in his life (6:29 minutes *Traffic Cops* broadcast 14 August 2008).

Hurrying to the scene of a serious crime, questioning distressed victim(s); with the assistance of forensic investigators and detectives, gathering evidence and commencing an investigation; should all depict the police in their most heroic role. Whilst much of the focus group discussion was positive, the picture is more complicated than might be supposed. The overall time spent praising and criticising the officers was approximately the same. The discussions in focus groups concentrated on three principal themes, all of which were contested. First, was the elderly man shown sufficient respect by the officers? Secondly, were officers sufficiently attentive to the *health and wellbeing* of the elderly man? He was obviously frail—using an inhaler—and was eighty-two years old. Should the officers have insisted upon a medical assessment and treatment despite his having rejected it when it was offered? Lastly, *investigative competence*, which for many participants relied on their own suspicions surrounding the young woman who had opened the door to the assailant and allegedly received injuries from the robber's knife. There was a wide consensus that she *was* implicated in the robbery, and we will return to this in Chapter 4. Meanwhile, there were concerns regarding whether the police took the alleged offences seriously enough or not and whether they acted with sufficient urgency.

Respectfulness

The importance of respect for fostering positive police–public relations is the principal emphasis of 'procedural justice' and it was foremost in the minds of our focus groups. In the video clip, one of the officers is shown taking a statement from the elderly man, who was reminiscing about his time as a prisoner of war held captive by both the Germans and Japanese during World War Two. In the *original* broadcast, the officer observed in a voice-over that 'It wasn't the easiest statement to take', but in the version shown to focus groups, this was muted. Despite this, there were many who sympathised with the officer on this point without them actually hearing this remark.

There was general agreement that officers were 'sympathetic', 'compassionate', 'caring' and attempted to 'calm' the situation, all of which was praised. Other attributes evoked more discussion. The fact that the police were patient with the elderly man when he digressed into recalling his wartime experience, and officers did not become irritated with his meanderings, was praised. For example, a group of young people, of mixed ethnicity and gender, attending a further education college, took the view: 'Not once, when the old man was going on, did he tell him to get to the point' and later officers 'showed a lot of patience with the elderly gentlemen, when they got there' (WS330028–29B). Another mixed ethnicity and gender group of young people who volunteered for service in the community took a similar view: 'I thought they was patient, because they listened to his war stories ...' said one of them, which elicited the remark '17 years!' and 'All the Germans', all of which was accompanied by laughter (WS330080).

A mixed ethnicity group of adult race equality activists appreciated how the elderly man's reminiscences must have conflicted with other demands on officers' time.

> P1:[1] It could be argued that they didn't seem to come across as very sympathetic towards the victims, but when you've got a chap who wants to tell you about when he was 17 and you're under time constraints, so they've really got to keep it to the facts. So, it's a juggle really between being sympathetic and listening to the story, but then you've got to get the facts down because you've got to be somewhere in 10 minutes. So, I think that balance was quite good.
>
> P2: I don't think it was that bad because he was telling him about when he was in the army
> [Greeted with indistinct interruptions indicating agreement.][2]
> So, I don't think it was that bad. I think they handled it good.
>
> P3: I think they were really good. In the sense that they were very mindful of the old man's health. They kept checking, 'Are you alright?' ... Considering, ... on the information they've got, I think that if there's somebody out there with a knife I thought they were incredibly patient [...] trying to get a statement, trying to get some facts down. I think that came across ... they came across in that. (WS330077)

Apart from patience, there was a question about courtesy. Just one participant in all of our interviews took exception to the officer addressing the elderly man

---

[1] For each quoted portion, participants are distinguished by a numeral.
[2] Editorial comments are enclosed in square brackets. Ellipses not in square brackets reflect incomplete speech.

as 'George' (WS330048) (cf Southgate and Ekblom 1985). A group of mid-career professionals in a desirable rural dormitory town felt that the officers did well. '[The elderly man] was treated very courteously and gently', to which someone else added 'Hmmmm, absolutely, yeah.' (WS330083)

However, some participants were attentive to mannerisms that might otherwise be inappropriate when holding a conversation with someone, such as looking at one's wristwatch. This was raised by a support group for those caring for disabled relatives at home: 'Well, OK. They done their job. Apart from the [officer] keeping on looking at his watch! (laugh) ... when he was taking that old man's statement.' This was followed by indistinct agreement from one other person. Someone else added: 'The thing is, you have to do that ... writing down and writing the time as well. That's probably why.'(WS330090) Sixth formers in a very deprived area discussed the same issue:

> P1: The police officer kept checking his watch. So, it looked like, he was trying to rush it along. I mean, I know that he was old and it was ...
> P2: He was just writing it down on a piece of paper.
> P1: Like he should have just let him, because you know what they're like, they like to tell their stories.
> P2: He was just writing it down on the paper. (WS330084)

What this so vividly highlights is the question of 'motive-based trust'. The officer taking the elderly man's statement undoubtedly looks momentarily at his watch. To one of our participants this appears to be 'trying to rush it along', but to another it was some administrative requirement. The behaviour is identical; the inference lies entirely in the attribution of intentionality. In general, our participants commonly felt that officers dealt with the elderly man in an appropriate manner, even if they recognised conflicting pressures under which the officers worked. There was more debate about how officers juggled competing obligations.

Health and Welfare

It was frequently remarked that the elderly man also suffered frail health and was thereby vulnerable. At one point, he became a little emotional recalling the incident and was seen to use an inhaler that lay on the sofa beside him. There were two moments that aroused debate: first, when officers arrived and surveyed the scene. Could or should they have insisted on the man receiving medical attention? Secondly, as the officers bade the elderly man farewell, should arrangements have been made for the man's continuing aftercare?

Considering the first issue: should the officers have insisted that the elderly man went to hospital or at least be given a check-over in his bungalow by a paramedic or other health professional? This divided opinion over the question of 'consent' to treatment. It has been noted by some observers that officers can assume ownership of a situation to which they have been called and that this may result in the police taking actions that callers did not necessarily want or did not meet with their approval (Shapland and Vagg 1988; Ericson 1982). Typically, many people fear that the police will 'go too far' in dealing with a minor issue more seriously than callers had wished. Such an experience, whether suffered directly or vicariously, could also lead to members of the public hesitating before involving the police at all. Here, few of our participants felt that the man did not require medical examination, but the issue was whether his express consent was required before any such examination could be conducted. For many, this posed a dilemma for the officers that was not of their making.

A mixed ethnicity and gender youth group who did volunteering work in the community thought that the trauma suffered by the elderly man required urgent medical assistance:

P1: Well, they asked him if he wanted an ambulance and he said 'No'. So, what can they do? Can they call it without his consent, really? …
Res: Do you think that they should have insisted that he got medical treatment?
P1: Yeah, checked out.
P2: At least get checked.
P1: He's elderly, so he's a lot more frail than people younger than him.
P3: He knew how to manage himself, like, taking his nebuliser and that, wasn't he?
P4: If he had suffered a heart attack later and sort of, y'know what I mean? Then, how would that stand with the police? [indistinct] Get checked over, sort of thing! (WS330080)

Asked directly whether he should have been taken to hospital, a neighbourhood watch group in an area of mixed housing were also divided on the issue:

P1: But they can't insist … can't insist. If he said 'No', they can't insist.
P2: They'd be abusing his human rights.
P3: It's horrible isn't it, 'human rights'?
[This was greeted with laughter and indistinct multiple voices in agreement.]
P4: … later on, then everybody would be blaming the police for not calling them—paramedics.
P2: But they asked him, didn't they? They gave him that choice.
P4: I don't think it works like that, does it? I think it's down to them to call the paramedics …
P5: If a person says they don't want anything, then they can't make them do anything.
P1: If they'd have gone over his head, then they'd have said that they were in breach of his human rights.
P4: … he might have collapsed five minutes later. (WS330052)

Another issue for debate was whether steps should have been taken to help and protect the elderly man once the police had left. Some groups were concerned not only about the man's health, but also the continued presence of the young woman, about whom many harboured the suspicion that she was impli-cated in the robbery. The neighbourhood watch group quoted above continued:

> P1: I thought the young girl […] it seemed strange for her to be there.
> P2: […] I thought the police would have said to him, 'You need someone to stay with you tonight.'
> P3: So would I.
> P4: You don't know how far they'd got through the conversation, because of the investigation, do you? It was cut short.
> P1: He said 'No, I'm alright here. I'll be here on my own.' Which, I would suggest, they would suggest he had someone to stay with.
> P2: It's the aftercare, after, that follows that up. Such as [my daughter] was given a panic thingy—panic button. They do follow up aftercare, don't they? Victims! Like you don't see that do you? …
> P2: They probably would go around the next day and ask again. (WS330095)

Again, this raises the issue of how far police officers should go in assuming responsibility not only for the alleged crime, but also in taking responsi-bility for all those involved. Like any public official, a police officer who intrudes into the lives of fellow citizens acquires thereby a 'duty of care'. The officers in this case needed to juggle this 'duty of care' and the 'right to a private life' (Article 8 of the European Convention on Human Rights) of the victim and the requirement for the victim to give consent for medical treatment, provided they are competent to do so, which this elderly man clearly was. Officers were judged by our participants in terms of how well they thought they had juggled those various obligations. Generally, their actions were praised, but for some their actions and inactions were, at the least, questionable.

Investigative Competence

The third theme to emerge from our focus groups was the extent of investiga-tive competence displayed by the police. The video opens with one officer going to the premises, briefly examining the elderly man and his young female companion for wounds the woman said they had both suffered, but in a voice-over he explains that he could see nothing. He then took an initial statement from both the victims together. The video then cuts to a male forensic exam-iner 'dusting' the door for finger or palm prints. He explains, to camera, how the powder functions and his reasoning that if the robber had pushed his way into the house he was likely to have used his open hand on the exterior of the door. In a voice-over, the other officer explains that 'due to the severity of the offence', CID officers were deployed on 'house-to-house' inquiries in the immediate vicinity of the man's dwelling. The video cuts back to the elderly man's sitting room where a young female forensic examiner was kneeling at the feet of the elderly victim and photographing something on the floor. The elderly man jocularly asks: 'Are you photographing all my rubbish love?' The woman laughs and replies, 'Just your telephone, that's all I'm interested in! No worries!'

The discussions of our focus groups can usefully be considered under three sub-themes: first, whether the emergency call was responded to with sufficient urgency; secondly, because so many participants were suspicious about the girl's complicity in the offence, the issue arose about whether officers were too dismissive of the allegations or investigated the situation sufficiently thoroughly as a scene of genuine crime; and, finally, given the suspicions that clung to the young woman, whether she had been appropriately questioned.

First, there was general agreement that the police had responded with sufficient urgency and commitment of resources. A mixed ethnicity and gender youth group held in a community arts centre (unfortunately, in a room with awful acoustics) tended towards a favourable view.

P1: The police handled it really well.

P2: I think the police got on the scene pretty quick.

P3: Handling the situation quickly, I think, is the way to do it, because we've been in experiences where we've wanted the police to deal with something quicker than they have done and we've been waiting around for hours for them.

[The researcher asked people to show whether they think this was a better service than they would receive locally. Then he asked, what explained the difference between what happens locally and this situation?]

P4: I think it's the actual seriousness of the situation—get there NOW.

[The researcher pressed the group about 'urgency' and they replied:]

P5: No because ...

P3: No, because they didn't know who they were.

P5: Apart from that you've got to have a proper brief ... detail before you can ...
   [Followed by indistinct discussion.]

P3: Yeah, that's right. Once they had the description that could have radioed someone with a description of the person. [...]

P1: In a car as well [...]

P3: Yeah, but it's good still to have a scout around and see if there's someone ...
   (WS330071)

An all-male youth group living in a desirable rural dormitory town tended to be more sceptical:

P1: Yeah. I think at the time they acted very quickly, according to what the video said, anyway. So, I don't think they could have done a lot more at the time.

P2: Two officers arrived while they were interviewing, so they were searching around the area. So [...] didn't seem to be urgent.

Res: How do others feel about that? ... Do you think they were ...?

P3: It didn't seem to be so urgent, really. It had already happened, so ...

Res: The girl said that it was only a minute ago that somebody had burst it their house.

P3: Yeah, but they probably didn't get there within a minute. (WS330089)

Elsewhere, there was mild, but discernible, disputation. A group concerned with community safety in an economically depressed area illustrated this:

P1: The operator said, 'Priority'—priority call—and the officer just walked up to the door and [makes the noise of knocking].

P2: I find that OK ...

P1: I'd expect police officers to be running.

P3: Basically I think the police acted accordingly, however they've got these regimes of what is a priority and what is not a priority ... If somebody's got a knife and waving it about then that's a priority ... High priority! ... If it had have happened to me I'd have expected ...

P4: The whole force to be out.

P3: Exactly! The whole kit and caboodle to be there.... If someone's brandishing a knife—whether it be true or false—you have to be going with the view that there is somebody using knife and somebody's been robbed. It may be that it was a little bit laid back with respect to that, but it's what you would expect in this day and age.

P5: Did I miss it? Did anyone see that whether they called for backup to do a search or anything?

P6: CID.

P4: Scenes of crime, CID.
[Followed by several voices offering corrections.]

P5: But was anyone looking for a hooded man waving a knife about?

P4: No, but they were investigating the site of the crime.

P5: But if there is a crime committed a second two ago wouldn't you ...?
[Followed by several indistinct interruptions.]

P6: They did house-to-house ...

P3: Neighbours, they said 'neighbours'.

P7: You're not actually told how many officers attended, or in fact how long it took them to get there.

P5: Okay.

P7: They said it was committed a minute ago, but it took her a minute to open the door! [Greeted with laughter.] (WS330043)

Urgency was one indicator that the police took the alleged robbery seriously enough. The mobilisation of specialist resources—SOCO and CID—was another. For instance, participants who were members of an association representing security firms in the area of a city centre shopping mall thought that the response was appropriate, albeit that there was some question about just how seriously the police took the allegation:

P1: They involved CID ... Scenes of Crime were involved. Then the first two attending officers remained, taking statements, taking details.

P2: There was a lot of resource, when the police …

P3: They did a lot for the old man's sake. They put wheels in motion so that they could say 'we put wheels in motion'. I don't think there was any real urgency about what they were doing. (WS330021)

We shall return to this issue in the next chapter, but suffice to say that many of the participants were of the view that the elderly man's young woman companion was implicated in some way with the robbery. In which case, the question arose whether, in their investigation, the police interrogated her with sufficient vigour. This is a major dilemma in policing: should those presenting themselves as a 'victim' be treated as such, or should they be regarded as a potential 'suspect'? Some appreciated that there was a dilemma. For example, the following contribution was made during a focus group comprising a local community group in very deprived area:

I think when they first got there, they had to take it on face value, I think. It would be difficult at that point. If you treated them as a hostile immediately (a) you're going to get a very different response from the person, and (b) they're going to let themselves out for a lot of criticism if it was unfounded. I mean, you'd see a lot going on afterwards. I mean, if we could see what happened two or three days later then we'd see a very different, y'know … (WS330039)

Others felt that the officers in the video clip were sceptical, but hid their scepticism. A young person in a desirable rural dormitory town said:

The girl was exaggerating everything. So, I thought he handled what she was saying pretty well. Not like getting too carried away with it all.
[Asked whether he thought the girl was exaggerating, he replied:]
Yeah. I think she was exaggerating what happened, making it sound worse than it probably was. (WS330083)

Many felt that the officers were justifiably suspicious of the young woman and that explained why they interviewed the girl separately, in another room. This was the view in a neighbourhood watch group in an area of mixed housing.

Res. 'Do you think they pushed her enough? Should they have pushed her a bit harder?'

P1: I think that's why they took her in the other room to get her … to get the old man's statement.

P2: Y'see, he was talking and she … Didn't he? 'He took a £5 note off you' and all the rest of it. So she was putting words into his mouth. Trying to throw us off the scent that's what … (WS330078)

A neighbourhood watch group in an area of mixed housing took the view:

They obviously split them up and interviewed them separately to see if they tallied … or they … or there were two completely separate … or the whole thing was fabricated.

A woman participant referred to the absence of knife marks on the girl and said how officers continued to interview the girl without 'judg[ing] at face value what had gone on' (WS330052).

Some were critical of the officers for taking the initial account of what had occurred from the man and young woman at the same time, but approved of them splitting the two victims up and taking full statements separately (the camera witnessed only the interview of the elderly man) (WS330089).

The researcher posed a summary of the discussion amongst representatives of local authority 'service users' and asked: 'A number of you have said that you were not convinced by the young lady's account about what took place.' There was general assent to this; the researcher continued, 'Are you satisfied that the police investigated thoroughly enough?'

P1: Not as individuals, but they probably had the same inclination as we've got here, and we can't speculate on what the policeman would be thinking, because he's not there to cast judgement, he's there to investigate crime.

P2: I think it's always going to be in the back of his mind because of the way she reacted. Though it may not have come out at that time, it would have come out later.

P3: I think it was good that they took her to one side and asked her things, because I think that's when cracks might have come in the story. So, the way that they asked them together, then took her to one side ... if she gave the same version of events, I think that's y'know. So, I think they did that well.

P1: As I say, we can't speculate on what the policeman thought, but we can speculate on what *we* thought. But at the time, he acted on the correct procedure, at the time. And the investigation would have been ongoing into her statement. (WS330082)

This discussion shows that despite the consensus that officers had responded appropriately, there was acknowledgement that officers faced dilemmas that were not easily resolved—whether to insist on a medical examination of the elderly man or whether to treat the young woman as complicit—that remained debateable. Officers were respectful of the elderly man, displaying patience when he digressed into his 'war stories', but should they have shown more urgency and devoted more resources, for example, asking for other officers to search the area?

Motorway Stop

In this video clip (the third to be shown to the focus groups), motorway patrol officers were alerted that a vehicle with a particular registered number had driven away from a petrol filling station without payment. Soon afterwards the officers were passed by the vehicle, which they began following. As they did so, they received information that the number displayed on the car's registration plate was unrecognised by the official database of all registered vehicles,[3] which led them to suspect that the car was stolen. They continued to follow the car whilst attempting to assemble other patrol cars so that they could surround the suspect car and bring it safely to a halt, but without success—other patrol cars were unavailable or too distant. The officers decided to stop the suspect car themselves. In the words of one of them, they considered themselves now to be 'the lone rangers'! As traffic became more congested, the officers turned on their warning lights and siren, and closed in on the suspect car, whilst giving a running commentary to the control room. The suspect car made no attempt to flee, but signalled left and gradually came to a halt on the 'hard shoulder' of the motorway. As the patrol car pulled up in front of it the police passenger leapt from the patrol car and ran back to the suspect car. By the time the camera arrived, this officer was tussling with the young male driver and could be heard to say: 'Get out before I drag you out'. The two men continued to struggle against the driver's open door before the driver of the suspect car raised his hands in a gesture of surrender and was escorted to the police car and placed in the rear seat. A few moments later the officer who arrested the driver knelt on the front passenger seat of the police car and explained to the young driver why his car was suspected of being stolen and why 'we arrested you the way we did'. The young man began to respond, but the officer did not allow him to finish.

Meanwhile, the police driver pursued inquiries over the radio and it emerged that the report of a 'drive off' had been withdrawn by the petrol station and a number identifying this specific vehicle (the so-called 'vin' number) confirmed its ownership by the driver, which together caused the twin suspicions of theft of petrol and of stealing the car itself to evaporate. There remained, however, a discrepancy between the registered number recorded in the database and the number displayed on the car, which the driver explained was the fault of the vehicle supplier. He also admitted to having been previously issued with a notice under the Vehicle Defect Rectification Scheme (VDRS) by another police patrol approximately a week earlier, requiring him to correct the erroneous and misleading number. An increasingly exasperated police driver asked the young driver why he continued to drive the car with inaccurate registration plates when he had received a VDRS notice. The driver claimed that he had been given 'fourteen days' in which to make the rectification, which had yet to expire. The police driver observed that 'any decent member of the public' would have made the rectification at the first opportunity, but the car driver argued that he was misled by the police officers who issued the notice (whom he described as 'you lot'). Nevertheless, the police driver informed him that he was committing an offence each time he used the car with the incorrect plates and that he was being issued with a fixed penalty notice in the sum of £30. As the officer completed the paperwork, the exchanges between him and the young driver became increasingly and mutually acrimonious. The scene concluded with the officer sarcastically bidding the car driver 'Have a nice journey' as he was released from the rear of the patrol car (9:42 minutes *Motorway Cops* broadcast 18 September 2008).

---

[3] PNC: Police National Computer.

This video clip is an example of stop and search that, as we have seen, is a prime example of 'police-initiated' contact and a frequent cause of dissatisfaction amongst those who have experienced it. Many stops and searches involve the stopping of motorists by police in vehicles.[4]

The circumstances depicted in this video clip also highlight another, usually somewhat obscured, aspect of routine policing—the so-called 'attitude test'! Officers in many jurisdictions refer to the 'attitude test' as a determinant of how they deal with people: those who do not challenge the officer's authority and comply readily with their requests and commands, are treated reasonably respectfully. On the other hand, those who do *not* can expect more robust treatment, including the imposition of a more or less arbitrary penalty, including arrest (Sykes and Clark 1975). This video clip illustrates precisely this type of exchange: the young driver, erroneously suspected of stealing petrol from a filling station and also driving a stolen car, *had* committed a minor offence of driving on false number plates. Despite having been issued with a VDRS, he blamed his tardiness[5] on the officer who had issued the notice and showed no remorse for having caused the officers to stop him. In short, this was a classic case of 'contempt of cop': a non-deferential, young, articulate, and apparently affluent, middle class man, who repeatedly challenged officers thereby failing 'the attitude test', resulted in officers imposing a discretionary penalty (what Chatterton (1976) refers to as a 'resource charge'). Incidentally, he fits the profile of one of the two categories of people that Sykes and Clark found (1975) to be most likely to challenge officers' authority, that is, members of the affluent middle classes who 'know their rights'. The video clip was capable of fuelling many other interpretations. Perhaps having discovered that the theft of fuel had been withdrawn and that the suspicion that the car was stolen was untrue, the officers felt it necessary to find something amiss that would justify the action they took. We can endlessly speculate. What we are interested in here (and in the following chapters) is how did *members of our focus groups* interpret what they had seen and how did that justify their evaluation of police action.

---

[4] Stops of vehicles are conducted under legislation distinct from that used to stop and search pedestrians. The difference is crucial, but often overlooked by those who conflate all 'stops' into a single category. Section 163 of the Road Traffic Act 1988 grants police the power to stop vehicles. It states:

(1) A person driving a [mechanically propelled vehicle] on a road must stop the vehicle on being required to do so by a constable in uniform.
(2) A person riding a cycle on a road must stop the cycle on being required to do so by a constable in uniform [or a traffic officer].
(3) If a person fails to comply with this section he is guilty of an offence.

As the Home Office website explains: 'The police have the power to stop anyone at any time—they don't need to give you a reason—and failing to stop is a criminal offence' (<https://www.gov.uk/stopped-by-police-while-driving-your-rights/overview>, accessed 23 August 2013).

[5] If, indeed, he was 'tardy' at all, since he did have fourteen days in which to make the rectification; however, the forms issued by most police forces stipulate that the car can only be used within this period for the purpose of making the rectification.

Consensus and Dissension

The most important feature of the views expressed in the focus groups is dissension: focus group participants who had viewed exactly the same video clip of this encounter could not agree about either the facts of the case or how they should be interpreted and evaluated. Whilst there was an overall preponderance of negative remarks regarding the conduct of the officers, there were two moments during the unfolding encounter that became the focus of *both* agreement and disagreement amongst our focus groups. These two moments were: first, forcefully arresting the resisting driver on the 'hard shoulder' of the motorway, which will be considered when we examine attitudes towards the use of 'force'. Secondly, the period following the discovery that the allegation of theft was false and the car was not stolen, but the number plates on the car were incorrect. The police driver berated the young driver for not rectifying the defect immediately, to which the young driver was casually dismissive and blamed the officers who issued the VDRS for misleading him. The exchange between the two men was described by our focus groups as 'petty', 'tit-for-tat', 'childish', 'bickering', 'banter' and a 'slanging match'.

One issue embedded in attitudes of our focus groups was whether or not the young driver was telling the truth in saying that the officer who issued the VDRS told him that he 'had fourteen days' in which to change the plates *and didn't warn him not to use the car in the meanwhile*. This involves imagining what might or might not have occurred in some past encounter with other police officers to which only the young car driver was privy. Was the car driver's account accepted or not by the focus groups?

Some participants accepted without qualification that the officer who issued the VDRS *had* misled the young driver. Perhaps predictably, a group of young offenders[6] thought the young driver was entirely justified:

> Yeah, the kid's saying 'Why give me fourteen days, if you want me to pay it on the same day?' Do you know what I mean? It's like a train ticket: if you want to go on a train its £20 and they give you a certain amount of time. So, if the police pull you and say 'Why haven't you paid this fine?' and you say, 'Well, I've had fourteen days'. What? Are they going to fine you even more. It's taking the piss, man! (WS330055)

A group of women attending a mother and baby group for émigrés from a war-torn country in the Middle East were asked whether they thought the imposition of a fine was justified, which evoked a chorus of 'No!':

> P1: Because he was told he had fourteen days.
> P2: Exactly!

---

[6] A comprehensive list of the general characteristics of all the focus groups can be found in the Appendix ordered by the audio recording number, which corresponds to the ID of files held by the Economic and Social Data Archive.

P1: Fair enough, y'know, they should give him fourteen days.

P3: If after the fourteen days [...]

P4: Yeah, fair enough.

P3: ... but why give him the fourteen days? [Which was greeted with a chorus of assent.] (WS330059)[7]

It might be imagined that a Neighbourhood Watch group in an area of mixed housing would discount the young driver's claim that he had been misled by the officers who had previously issued the VDRS, but this was not so. A young woman said, to murmurs of assent from others:

P1: When the kid was saying, 'Look, I've got fourteen days to get it solved; I didn't know ... he actually seemed genuine. He didn't seem ...

P2: He tried to explain himself.

P1: ... he explained himself quite well. I thought. If he ain't been told originally that if he drives within those fourteen days ... But it just seems that they're treating him that way because of his age.
[Later an older women added.]

P3: There are two problems: one, the information given out at the beginning and, two, when the lad originally had his notice over his car number plate, then should somebody explain to him *exactly* what the legal position was and if they don't, then you've got to go back to them and say 'You've got an issue there, on those who gave it out, and they've got to be put right on that for the future, because it'll happen again!'
[Later still, an older man added.]

P4: Would there be justification that he didn't know? He didn't know that if he drove with that notice he'd get a fine. Isn't there any ...

P3: No, because you can't prove it. You can only evidence something you can prove and if he hasn't been told, it's hearsay. You can't use that. You've got to have something factual. If you've got it in writing, you could argue ...

P4: Yeah! (WS330052)

Others rejected the young man's explanation, although often not without challenge from fellow participants. Their view was that the car driver had clearly committed an offence of driving with incorrect number plates for which he should be punished. Some members of a neighbourhood group in a deprived area took such a robust view:

Res: Do you think it was fair that he gave him a ticket?

P1: Yes!

P2: That was frustration.

P3: No, I think it was fair.

P4: I think it was fair to give him a ticket seeing that it's two weeks ago that he knew that the plate was wrong.... These people who make the number plates are professional people, because now you have to go to a registered place to make a

---

[7] In each extract featuring more than one person, participants are distinguished by numerals, but only for the extract in question.

number plate. They should have gotten the proper documentation before making the number plate. But now that he *knew* it was the wrong plate, he should've taken it back ... and get it sorted.... I would give him a maximum three days to get it sorted.

P3: Yeah, as I said, yes he's got the wrong number plates. He admitted it. It wasn't like, 'Oh no, I didn't know!' Then they'd probably have said, 'Yeah, it's a bit unfair ...', but he said, 'Yeah, I know', and he gave all that lip about 'I ain't going to pay, the car place will pay'. So ... (WS330037)

In a group of race equality workers and activists there was dissension regarding the recall of the young driver and his motives:

P1: That fine he give him; I don't think he should've given him that, because ...

P2: Yeah, he's already had it ...

P1: Yeah, and he said they didn't tell him he couldn't drive his car when he received the first fine.

P3: How do you know that?

P1: That's what he said.

P3: He's saying that to get out of a £30 fine.

P1: But he gave him the fine after he said it.

P4: He already received a ticket a week before ...

P1: ... and he said he'd got fourteen days in which to change it.

P3: You don't know it wasn't explained to him, he just chooses to say it wasn't ... You don't know it wasn't explained to him [...] it's just human nature isn't it?

P4: Don't get me wrong, it think it's up to him to know he's driving around with different number plates to what should be on there in the first place.
[Followed by an indistinct objection.]

P5: Yeah, but that's just his word against his. If you can get away with it, I would ... (WS330077)

What is at issue here is more than believing or doubting the young driver's account of the occasion when he was issued with a VDRS, but a wider issue of responsibility for the whole episode. Was the driver responsible for using a vehicle knowing that its number plates were incorrect, or were the police wrong to treat him as a suspected car thief and imposing a fine for an administrative offence quite arbitrarily? Participants were equally divided about this.

Some of those who were critical of the police interpreted the officers' actions as the product of prejudice and baseless stereotyping. This view was forcefully expressed by mothers of young men who had a history of conflict with the local police:

P1: It's the uniform, y'know, 'We've got the uniform; we can do what we want.'

P2: 'Have a nice day', with your sarcasm.

P1: Yeah. When he's giving back the attitude they don't like it. They're dishing it out themselves [...]

P3: In the first instance, they approached him wrong anyway. There was attitude: 'young ...'

P1: Straightaway.

P3: Straightaway.

P4: I think I'd have behaved just like the young man, I would (laughter). (WS330025)

Others felt that the young driver was the author of his own misfortune. Residents in a hostel for the homeless felt that the young driver had brought the situation upon himself:

P1: He'd done it himself, the kid did, by not putting the number plate right.

P2: He said, he'd got a fortnight, fourteen days.

P1: He shouldn't have a fortnight. He should have done it there and then.

P2: If there had been an accident and they were searching for a car, they'd never have found it. Would they? (WS330079)

Some participants had experience of vehicles with incorrect number plates and drew a contrast between their own circumstances and those of the young driver in the video clip. Amongst a community safety group in an area of mixed housing some criticised the car driver for his lethargy:

P1: Now, I drive a company car and they went to change the tax disc on it one year and the number plate on my car was wrong. They wouldn't let me in that car. They were running around like scalded cats and … the right plate was on that car within an hour. The car was where it was—it stayed. It didn't move. He would have known … he would have been told that 'you need to change that plate straightaway', when they gave him the fine to start off with.

P2: He should have taken the car straight back to where he bought it from and they would have sorted out there. (WS330045)

Some groups could not agree whether it was or was not reasonable for someone to be unaware that the registration plates on their car were inaccurate. The following discussion occurred within a Neighbourhood Watch Group in a suburban area:

P1: The fact that you've got 'dodgy' plates on your car doesn't always mean that it's your fault: it could be somebody else who's done it.

P2: Yeah, but …

P1: … the police, the police.

P2: … but it's usually the pointer.

P1: … they didn't know the reason then for the dodgy plates, did they?

P3: I ain't being funny, but if it's your car shouldn't you know what the number plate in the registration book is? And you say 'That's wrong!'

P4: That's …

P5: Having said that, we chop and change our cars that much now, if someone said to me …

P6: I'm glad you can afford to chop and change so much! (laughter)

P5: Yeah, but what's the registration number of your car! Y'know!

P6: I've got me voucher! (laughter)
P7: I don't know. I'm changing it all the time and I don't see it often (laughter). (WS330078)

Others felt that the police officer mishandled the situation and escalated the conflict by insulting and demeaning the young driver. A race equality activist group felt:

P1: Towards the end, I felt that the police officer was being ... escalated the situation by responding in the way that he was and I think that made the other chap aggressive ...

P2: The police abused their power as well at the end by deciding he would be fined for apparently for nothing [...] depending on the situation. It was like 'Well, we're going to fine you now', for what? I think it escalated and they couldn't manage the situation and [the police driver's] way of managing it was 'OK, we'll give you a fine then'. So that was more abusive than managing *that* situation, which [called for] an apology really, it was a genuine mistake 'This was the information we received. Clearly, it's not what we've got from you. Thanks for your cooperation.' It got to the level where [the car driver] retaliated; I was getting angry myself. It wasn't dealt with appropriately.

P2: They didn't need to use the fact that he was eighteen as well. He started dwelling on the fact. 'Grow up little boy' and that sort of thing. Totally unnecessary, I thought. Lack of respect. ...

P3: I thought the lad exacerbated it towards the end. They hadn't apologised and I do think they should have said, 'We do apologise for the misunderstanding, but thank you for your cooperation.' But to be winking at the camera and going ... He was exacerbating the situation a little.

P4: It must have been quite frustrating, but that's their role isn't it?

P3: Of course it is, yeah! (WS330075)

Even if, in the view of some, the police understandably 'got it wrong', they felt that the officers should have quickly apologised.

P1: The car wasn't stolen. Was it? It wasn't stolen!
P2: Then they should have apologised. (WS330021)

On the other hand, two young women attending a community safety group disagreed remarking:

P1: I always believe that if you act in a certain way, you get treated in that way. He acted like a little boy and got talked to like a little boy.
P2: I thought that if he wanted respect, I think he should've shown more respect ... The language he was using ...! (WS330045)

Some felt that the police officer and young driver were equally responsible. Young people attending a church youth club in an area of mixed housing likened it to an exchange between children, or even worse, 'politicians'! (WS330060)

Whether or not participants believed the young driver's account of the occasion when he was issued with a VDRS, all those expressing an opinion rested not on what they *witnessed* directly, but what they *inferred* had taken place on a previous occasion. However, it was not only their belief or disbelief of the driver's account of being given 'fourteen days' that relied on such inferences. Sometimes participants were willing to speculate quite extravagantly beyond what they had witnessed. In the following exchange amongst a neighbourhood watch group, the participants speculated about what might have justified the arrest of the driver.

P1: Why are the police so concerned about getting them out of a car and into a police car? Where, in fact, they're in a locked situation. I've been in that situation; you can't get out of the car because the back doors are locked. They seem to want to get you into their own environment before they start questioning.

P2: There could be a weapon in the car.

P3: Yeah!

P2: There could have been a weapon in the car.

P4: It's a very dangerous thing to do, to stand on the hard shoulder trying to talk to people.

P2: Yes, I was just going to say ...

P4: With artics going past, you're not going to hear ... I'm not going to hear in that situation. So, they get you in the car so that they can hear every word you're saying. If it's me, I'd want to be in the back of the police car ... because if something runs into the back of the car, you're not going to stand much chance of surviving. The safest place to be there is in the back of the police car. (WS330052)

Such reliance on imagination was not restricted to envisaging how the situation might unfold (e.g. the presence of weapons in the car). Some expected that the police had more IT capacity than they actually possess. A group of mid-career professionals imagined that the VDRS issued to the driver previously would be available on a police computer accessible to the patrol crew. Those who took this view concluded the whole incident could have been avoided because the suspicion that the car was stolen depended on the incorrect registration plates displayed on the car. The only IT specialist amongst them was more sceptical about police information systems.

P1: (Heavy sigh) Thoroughly over the top.

P2: Yeah, agreed, agreed!

P1: Thoroughly over the top. Ludicrous, ludicrous.

P3: The fact that he'd been given a ticket before, should be on the police computer, and the reason why he'd had that ticket. That would have solved everything there, wouldn't it? Everything would have been solved: they'd have known exactly what was going on. They'd have just pulled him over, 'Don't you think it's time you changed your plates, mate?'

P1: Yeah, yeah!

P3: Job done!

P1: I mean, where was it? They were at junction 6 or 7 and they're now near Gloucester. That's about half-an-hour away, so they had plenty of time to check that up, didn't they? Yeah? Whilst they were driving down. That was unbelievable.

P4: But they couldn't check that because the plates were coming up with nothing. They had no idea.

P3: Yeah, but they had a ticket—he'd had a ticket about a week before. His name should be on the police computer.

P4: Yes, but his name wasn't coming up on those plates.

P3: Yeah, but the fact that he'd had a ticket a week before on those false plates.

P5: Surely the number plates would have linked to the fact that they had pulled him over. Whether those are false plates or not, that information has got to be logged in the police computer somewhere. Surely? I don't know!

P2: Clicking the wrong buttons.

P4: I don't think their information is going to be that good to be honest. (WS330083)

A young adult studying for business qualifications asserted with confidence that 'He wasn't given a prohibition notice. He was just given a normal producer and instructed—as far as I understand from this—he was instructed, 'You've got fourteen days. There's a problem with your number plates. Sort that out' (WS330067). This would appear to be an error: a 'producer' normally refers to a form[8] requiring the production of crucial documents, such as a driver's licence at a police station, but the form in question here was a VDRS notice instructing the driver to rectify the erring number plates. This illustrates how procedural niceties are not only poorly understood, but can also give rise to misunderstandings, even those firmly held.

Sociologists have long appreciated how making sense of others' behaviour requires us to 'take the role of the other' (Mead and Morris 1934). How focus group participants judged the actions of the officers depended heavily on whether they took the perspective of the officers, or that of the suspected car thief. Those who took the officers' perspective accepted the good faith of the officers and appreciated that whilst they acted in error, their actions were understandable, prudent and justifiable given that they believed the car to be stolen. Others identified themselves with the car driver who was aggressively arrested on suspicion of stealing a car, of which he was innocent, and then fined for a minor administrative infringement about which he believed he had been misled. This was captured during a discussion amongst a group of young men who lived in a desirable rural dormitory suburb:

P1: You have to put yourself in the situation where it was your car that got stolen. Would you want the police officer to talk to the robber like ...?
[This was followed by indistinct interruptions.]

---

[8] Officially a 'HORT1', known colloquially as a 'horty'.

P2: But the car wasn't stolen …

P3: It wasn't stolen!

P4: Ask him a question to find out…. The way it escalated …

[…]

P5: They checked his tax disc […]

P3: To be honest if they said you'd done something you hadn't done, how would you feel about that?

P2: If the police come up to you, dragged you out of your car and started talking down to you like that …

P5: No, the question is, how would you feel if the number plates got mixed up on your car; you weren't aware of it; and the first you're made aware is when the police pull you over and start being rude to you? How would that make you feel? Y'know! (WS330071)

This is also telling confirmation of Tyler's view that trust is 'motive-based', but also that the inference of motive is highly problematic. As we shall discuss in the next chapter, police are required to act on suspicion, which is an error-prone basis for action, especially when that action is likely to be unwelcome. When they make such a mistake public sympathies are divided, because the consequences of that mistake are immediate, apparent and disagreeable—such as being dragged from a car and locked inside a police vehicle. The question that arises for witnesses and bystanders is whether the officers' motives and actions were reasonable, or reckless. This can only be answered by inferring the officers' state of mind.

Conclusions

In this chapter we have compared the reaction of our focus groups to two video clips that were rated on our crude scale at either extreme: the investigation of the robbery of an elderly man gave our focus groups the most favourable impression, whilst the motorway stop was regarded as the episode that left our focus group members least favourably disposed to the police. Moreover, assessments of the motorway stop showed the widest dispersal of overall evaluations, whereas the robbery of the elderly man yielded the least dispersed scores on the scale. Yet, the differences between these scores are not accurately reflected in the discussions that our focus groups held. Not everything about the response to the elderly man's robbery was regarded favourably and there were some things that the focus groups felt were laudable about the motorway stop. Whilst the motorway stop produced very different and often hotly debated points of view from our focus groups, so too did aspects of the response to the elderly man's robbery.

The complexity and ambivalence of our focus groups' evaluations of these two video clips was repeated in their discussion of the remaining video clips, *all* of which contained periods when groups expressed both positive and negative views. Indeed, considering all four focus groups, we might characterise *all* the video clips as divisive to some extent (see Appendix). There were three aspects of this dissension: first, participants simply disagreed about whether specific features were reason to criticise or condemn; secondly, disputes arose about what had occurred and why; finally, many individuals found reason to both praise and condemn, for instance, by approving of how the motorway patrol tried to enlist the support of other patrols to safely stop the suspected driver, whilst condemning the badinage between the driver and the officer. There were only two aspects of our focus groups' discussions which were common to all: first, was the intensity of the discussion that followed both video clips, but especially the stopping of the suspected 'stolen' car on the motorway. One might observe *plus ça change*: attitude measurement does not imply that there will be total agreement, only that the arithmetic mean of a sample is of a particular value, or that a certain proportion of the sample used one category rather than another. However, it is the mean values and highest proportions that tend to attract most analytic attention, especially when they are statistically significant. Statistical significance is an index of how likely or unlikely it is that a result has occurred purely by chance and fails to reflect underlying reality. Yet, perhaps the 'story' told by the dispersion of individual outcomes *is 'the story'* and not just an inevitable artefact of sampling methodology! Perhaps it could even be the case that attitudes are not something that people possess, in the way that they might be said to possess physical characteristics like height and weight, which vary but only within a narrow range. Maybe (and we do not pretend to be in a position to resolve these issues) 'attitudes' to the police and possibly other matters are intrinsically fluid, responsive to a persistent stream of prompts. When they are asked by researchers and pollsters to commit themselves to some composite overall assessment, say, of the police, they then enter a distinct universe of meaning. Secondly, amid all this dissension, there was considerable agreement throughout all focus groups about *what* was controversial in the video clips they had watched. The same moments and aspects were repeatedly the focus of attention, whether to praise or condemn. Instead of claiming that members of our focus groups, or some proportion of them, approved or not of how officer(s) conducted themselves, in the remainder of this book we will focus on those areas of controversy. For it was the *intensity* of discussion and debate that was such a prominent feature of our data.

4

Suspicion

Introduction

'Reasonable suspicion' is the bedrock on which police officers execute their legal powers,[1] but what does 'suspicion' mean in practice? What prompts 'suspicion' in any specific situation? 'Reasonable suspicion' is more than a legal threshold, it is a claim to propriety: the officer is not, say, stopping and searching someone whimsically, or because of bias and prejudice, but is acting 'reasonably' in response to actual or potential wrongdoing. Yet, officers find it difficult to articulate what precisely it was that aroused their suspicions. Officers are often heard to say in videos such as those selected for this research, how there was something undefinably suspicious about the situation, even if they could not identify or articulate it. Yet, objective evidence leads to doubt about the value of officers' intuition (Alpert and Noble 2008). Stop and search is a supreme example: the so-called 'hit rate' is less than 10 per cent. This has fuelled complaints that the ethnic disparity in stop and searches is the product of 'institutional racism' (Macpherson of Cluny et al. 1999; Home Office/College of Policing 2014). This raises a wider point of direct relevance for the notion of 'procedural justice', which places a strong emphasis on the need for officers to be seen to act fairly: can it ever be *fair* to suspect wholly innocent people of wrongdoing? In other circumstances, to suspect/accuse someone of wrongdoing might amount to defamation, and certainly most people are likely to find it offensive and would likely be indignant towards their accuser.

How satisfied were our focus groups that officers depicted in the video clips were executing their legal powers 'reasonably'? Did they agree that the actions of 'suspects' were, indeed, suspicious? Three of our video clips created debate about the issue of suspicion. First, the stopping of the suspected car on the motorway. We saw that most participants agreed that the officers had ample

---

[1] In the USA the standard is 'probable cause', which—for all practical purposes—is the same.

reason for believing that the car might be stolen: it had been reported as driving away from a petrol filling station without payment and the registration number displayed was incorrect. The fact that officers suspected it was stolen was not seen as problematic, it was what happened subsequently that proved controversial. We will address this issue more deeply when we turn to the use of force by officers. Here, we limit ourselves to the issue of whether our focus groups believed that suspicion was justified or not and since the remaining two video clips aroused most debate will concentrate on those. We are already familiar with one of these: the video clip depicting officers dealing with an alleged robbery at the home of an elderly man, which left many in our focus groups convinced that 'Chantelle' (the elderly man's young companion) was complicit in the robbery. The issue of suspicion also arose in another video clip yet to be considered in detail; this video clip showed three young men breaking into a car in a superstore car park. We will consider this in detail later in this chapter. First, let us consider the robbery at the elderly man's home, discussed in the previous chapter.

Robbery at Home of Elderly Man

Unlike others, the outcome of the situation depicted in the video was not concluded within the duration of the video clip. What had actually occurred at the home of the elderly man remained for focus group participants to resolve for themselves. On the whole, they were highly suspicious of 'Chantelle's'—the young woman's—role in the whole affair. How, then, did *they* construct their own suspicions? How did this affect their evaluation of the police officers who investigated the alleged robbery?

Two main themes emerged: first, Chantelle's credibility and the suspicion that she might, in some way, be implicated in the robbery; and, secondly, the relationship between the elderly man and Chantelle, which many found to be suspicious. Before proceeding with the analysis, it should be acknowledged that a few focus groups contained people who recalled viewing this incident on television when originally broadcast and were able to remember the outcome—Chantelle's boyfriend was convicted of the robbery. Although only a couple of those who could recall this episode disclosed it to others in their respective groups, it possibly biased discussion.

Chantelle's Credibility

For many focus group participants Chantelle's (and to a lesser extent, the elderly man's) credibility relied on what participants expected to be evidence of distress. Does the coherence with which an account is rendered confer credibility or detract from it? Does confusion about detail undermine credibility or is it explicable as evidence of shock and distress? Do inconsistencies between the account given by the putative 'victims' and objective evidence cast doubt?

For some participants, the way in which Chantelle related the story of what had allegedly occurred had the hallmarks of being rehearsed. Young men attending a further education college took this view.

> P1: When he [the officer] asked 'What did he look like?'
> P2: She said, 'Five foot five'. She come up with a measurement!
> P1: Yeah, she came up with a measurement! (WS330006)

A neighbourhood watch group in a residential area of private housing also thought that Chantelle was too rehearsed about some matters and inconsistent about others. Either way, it undermined her in their eyes.

> P1: That girl's a liar, 100 per cent! She tells lies. She's in cahoots with the chap who ...
> P2: It's her boyfriend!
> P1: ... on that old guy! To get in there. Her story was changing from time to time. He's put a knife to my throat ... to my arm. There isn't a mark on them. Liar!
> P3: Liar!
> [...]
> P3: Surely, I don't think all those bolts on the doors were not for a stranger. I think they opened the door and then they entered.
> P2: You might be saying afterwards 'Don't jump to conclusions.'
> P1: So, I think she knows [indistinct agreement].
> [...]
> P1: So that's why they're not worried about her. They know that she's a liar.
> [This was followed by a general, but indistinct, discussion agreeing. One voice says 'Too many details' and another replies:]
> P2: She's a storyteller. Every time she opened her mouth there was [...] 'Then he did this' and 'Then he did that'. (WS330078)

The reason for doubting an account that was too coherent is that most participants were looking for evidence of overt distress, which in their view was absent. Being threatened at knifepoint was expected to leave the victims fearful and agitated, all of which would preclude the composure that Chantelle displayed in offering a coherent account. For instance, amongst a group of professionals and volunteers promoting racial and sexual equality in a very deprived area, some were sceptical.

> P1: She didn't look that distressed!
> P2: No, she didn't, did she? So that's what I thought: did someone follow her to the house, or did she play some part in setting it up? But towards the end ... When they said, 'We've found the money, all £45 of it' in a bag[2]—they found all the money, didn't they? Then I started to think otherwise. Was it a robbery gone wrong or a (laugh) or whether it was planned or what? (WS330047)

---

[2] Actually, the voice-over explained that the bag containing the elderly man's pension—'All £45 of it'—had been found, but empty of its contents.

Not everyone agreed that Chantelle's behaviour was suspicious. At a consultation group in a multi-cultural area conflicting interpretations were aired. When one participant thought Chantelle must have been very shocked, another replied:

P1: She didn't seem very shocked.

P2: Shock in different people means different things and to me, the concern has got to be that *both* of them are victims, but they seemed to be concentrating on the one rather than both of them—both of them are victims in this. Sympathy goes out to the gentleman because of his medical condition.
[A little later the group returned to the theme.]

P3: She kept forgetting her name—'Chantelle'!
[This remark was greeted with general jocularity.]

P4: She's not telling the truth.

P5: No, she's making it up. (WS330050)

Some members of a church youth club in an economically deprived area not only thought Chantelle's appearance betrayed her, but also implied that the police officers should have questioned her more closely:

Her eye make-up was all intact; she wasn't distressed. If that would have been a knife to my neck, I would have been distraught. When the police knocked on the door, she went, 'Who is it?', 'The police'. Well, I wouldn't have taken anyone's word for it. You'd be looking, wouldn't you, out of the curtains? She opened it straightaway. So, obviously, I would have liked them to question *her* more, even to see how she was. Because, y'know, I think she was lying. (WS330060)

Amongst some of our focus groups there were individuals who had direct experience of being robbed, one in circumstances eerily similar to those depicted in the video clip. Yet, they remained sceptical of Chantelle and felt that her account of the robbery should have been probed by the officers.

P1: [...] then again the girl might be in shock. Indeed, everyone could have been in shock.
[...]

P2: The description wasn't great, was it? They said, 'Oh, his face was covered'.

P3: What about his hands?

P4: When you're being robbed, you don't look at these things. We was robbed in our own bedroom ...

P5: It's their job to ask: 'Is there something distinctive about him that might ... '

P6: That would have been left for the detectives.

P3: When they were asked about his age, they said 'No, no eighteen'. Well, if he'd got a hood on his face how would they have known? You can't really tell, if someone is hooded, how really old they are. So, I thought that was strange, but you know ... stress?

Res: Some people have been rather doubtful about the story ...

P5: I was! I was thinking, 'This girl doesn't add up to me! It sort of set something up ...'

P7: When she said she wasn't a relative, but 'good friends'. I thought that was strange.

P4: I don't think she was there to look after him or to drink his cans.

Res: Do you think, therefore, that the police should have probed her story more?

P5: I do. I actually thought it took a long time for him to establish exactly who she was (laugh). I thought, 'Why haven't you asked, "Who are you?" '. It was quite a long way down the line, when they took her into a separate room, I thought, 'Why hasn't he established straight away who you are and what relationship you are to this man'. (WS330090)

Many participants drew significant conclusions from two aspects of the situation: Chantelle's confusion regarding the name that the alleged intruder used to gain entry—'Chantelle' or 'Kayleigh'—and the apparent absence of knife marks on either of the alleged victims, despite Chantelle's claims to the contrary.

Turning first to the question of names: the video clip shows the young woman answering the door to the first officer to arrive. She says that a man had come to the door and asked to speak to 'Chantelle', but then corrects herself and says that he had asked for 'Kayleigh', a friend of hers who also visits the elderly man. For many participants, this confusion over who the man had asked to speak to was evidence of the young woman's unreliability.

Worshippers at a Sikh temple (interviewed by a Sikh and the conversation lapses into Punjabi from time to time) considered this confusion of names to be suspicious.

It could have been somebody she knows. The thing is, right, that she said ... at the beginning she said that he shouted out a different name. Then if he shouted out a different name, why did she let him in?

[...]

The suspicious bit is that he ... she said 'Chantelle' and her name is something else ... right ... and she ... she shouldn't have let him in anyway. Shouldn't have opened the door ... y'know, if it's somebody you don't know. (WS310027)

Students attending a school in a very deprived area of public housing were equally sceptical.

P1: When she unlocked the door she was on about 'Chantelle' and then it was 'Kayleigh'—that's who she was. She was 'Kayleigh'. Then when they asked her her name no it wasn't, it was 'No I'm Chantelle'. So, what is her name 'Kayleigh' or 'Chantelle'? Then it was 'Oh, he looked about 20', you know, then in the next breath she says she didn't see his face.

[...]

P2: She kept on changing her story!

P3: She didn't even know her name!!!

[This was followed by general laughter.] (WS330084)

On the arrival of the police, Chantelle claimed that a knife had been pressed against her flesh, leaving marks. Later, the elderly man said that a knife was held against his throat. The officer is seen examining the arms and shoulder of Chantelle and the elderly man's neck, but reported, in a voice over, that he could see no marks. For some, this was reason enough for suspicion. For instance, amongst a second group convened at the Sikh temple it was said 'She said she had marks, but I didn't see anything.' (WS310030)

A regeneration action group in a deprived area also focused on the absence of any marks:

P1: They did mention, she'd got no marks.
P2: They did say, that they'd noticed that. It would be things that …
P3: You'd have some sort of a scratch or mark there.
[This was followed by general, but indistinct agreement about the lack of marks.]
P4: … They did mention it. They couldn't see any marks. Obviously, if you look at it one way, you could say that it looked suspicious. (WS330059)

A group of mid-career professionals concurred:

P1: I think she's in on it. I think she's in on it.
P2: All these bruises and knife marks, but there wasn't any, was there?
[…]
P3: I think she got into a muddle with her names right at the beginning, which turned me off. Who was who? It was all a bit … She didn't seem that distressed—if you think how I was! (WS330083)

Some others drew even more adverse implications. Amongst a youth group who met at an arts centre in an area of mixed housing, the absence of knife marks combined with confusion over names led some to the conclusion that Chantelle was 'on crack' (WS330071).

Chantelle's credibility highlights an issue to which we will return shortly: in assessing this (and many other situations dealt with by the police) ordinary people confront a situation of which they are largely, if not wholly, unfamiliar. How would someone react when faced with a knife wielding intruder? Would they have become 'hysterical'? Would eye make-up be smudged? Would they invariably scream? Research on 'mock juries' convened to adjudicate hypothetical rape cases concluded that 'jurors' rely on common-sense understandings of how sexual encounters 'normally' occur as a template for assessing the credibility of those claiming to be victims (Ellison and Munro 2009b). Deviating from that template helps to structure assessments of guilt and responsibility. However, the reasoning of these 'mock jurors' is incompatible with objective research on rape. These 'mock jurors' are, at least, likely to be familiar with sexual encounters of some kind. However, in this video clip the challenge is to imagine something that was utterly unfamiliar—being robbed at knifepoint by an intruder. It is interesting that amongst the young people at the arts centre one them *did* have experience of being threatened with a knife and this led another participant to be much less sceptical of Chantelle.

P1: To be fair. I was threatened on the bus with a knife once. It is quite scary! So, you would be shaky […]

P2: That's probably why you think of her as suspicious, because there's that shaky … she looks so suspicious because she's so shaken. (WS330071)

Moreover, expectations are not necessarily consistently applied: participants were suspicious of Chantelle because she appeared too calm, but *also* because she was flustered and unable to recall the name used by the robber to gain entry ('Kayleigh' or 'Chantelle'?).

Relationship Between the 'Victims'

Apart from the appearance and behaviour of Chantelle, many participants were attentive to the contextual cues arising from her presence in the elderly man's flat, where she was drinking beer with him. In the video clip the officer asks about their relationship and Chantelle replies that they are not related (presumably in a familial sense), but the man is a 'friend of the family'; at which point she fondly strokes the man's cheek with her hand. Promoters of equality issues in a deprived multi-cultural area spoke for many in expressing disquiet. One participant drew attention to it:

It seems to me to be strange to have a young person who is a 'family friend' on an evening.
[This generated an animated—and therefore impossible to transcribe—discussion of suspicion, which concluded with another participant observing.]
You wouldn't do it [affectionately stroke the man's face] to a 'friend of the family'(WS330050).

This was not the only occasion on which the phrase, 'a friend of the family' was repeated. A group of Sikh worshippers did so derisively (WS310031). They were joined in their ironic laughter by members of a trade association concerned with the security of a local city centre, one of whom also noted: 'She wasn't the only young girl to go there as well. She was "a friend"' (laugh) (WS330021).

Implicit in the response of many participants was scepticism about the propriety of the relationship between the man and the girl that some believed to be sinister. For instance, members of a community action project in a deprived area took this view:

P1: Perhaps it's just me being a bit cynical but I would have talked to her a bit more?
[This was immediately followed by an excited jumble of conversations that defied transcription. One voice referred to marks and doubts that there were any.]
Res: So there seems to be a certain cynicism around the table …
[Which was greeted with laughter.]
Res: What are you cynical about?
P1: The girl's story. I think it was a set-up.
[Again, there was an excited but indistinct cacophony of shouted competing claims.]
P1: I didn't think that at first,
P2: … they were claiming it on the 'Social' or something.
[Further indistinct, but excited chatter.]

Res: When you say it was a 'set-up', are you saying it didn't happen at all, or …
P1: That's how it seemed to me.
P2: … or she was part of it.
P1: Yeah, yeah! (WS330025)

Most participants imagined that 'Chantelle' was exploiting the elderly man's desire for company, but others elaborated the conspiracy theory to embrace not only Chantelle, but also the elderly man. For instance, a multi-cultural group of young professionals ventured an explanation of what might have occurred.

P1: I think they were in this together, together.
P2: Collaboration of some sort…. Like I say, if someone is having a party and it's gone wrong and somebody takes the money; or you've had an argument and you want to 'stitch him up' and you ask someone 'Will you help me stitch him up?' It can be anything because you don't know the true facts behind it. So, we could make as many judgements … Or it could be in shock. She could have been in shock. (WS330067)

How Should the Police Have Treated the Man and the Girl?

Given these suspicions regarding the girl (and in some cases also the man), how did participants in our focus groups expect the police to treat her (or them both)? In the previous chapter we considered the various criticisms of the police response that were voiced. Here we will focus on how those criticisms related to the suspicions that focus group members entertained.

Generally speaking (and not surprisingly) those who believed that one or both of the 'victims' were lying expected more vigorous and incisive questioning. Others were more willing to consider the possibility that the deficiencies of the young woman's account resulted from the trauma she had suffered, but often these were isolated remarks that were readily dismissed. Amongst volunteers at an urban regeneration consultative group in a deprived area doubts were aired but scepticism triumphed.

P1: I don't know how to say the lady was credible or wasn't credible because her statement was a bit … but she could be traumatised.
P2: I think it was right to treat her statement as suspicious. Her statement … she kept faltering this way and then … I think she might have had something to do with it. The relationship is a bit suspicious, let's be honest.
[…]
P1: My reaction was, 'Come on, Miss' (laugh).
P3: To me it was obvious that when he [the officer] didn't believe a word of what she's saying.
[…]
P1: Yeah, when he [the officer] entered the house it was obvious that he just asked … Yeah, yeah, his way of questioning, yeah. Well, I would as well, if I was the officer I'd think I don't think she is …

77

P4: I think the officer was very professional.

P1: He was very diplomatic, wasn't he? ... Yeah, he was 'very professional' with the elderly gentleman.

[Which was greeted with murmurs of agreement.]

P1: ... he was very professional, but I think ... It was obvious, as he was writing it down, the words were coming out, he was thinking 'I'm not believing you' [...] If we could pick it up ... I'm sure he could.

P4: First of all, I've got to look at it as the possibility ... There's a young lady in that episode that is, what is giving to me a big question mark. Said that she'd been ... with a knife there and there. I didn't see any visual reality of evidence of violence on that person. I was surprised that the officers who were dealing with the case didn't examine her more thoroughly as regards seeing knife wounds of that ilk, or what she claims to be. So, I'm looking at the possibility that it's a set-up. The other thing is, I've got to say is, that when the CID was brought in to take fingerprints and everything else. There's got to be a place for that, regards bringing them in so quickly as regards to a crime or major incident of that ilk. But I'm still questioning: is it a set-up which is trying—as I was saying—to fool the police in this incident. That's the way I feel about it. [...]

Res: You don't think they should have questioned the young girl more, in a more ...?

P4: Yes, I do. And I think the CID should have sat her down in another room and said, 'Look. This is just not adding up'. That is the way that I see the situation. Whether they did that or not, I don't know, but from what we were shown ... I feel there should have been some sort of dialogue between officers and that young lady in a private setting. And I think, to be perfectly honest with you, it would have left doubts in those officers' minds.

P1: I go along with that. You could see in the background that the officer said he could see no visible marks and the officer did take her aside, but I think the officer ... but I think the officer acted professionally because she was only a friend of the gentleman and the gentleman hadn't said that she *had* done it, then they had no avenue to go down, because when it happened, apparently both of them were in the house. So even so the old man ... he may ... I may say, he does ... he may have suspicions. He didn't say to the officer ... so the officer didn't know what to do. He might have his doubts, but he's got no facts.

P4: Bear in mind, that that young lady in her first opening statement she said that when she opened the door, she was pushed and then a knife was put to her throat, there were slashes on here shoulder and whatever ... The police officers had only got *her* word of what had took place. Nobody else's, but just her word. And I still say that there's a lot to be decided on that ... (WS330037).

Some successfully resisted the sceptical view that prevailed elsewhere. For instance, students at an FE college serving an area of mixed housing took the charitable view that the police should not have been suspicious of the young woman's account because 'She was all shook up' (WS330028). Members of a neighbourhood watch group in an area of mixed housing tempered their suspicions by acknowledging the possibility that the young woman may have been either adversely affected by the experience and/or was unable to articulate her experiences very well.

P1: My feelings were that if I was the policeman I'd be suspicious of the girl.
[Greeted by murmurs of agreement.]
P1: Was she making it up, and it was her boyfriend and they're after the old man's money?
[Further murmurs of agreement.]
Res 1: Do you think the police officer should have been more suspicious, then?
P1: Yeah
Res 1: ... and taken more action ...?
P2: We don't know what ... what ... He took her into another room to talk to her and we don't know what went on there, do we?
P3: She did seem genuinely strung–up at the beginning, didn't she?
P4: Agitated ...
P1: The problem was that she wasn't very articulate and that's the biggest problem—you've got to get past that. She was trying to explain what happened. She wasn't very good with her words, her choice of words. So, I think automatically you're going to drop down on the suspicious side, which may not be absolutely the truth.... I wasn't suspicious of her. I just thought she wasn't very articulate.
P3: Neither of them were! Plus the old man was taking medicines as well.
Res 2: Do you think they were probing enough of the stories?
P3: Not really.
P5: It's very strange: a young girl and an old man!
[This was greeted with general agreement.]
P5: What was she doing there in the first place?
P1: Not related.
P2: There wasn't much about the weapon ... There was no substantiation of that, was there? So, they could have asked more.
P5: It might have been her mother that went [to the old man's house] rather than her. If she has a mother, of course!
P1: No, they were up the pub.
[This was followed by general laughter.] (WS330052)

Others acknowledged the complexities of the case, but felt that these complexities did not absolve the police from rigorously examining the credibility of Chantelle. A local authority community safety group of local residents held this discussion:

P1: I was a bit concerned ... they were going to take the girl into another room and take a statement, yet she told the whole story in front of the old guy and the policeman anyway. Yeah, OK, I understand you have to have statements then surely ... No! That should be done .... I don't know.
Res: Are you saying that it should have been done earlier or later?

P1: Well I appreciate you have to give an overview of what happened, but she went through the whole thing and then had to make a statement. So if there was any—I'm not saying that there was any collaboration there (I don't think there was)—but if there was any collaboration at all, it had all been said before, so when the older guy was interviewed he could have said exactly the same thing if it hadn't ... That concerned me....

P2: Unfortunately, when they questioned the girl in front of the old man, he picked up on every answer she gave. At the end of the day, he was eighty-two and the only thing he remembered was what she had said.... If I was being cynical, she would have been the first to be arrested!

P2: Also, in a state of shock you say things ...

P3: Well that's true.

P4: Well that's another part of the equation, isn't it?!

P2: Are you saying that the girl should have been more shocked ... The more so in the way she portrayed herself ...

P4: They were both in shock. They gave the appearance ...

P2: She didn't seem to be that much worried, because I think (without spoiling it[3]), I think that she was involved in it.

P3: I think that the girl herself ... I think that perhaps she should have been interviewed with a female officer there as well as a male officer there ... to cover the police's concerns, because they were taking her into a room on her own and I was suspicious of the girl from the beginning—I don't know why—but there's just something about the story that just didn't ring true. If I was in that situation I'd want two colleagues there ...

P5: She was very confused as to who she was and perhaps there should have been a woman police officer to take the statement, but she didn't seem as upset ... if, what has happened to her ... I don't think she was as upset about the whole situation as the old man was, which was a [...] terrifying thing. I think she composed herself quite well really.

P2: She had too much to say for herself, really.
   [...]

Res: Given what you have said about your scepticism about the young lady, do you think the police should have interrogated her more firmly?

P2: Yeah.

P5: They might have done after for all I know.

Res: At the time, from what you saw, did they ...

P1: Given the age difference of the two people and no relationship between them ...

P4: She might have been known to them [the police] for all we know.

P5: Initially, at face value, you've got to treat them as 'victims'. What comes from the outcome of the investigation: that determines whether she was [...] part or not. But initially she's got to be looked upon as a 'victim'. (WS330043)

Three striking conclusions can be drawn from this data: first, despite the sometimes explicitly acknowledged complexities, all but a very few of our

---

[3] This participant recalled having seen the episode from which this clip was taken.

participants were robustly confident that their suspicions were correct. They expected the police to treat Chantelle, not as a 'victim', but as a 'suspect'. Secondly, they believed that they shared these same suspicions with the officers dealing with the case. In other words, in their view, there was ample justification for the police actually treating Chantelle as a 'suspect', rather than a 'victim'. Indeed, they expected the police to do more in this direction than was evident in the video clip. This is an issue that goes to the heart of contemporary policy debates, especially those concerning crimes against women (Her Majesty's Inspector of Constabulary 2014) and children (Jay 2014). The complaint is repeatedly made that police officers do not accept what victims allege. Yet, in this video clip very few people accepted that the putative victim, Chantelle, was an innocent party and many seemed convinced that she was in some way implicated in the offence. Should the police officers have accepted without scrutiny what Chantelle alleged? There was a remarkable level of agreement amongst our focus groups that they should not.

Theft from Parked Car

In the previous example, the focus groups did not know what had actually occurred at the elderly man's bungalow a few minutes before the police attended. Their suspicions of Chantelle's complicity relied on their assessment of her account, lack of evidence of knife marks, to support it and they drew upon the context of a young woman apparently befriending an elderly man and her displays of affection. However, what if there is clear evidence—caught on CCTV—that three young men have broken into a car parked at a superstore? Does this prove their guilt?

In the video clip we discuss next three young men were seen on private security operated CCTV breaking into a car parked in a superstore car park. A plain-clothes, on-site police officer, assisted by private security guards, challenged the young men (who made no attempt to escape). The young men claimed that they were doing a favour for a girlfriend of one of them who had locked her keys in the car. The officer arrested all three men until their account was corroborated by the arrival of the girlfriend, but one of the men objected strongly and vociferously, and was arrested after a brief struggle. Once the girlfriend arrived, proved her valid ownership of the car, and corroborated the men's story, the two compliant men were de-arrested and left the scene, but the other young man remained truculent and was rearrested on a public order charge. As the officer transported him to the police station, the young man accused the officer of racism on the grounds that 'He saw me, the only Paki ...'.

In deciding whether or not the young men's behaviour was sufficiently suspicious to justify their arrest, our focus group participants relied on cues relating to the young men's behaviour; their appearance; and other stereotypical characteristics. On most of these issues, focus group participants largely agreed, both amongst themselves and with the officer in the video clip, that the young men's behaviour was suspicious. On the remaining issue—the one youth's agitation—there was a division of opinion.

Breaking in

Some actions committed in particular circumstances are so anomalous that they become noteworthy—'peculiar', 'odd', 'strange'—and call for some explanation. Some of the explanations that jump most readily to mind suggest wrongdoing. Hence, seeing three men standing beside a car and smashing its passenger door window was uncommon enough to invite the inference that they were trying to steal the car. Almost everyone agreed that their behaviour was suspicious and justified police intervention. For young men at an FE college in an area of economic deprivation it was obvious that police would want to 'see what's going on, really' (WS330006). The likelihood that the youths' story was true was thought to be small (WS330090).

Nevertheless, forming a suspicion still requires connecting the 'dots' so as to create a coherent picture, however rudimentary. Another 'dot' to which the first could be connected was that the police officer did not unilaterally form his suspicion, but instead was alerted by the superstore private security personnel. Young volunteers at an urban regeneration scheme in a very deprived area felt that this bolstered confidence in the suspiciousness of the youths' behaviour:

> Somebody's obviously reported it to the police. So, someone's obviously seen it as [...] assume that they have broken in. There's a group of boys all round this car who obviously aren't the car owner, who would have the keys. Assuming they've broken in. (WS330080)

Nevertheless, they appreciated 'that's a judgement, though, isn't it?'

And where was the owner on whose behalf the youths purported to be acting? Many felt that the owner should not have left the scene, but remained to establish the bona fides of the young men and their actions. Mid-career professionals in an affluent rural dormitory area, felt that there were many options that might have been taken to forestall suspicion.

> P1: It doesn't need to happen, does it? They could have acted totally differently, couldn't they? They could have gone to the security guard and said, 'Look. We're going to bust into this car. The missus has left the keys in there.' They could have called a locksmith, y'know. There's a whole different bunch of scenarios they could have used [...]
> P2: You assume they've got some level of intelligence in the first place.
> [This was followed by laughter.]
> P3: Or, perhaps she called them because they're already good at breaking into cars!
> [Further laughter.]

P4: I assume they would have a mobile phone on them to accept that call, to actually ring her back, 'Darling, could you please speak to the policeman?'
[Followed by indistinct general agreement.]

P4: ... which would have taken thirty seconds. Then probably nobody would have ever got [...] handcuffed, or anything. (WS330083)

In fact, *had* someone phoned the police telling them that they planned to break into a car, the police would have probably warned them against doing so, since otherwise it would be tempting for a car thief to arrange for an accomplice to make such a phone call and thereby forestall police intervention. Members of a neighbourhood watch in a deprived area more credibly suggested that the better option was to go home, collect the spare car keys and return to the car park.

P1. Actually, one of the trouble is that one of the three turned around and said 'I am the boyfriend'.

P2: Hasn't he got a car key?

P3: Exactly! One would have gone home, get the key and come back.

P4: The trouble is you phone the police and say, 'I've lost my car keys' and they won't do nothing. That's the sad part about it: they won't do anything. They'll probably tell you, 'Oh, we can't help. Go and get your own car keys'. I hate to say that, but that is exactly what they would do.
[...]

P5: I can't understand—store security ... store security were on the scene. Why didn't he explain to them? Why didn't the lady whose car it was stop there and explain it to them? It could have stopped all that.

P2: She was as much to blame as anybody.
[Another voice urges that the woman was 'more' to blame.]
Yes, 'more'! She shouldn't have moved away from the car. (WS330095)

The previous focus group were not alone in blaming the woman owner for what happened. Race equality workers and volunteers agreed unreservedly.

They should have a word with the woman too: 'The next time you do that, don't phone up your friends to break into your car. Go and tell somebody.' Y'know, because she was the one who was responsible for the whole incident in the first instant. Y'know, if I'd have got my car there, then I'd have called either the AA or RAC, if I was a member, or gone to people in the car park, y'know, so that they knew what was happening, because it is just *bound* to cause trouble, isn't it? (WS330047)

Very few felt that the police were unjustified in being suspicious of the youths. However, an exception was a group of young people attending a community arts project who considered it unlikely that genuine car thieves would have been so brazen as these young men. They felt that the police should not have jumped to the conclusion that it was an attempted theft.

P1: To be fair, I thought they were trying to break in to the car (laugh).

P2: But you got to ask yourself: it was in a car park in broad daylight at a shopping centre ...

P3: Who commits crime with people watching you?
[This was followed by an indistinct interjection.]

P1: Desperate people!

P4: You wouldn't, like, look at the car for ten minutes, you'd take what you want and get out of it.

P5: They were trying to hold something down! If they were going to smash the window and get off, they would have done that within .... They would have been that quick.

P2: Ah! The police didn't assess the situation properly, that's another thing to think about, isn't it? (WS330071)

Whilst a minority view, this does highlight the scope for interpretative licence in the construction of suspicion, because suspicion is always contextual and involves the selection of some cues and inattention to, or rejection of, others.

Appearance

We have already seen how, apart from what the young men were *doing* in breaking into the car, their appearance confirmed the suspicions of many. One youth wore a hooded sports sweater with the hood up and one of his colleagues wore a baseball cap, at least one of them wore gloves, which many of our focus group participants equated with the stereotypical image of young criminals, especially in view of the sun shining in the background. Members of a trade association for a local private security industry felt that such an appearance confirmed their suspicions: 'he knew he was in the right, but the situation didn't look right from the start. Two guys in the middle of a car park; one with a hood up; breaking into a car—even a pedestrian walking past would think that is suspicious' (WS330021). So too did residents attending a 'safer neighbourhoods' meeting in a deprived area. 'The situation was: they were dressed in a manner with hoods on with devices to break into a car. So they gave the view that they're criminals about to commit a crime. I think that is something we can all be clear on' (WS330043). Despite some members of a 'mother and baby' group in one of the most deprived neighbourhoods having personal, albeit vicarious, experience of being unwarrantably suspected by the police, there was general agreement that the youths' appearance and resistance mutually reinforced their suspicions.

P1: They did look a bit dodgy, didn't they? Dark clothing; they had hoodies on, which is what [...]

P2: Wearing dark clothing with a hood. Does that automatically mean ...?

P3: They was trying to get into a car. That's what I'm saying. But if they walked into a shop with his hood up, he'd probably have security guards follow him (WS330049).

Very few comments suggested that reliance on appearance was likely to cause bias in who became suspected of what. This minority view was expressed most eloquently by equality workers and volunteers in a multi-ethnic area of acute deprivation:

P1: If they'd have been dressed in suits, who they have ... would what happened, have happened if they were dressed in suits? Has the way they were dressed have anything to do with the outcome of what went on?

Res: What do you think?

P1: I think if they'd been dressed in suits and listened to the story, they'd have been believed straightaway. Because the two gentlemen were dressed the way they was, *speaking* the way they was; that's why it took the route it did ...

P2: I was just thinking: it was their youth that was standing against them really. 'Ah yeah! Three young lads hanging around a car, likely story. As [name] said, if they'd been dressed in suits; if they'd been a bit older; if they talked a bit posher; whatever, they'd probably have been treated a little bit differently.

[...]

P3: I was just thinking: when you watch the video and them guys are by the car, they did look a bit suspicious. They're standing there [...] with their hats on. So, I don't know.

Res: Who thinks that that initial shot from the CCTV justified taking action? [Answered by various cries of 'Oh yeah', 'Definitely' and indistinct tokens of agreement.]

P4: 'Course with hats on, they just looked a bit ...

P5: Break into a car. Oh yeah!

Res: Do you agree? Do you?

P1: Oh yes, because of the way they were dressed and the way they was coming across, yeah (WS330077).

No Escape

If our focus groups frequently mentioned the three youths' appearance, one feature of their behaviour that largely escaped mention was that they made *no attempt to escape* when the private security guards (who were first to arrive) initially accosted them.

I thought it was interesting though, as a police officer, he's walking up ... scarper. If they were up to something, just looking back on it ... then they're going to run off, they're going to run. But they were saying, 'Alright, just let us stand by the car, lads, until she turns up ... not needing to ...' (WS330047)

Those few who did feel that this failure to escape was indicative of innocence, tended also to be critical of the officer for ignoring this cue and treating the youths as if they were suspects. Amongst race equality workers and volunteers in a very deprived area some thought the police action to arrest all the young men was unduly hasty.

I thought they made the arrest rather too quickly, before they'd had the chance to prove that story ... They didn't give them any chance to [...] I thought that was a bit too soon really. They hadn't tried to escape at that point, so ... I didn't think there was any reason to arrest them until ... (WS330075).

A group of predominantly (if not exclusively) black and exuberant young men attending a city FE College took the same view:

P1: ... The policeman come and goes in there with no facts.
P2: Actually, the policeman come in guns blazing ...
P1: That's true! He didn't even ask Security 'What's going on?' He got no information he just wanted to go on with it himself (WS330006).

Racism

The belief that the officer acted precipitately was a view held by only a few of our focus group participants. By contrast, the response of our focus group participants to the arrested youth's accusation of police racism was nearly unanimously dismissed. The idea had little traction amongst both groups of young offenders serving community penalties, most of whom were non-white (WS330055 and WS330057). Worshippers at a Sikh temple joined them in dismissing the accusation almost without any discussion (WS310031). So too did attendees at a mother and baby play group provided for Muslim émigrés from a Middle Eastern war-torn country (WS330060), with whom members of a youth club serving the same community agreed (WS330069). This was also the view that members of an all-white youth arts club also shared (WS330071). Two groups representing professionals and volunteers promoting race equally in a very deprived multi-ethnic area were equally dismissive (WS330075 and WS330077). Members of all-white neighbourhood watch groups in relatively affluent areas took the same view (WS330052, WS330078, WS330095); so too did members of an urban regeneration consultative group in a deprived multi-ethnic area (WS330037); as did young volunteers in a similar scheme in another area (WS330080). A support group for carers in an area of multiple deprivation agreed (WS330090). Members of a youth club in an affluent rural dormitory town also agreed (WS330089). The young man was frequently accused of 'playing the race card' and there were repeated expressions of sympathy for what the police are obliged to tolerate from those making such accusations (WS330043, WS330078) and regret that there has been a general decline in respect shown for 'authority' (WS330045).

The accusation was attributed to a variety of motives: the young man was said to be 'taunting' the officer (WS330083); seeking compensation (WS330077); attempting to 'hurt' the officer and cause him to hesitate in taking action, or 'playing to the camera' or inciting bystanders to intervene on his behalf (WS330035); detecting racism where none existed (WS330095).

Perhaps a flavour of the widespread dismissal of the accusation of 'racism' can be gleaned from the discussion held amongst multi-ethnic representatives of local authority 'service users'. In the context of a discussion about the exchange when the arrested youth accused the officer of not speaking plain English; mishearing what the youth has said, the officer replies, 'I have no trouble with your English', the following discussion occurred:

P1: He was using the race card against the gentleman ... the police officer.
P2: I think the police were doing their job and it's their job to check out the ownership.
[...]
P3: I think they may have been a little bit over aggressive, but then again, the suspect didn't help and he started using his colour as a reason for police harassing him and sort of making out that it was a racist thing.
[...]
Res: At the very end ... Some people have already mentioned it as part of the discussion, but at the very end the young man says that this is an act of racism. Does anybody agree with that or ...
P4: I think he has a complex.
[This was followed by an indistinct, general conversation rejecting the accusation of racism.]
P1: There was no racism in the video.
P5: I don't think there was any racism at all. (WS330082)

The most sympathetic view of the accuser—albeit a small minority viewpoint—was that police generally are racist and the youth's opinions may reflect prior experience (see WS330069, WS330059).

P1: The only thing is: that person's probably had a very bad experience previously ... with a police officer. 'I'll have a go back now. This is my opportunity to go back'. Sometimes, I know, that very often the perception is that people use the race card, but unfortunately the police do have a habit of stopping certain categories of young people, ethnic groups, just because the perception is they may be causing problems or they may be engaged in some anti-social behaviour, unsociable activity. You can't dismiss that.
[This was followed by indistinct conversation.]
Res: Do others feel that?
P2: Some police officers do do that but not, but not all of them. You can find the rare few who are not unexceptionable [...] not by race or gender.
P3: I think the police just [...] young people, because they always seem to be causing the problem all the time.
P2: So age [...]!
P3: Yeah! (WS330050. See also WS330069, WS330059.)

Several participants referred implicitly to the ethnic disproportionality evidence in statistics on stop and search (WS330049).

Perhaps the strongest evidence for the dominance of the dismissal of the accusation of racism was that *no* group raised the accusation of racism made by the arrested youth without being prompted to do so.

Becoming Agitated

Hitherto, one might imagine that our focus groups were of one mind in evalu-ating this video clip and were pretty favourably disposed to the police. Despite the officer's suspicions proving groundless, most of our participants felt that his suspicions were justified: the youths *were* breaking into the car and conformed to the appearance of stereotypical car thieves. Very few drew attention to the fact that the youths made no attempt to escape, as would be expected of genu-ine car thieves. If the youths had been erroneously suspected of car theft, it was not the officer who was to blame, but the youths themselves or the woman who had asked them to break into her car and then departed. Accusations that the police had been 'racist' in arresting one of the youths was roundly dismissed by most people as 'playing the race card'. One might, therefore, expect that this video clip would arouse least contention of all and yet in the approval scores that participants recorded after viewing the video clip there was, in aggregate, markedly more dispersion than for the 'robbery of the elderly man' video clip and it was on a par with other clips. What accounted for this level of evaluative disagreement? The answer lies in a brief exchange between the officer and the one youth who was arrested only after a struggle.

Allow us to describe in detail what occurred in the video clip. On arrival at the scene, the plainclothes officer found several private security guards already talking to two of the three youths, whilst another guard was engaged in a conversation with the third a few feet away. The officer initially talked to the two youths, one of whom explained that they were breaking into the car as a favour. The officer decided to arrest all three youths until their explanation could be corroborated and the two youths were each handcuffed without resistance and led away to the security guards' patrol vehicle. Meanwhile, the third member of the group began to object to being arrested and the officer shouted to him to 'Watch your language! Watch your language now!' The officer strode over to where this youth and the security guard were now loudly arguing, announced that he was a 'police officer' and warned the youth that he was committing a 'criminal offence'. The youth demanded to know what offence he was committing and the officer replied 'a public order offence', which elicited a riposte from the youth about his grasp of English. The officer replied, 'I don't have a problem with your English'. The two men were now almost nose-to-nose and the youth stepped back with the officer following in a mutually hostile exchange. The officer then instructed the youth, 'What I'm saying is, "Don't tell me my job"'. The officer then took hold of the youth's clothing, but the youth shrugged his hand away and stepped further back, telling the officer not to touch him. The officer said, 'I'm going to touch you because you're committing an offence. I'm warning you under section 5, if you carry on, you'll be under arrest'. The youth then asked aggressively, "Section 5', what's that?' Then mockingly referred to 'Section 7 ... or 8 ... or 9'. Meanwhile, the officer instructed the youth to 'Chill out'. The youth turned and began to walk away. The officer instructed him to 'Come here! You're going to end up getting locked up in a minute'. The youth continued to shout and ignore the instructions of the officer. He was then arrested for 'suspected theft from a motor vehicle', whereupon he passively resisted. With the assistance of the security guards, the officer pushed him to the ground and after a brief struggle handcuffed him behind his back. Once handcuffed, the youth was brought to his feet and led to the officer's car. As they walked, the officer said, 'This could have been sorted civilly, but due to your manner you're under arrest'. The youth continued to protest, complain about his treatment and make accusations. This whole exchange took just seventy-five seconds, but we have described it in detail for two reasons: first, it is a pivotal moment in this encounter that divided opinions amongst our focus group participants. Secondly, we will return to it later when discussing the use of force by the police.

How did our focus group participants interpret and evaluate this exchange? There were three discernible approaches: first, a majority interpreted the youth's behaviour as evidence of a 'guilty mind'. Secondly, others could understand why the youth became so annoyed, but considered his actions imprudent. Thirdly, a minority view was that the youth was perfectly justified in expressing his annoyance and the officer was acting oppressively in arresting the young man and his companions. In many groups there were strong divisions of opinion as participants took different views. Let us consider these competing viewpoints.

He deserved it!

Many of our groups agreed that the youth who was arrested brought his misfortune upon himself. Middle Eastern migrants attending a community 'mother and baby' group took an uncompromising view. They drew an invidious comparison between the two compliant youths and the third, who resisted. 'But if you're telling the truth, you're not going to be like that chap. Of course, the police have to think that that chap was doing something wrong because of his attitude.' (WS330059) One member of a multi-ethnic group of final year pupils in a school serving a very deprived area of public housing expressed this view in equally uncompromising terms: 'There was just suspicion at first, yes, but then he started being rude, so they just bang [arrested] him.' To which another added: 'If he had nothing to worry about, he wouldn't be making a fuss in the first place.... At the end of the day, if they're telling the truth, she's going to come back in the end.' A third confessed that he was unable to understand why the youth became so upset (WS330084). A member of a church youth club was unequivocal that the arrested youth brought his misfortune on himself: 'And if they'd have remained calm—that boy that got arrested, was getting quite aggressive—so, if he'd have remained calm, it would probably have been dealt with ... quick, really.' (WS330060)

Not only did 'race equality' professionals and volunteers also think that becoming agitated was evidence of a 'guilty mind', they wondered whether the youth had more to hide: 'You look more guilty if you're aggressive and trying to fight with police, don't you?' A further (but unfortunately indistinct) contribution wondered whether the lads who were giving the problem, or 'mouthing off, or gobbing off or whatever' have previous convictions, criminal records, which put them at ease, or which prompted a change in their behaviour? (WS330047)

Members of a 'safer neighbourhood' consultative group in a very deprived area felt that aggressive behaviour would appear to confirm the youths' guilt even if they were innocent. One of its members drew on past personal experience to make the point:

> P1: I think, as the man was being so aggressive, it almost looked as though he was guilty.... Y'know ... it made it more ... He didn't do himself any favours (laugh), y' know.
> P2: But if you're innocent, you don't go off the deep end like that, do you? [Followed by indistinct general agreement.]
> [...] got to be a mouth. [...] there's always got to be one ... (WS330045).

Empathy

Some focus groups agreed with a contrary view: they could empathise with the youth who resisted and was arrested. What weighed on the minds of many was that the youths themselves knew that what they were doing was not only innocent, it was also virtuous—helping a friend in distress. They appreciated how traduced the youths must have felt at being accused of wrongdoing. Residents in a hostel for the homeless took the uncompromising view that right was on the side of youth, who was entitled to feel aggrieved:

> P1: The police officer was in the wrong and the other geezer was in the wrong. Two wrongs don't make a right!
> Res: So, were they equally ...?
> P2: It's the coppers that is [...] he's going to get defensive and he's done nothing wrong ...
> P3: When he's pointing at him, y'know, his back's going to ... (WS330079).

This view was also voiced clearly at a 'safer neighbourhood' group in an area of deprivation:

> P1: I can understand from the bloke himself's perspective, 'I'm angry, I'm upset, because I've done nothing wrong'. And I feel myself that in that situation I would be angry and upset because I've done nothing wrong. But I think it was ... and I think possibly afterwards, if he saw that footage he'd say, 'Yes, I can kind of see why you came along and why you thought what it was, and I did kind of react and why ...'. You'd probably say, 'You were wrong to arrest me in the first place because I'd done nothing wrong, but my reaction didn't help the situation'.
> P2: He was obviously aggressive himself, because if, y'know, he's helping a neighbour, he shouldn't carry on like that really. [...] but at least the police say, 'Calm down' ... (WS330039).

Dissension and debate

The brief exchange between the youth and the officer provoked more or less heated controversy amongst participants. In many groups there were more or less passionate debates between these competing views. Divisions emerged even amongst representatives of security companies in a meeting of a trade association, who might have been expected to adopt the perspective of the police officer:

P1: I think they just made assumptions. I think police officers just made assumptions as soon as he got there, because the first thing he said was, 'What's the crack?', assuming that ... something. Instead of saying, 'Hello, what's going on? Can you explain?' He put them under arrest, all three of them, before they had found ... Oh no! Whether the car was being stolen. Didn't check out their story and he'd got them all under arrest. I think he provoked the reaction that he got.

Res: Interesting! Do other people agree with that?

P2: I agree with [name]. I think they was too heavy-handed, I think.

P3: On discussion, you're probably right, but I paid more attention to the body language: I mean, the police officers were quite calm and collected when they started talking to them ... the perpetrators—the alleged perpetrators—so, I thought straightaway I thought they behaved how they should behave, but they just hurled abuse at them—didn't they?—so, the situation just got a bit out of control because they were quite abusive in their language. Yes, so, I think they did behave OK.

Res: Yes, well, OK.... What did you think about it?

P4: Well, I thought the police was a bit heavy-handed. They didn't sort out the problem properly, before they—you know—arrested him. You know, get the lady before—y'know—or do something before they done that.

Res: OK. Which side do you fall down on, then?

[Followed by general laughter.]

P5: I think ... yes, I think ... the police officers and security approached the situation right—y'know, in the correct manner, ...

P3: If he [the suspect] had remained calm throughout, there would have been no arrest in the first place. [The officer's] intention wasn't to arrest him, but to ascertain what happened.... With hindsight, I think that officer would probably think, 'Well, he was innocent after all; perhaps I shouldn't have done that'. But in that particular moment, I think I would have reacted the same, because the man was getting very aggressive. (WS330021)

Members of a neighbourhood watch in a relatively affluent area were also divided on the issue. In reply to another participant who was critical of the police officer:

P1: Well, I think he just tried to calm things down. Wasn't he? And this fellow was being irate and not being calmed down.

P2: He was acting guilty.

[This elicited background remarks agreeing.]

P2: His behaviour was 'guilty'.

P3: The policeman, to me, seemed to be just going at it, at it, at it.

P1: And was just trying to calm him down.

[...]

P4: I think because he wasn't doing anything wrong, he was more offensive. He hadn't done anything wrong and was wondering what the hell was going on. (WS330052)

Race equality workers and volunteers in a very deprived multi-ethnic area were divided:

P1: It was the security company that alerted the police officer, wasn't it?

Res: Yes.

P2: Especially when they started swearing at them and stuff, then I think you've got something to hide if you're reacting that way.

P3: If they'd cooperated then, obviously, they'd have pursued it. But because they weren't compliant that made it all the more suspicious.
[Later the group returned to the issue in the context of discussing the triggers for the young man's arrest.]

P4: I think it was because he was getting verbally aggressive, wasn't it?

P5: Yes, but wasn't that because his situation wasn't explained to him?

P4: I think, if I remember, when the guards came to him they did explain.
[The speaker then digressed to acknowledge the possibility that memories of the clip might vary. Continuing, he said]
… but I thought they did explain to them. 'What are you doing?' 'We need to find out who's the car is?' There was that explanation, wasn't there?

P6: Yes and then he broke away!

P4: 'If you're doing nothing, then you have nothing to worry about', I remember that comment. (WS330075)

A 'dog that didn't bark'

In his story 'Silver Blaze', Sir Arthur Conan Doyle explains why an investigator must pay attention not only to what *has* occurred, but also what *has not*: a guard dog that doesn't bark, suggests that it knows the intruder (Doyle 2011). Well, the 'dog that didn't bark' in this research was the part played by private security personnel in the arrest of the youths and subduing the truculent young man. Very few of our participants mentioned them at all and even fewer discussed them. There was some confusion about who or what these men were, but this was resolved by other members of the respective group. No one took exception to their helping the officer in making the arrest, apart from protesting that there were too many people involved—a topic to which we will return later when we discuss the use of force.

Conclusions

These two video clips considered in detail here, as well as stopping the suspected stolen car on the motorway, pose the central operational conundrum of police work—suspicion. All three situations are suffused by ambiguity and confusion that would permit them to be interpreted as evidence either of 'innocence' or 'wrongdoing'. Is a car reported to have driven off from a petrol filling station without paying and displaying a false registration plate likely to be 'stolen'? Are three young men breaking into a car in a superstore car park attempting to commit theft or helping a friend, as they claim? Is a young woman companion of an elderly man who has been robbed by an intruder an 'innocent victim' or complicit in the crime? To answer these questions implies that each of our focus group participants had also independently formed their own suspicions, allowing them thereby to compare the suspicions of officers with their own. If there was agreement, then presumably they felt that the officers' suspicions were justified, but if not they might express criticism that the officers acted 'hastily'. On what basis did our focus groups implicitly rely in forming their own suspicions?

First, they regarded certain behaviour as sufficiently anomalous to arouse suspicion. Breaking into a car in a public car park is so unusual that it invites suspicion. Driving a car with a false number plate likewise is so extraordinary that Automatic Number Plate Recognition technology is programmed to 'ping' such anomalies. However, as Ellison and Munro (2009b; 2009c) remind us even in these apparently obvious cases, the presence of an *anomaly* suggests a background knowledge of what is normal. On what is this background knowledge of normality based? Direct experience would teach us that few cars parked in a superstore car park are broken into, for whatever reason. However, *only one* of our focus group participants had experience of being robbed in their own home by a knife-wielding intruder, yet the remainder had little hesitation in voicing expectations about how those involved were likely to act and should have acted. For instance, it was asserted in more than one group that if someone intruded into the home of the speaker they would have created pandemonium and not meekly followed the intruder into the sitting room. Creating an imagined 'normality' is not only central to forming a suspicion of rape or sexual assault, it appears to be widespread, indeed it may be essential. 'Crime' is equated with a deviation from 'normality', but most criminals do all in their power to disguise their criminality and portray an image of normality. Police officers learn quickly that they cannot accept situations at 'face value', but should examine whether it is a disguise for criminality.

Secondly, such assumptions about 'normality' and how people would respond in extreme circumstances rely on stereotypes, but stereotypes have a much wider reach. Many participants freely admitted that it was the *appearance* of the three youths that confirmed their suspicions that they were committing a theft. What was it about their appearance that proved so persuasive? It was that one was wearing a 'hoodie', another wore a baseball cap, and one or more were wearing gloves on a sunny day. Is such an appearance evidence of criminal intent, or simply a fashion statement? Likewise, is it anomalous that a young woman spends some of her leisure time drinking beer and watching television with an elderly man? Many of our participants thought that it was, but perhaps Chantelle was a kindly person who took pity on an otherwise isolated elderly man.

Finally, as noted previously, forming suspicion involves 'joining the dots', a pre–condition for which is that one recognises all the relevant 'dots' and ignores irrelevant ones. However, it is even more important that 'dots' that are inconsistent with or contradict what is assumed to be the emergent picture are given due consideration and not simply dismissed as irrelevant. For instance, the driver of the suspected 'stolen' car pulled over immediately when signalled to do so by the officers. A few of our participants felt that this was evidence inconsistent with the behaviour of genuine car thieves. Was it inconsistent? Others amongst our focus groups pointed out that police reality TV shows often reveal how wrongdoers sometimes pull up in apparent dutiful compliance with police instructions, only to speed away when an officer steps out of the police car, thereby gaining an advantage as they attempt to escape. What our data indicates is not the superiority of police suspicion, but the extent to which *all* such suspicions of wrongdoing are founded on stereotypical assumptions and beliefs about what is 'normal' and hence also what is 'anomalous' in circumstances of which one is very unlikely to have direct experience.[4]

Police must not only understand a scene and the behaviour of those therein, they must also appraise the credibility of explanations and accounts given by 'suspects' and 'witnesses'. Is it credible that the driver of the car thought to be stolen was told by an officer a week previously that he 'had fourteen days' to rectify the erroneous registration plates and could drive during the interim? Was it credible that Chantelle could not see the intruder's face and yet be so definite about his age? Were the youths really doing a favour for a girlfriend? Not only must officers appraise all these and many more aspects of these relatively routine situations, they must weigh different elements against each other. For instance, even if some credibility is granted to the three youths' claim to have been performing a favour for a friend, is it likely that that favour would be performed wearing a 'hoodie', baseball cap and gloves?

Perhaps because the information on which suspicion is erected in a policing environment is so impoverished, many of our participants relied heavily on the corroboration provided by third parties, but this proved to be far from foolproof. The car driven along the motorway initially attracted suspicion because it was reported to have driven away from a petrol filling station without payment being made. The fact that it was also displaying a false registration number was taken by the officers in the video clip as corroboration for suspecting that it was stolen. Few, if any, of our focus group participants questioned this suspicion. When the allegation of driving off without paying for fuel was withdrawn many of them were incredulous at this reversal.

Given these uncertainties, should police be expected to 'get it right', or is it understandable that often they are likely to make a mistake? What is striking about so many of the focus group discussions is the unreserved confidence with which the suspicions entertained by our members were held. It was 'obvious' to many that Chantelle was complicit in the robbery of the elderly man. What all

---

[4] Indeed, all behaviour/interaction is founded on what Erving Goffman referred to as 'normal appearances': Erving Goffman (1971).

but a few (who happened to remember viewing this episode) were not to know was that Chantelle's boyfriend *was* convicted and imprisoned for the robbery, but no further action was taken against Chantelle. So, in this instance, our participants would have had their suspicions, at least, partially confirmed, albeit that the grounds for holding them on the information available in the video clip was open to much uncertainty. However, what did provoke sometimes heated debate were the actions taken by officers on the basis of equally slender suspicions. In the next chapter we turn to examine our participants' appraisal of that most distinctive police response—the use of force.

5

Use of Force

Introduction

Policing is distinguished by the power granted to officers to use force to accomplish a lawful purpose, most commonly to arrest suspected wrongdoers. Evidence from Britain and other democratic countries suggests that most arrests are conducted reasonably amicably, with the arrested person submitting without resistance (see, for example, Sykes and Brent 1983; Terrill and Paoline 2007; Chatterton 1976). However, in the event that suspects *do* resist, police officers in England and Wales are empowered[1] under section 117 of the Police and Criminal Evidence Act 1984 to 'use reasonable force, if necessary, in the exercise' of the powers contained in the Act. They also enjoy the powers conferred on 'any person' to use force for a lawful purpose contained in section 3 of the Criminal Law Act 1967.[2] They also, of course, can invoke the right to self-defence and the defence of others under the Common Law. The word 'reasonable' is one that is freely used in legislation and judicial decision-making, but rarely, if ever, defined in general terms. Instead, the concept is context-dependent, so that an application of a particular measure of force in one situation may be considered reasonable, but not when applied in another. This issue tends to achieve prominence in circumstances where either the police use novel or potentially very injurious tactics or equipment (such as firearms, incapacitating weaponry, public order tactics like 'kettling') or where the result of the police use of force proves fatal.[3] Chapter 1 discussed evidence

---

[1] This is not an exclusively *police* power, since it extends to 'A person', but it is overwhelmingly police officers who rely on this provision.

[2] Section 3 of the Criminal Law Act 1967 also grants to 'a person' the option to 'use such force as is reasonable in the circumstances in the prevention of crime, or in effecting or assisting in the lawful arrest of offenders or suspected offenders or of persons unlawfully at large'.

[3] Such as the deaths of Jean Charles de Menezes mistakenly identified as an escaped terrorist following the London bombings of 2005 and of Ian Tomlinson, who died after being struck with a baton and pushed to the ground during disorder in London in 2009.

that notable occasions in which police have used force in the USA—such as the arrest of Rodney King—produced a significant, but short-lived, decline in diffuse support for the police generally. However, the focus on particular tactics and weaponry, and seriously injurious outcomes, might distort our understanding of how the public view the exercise of this power to use force by officers making more routine arrests in the course of their duties (recent research published by the Independent Police Complaints Commission has made some attempt to fill this void. See IPCC 2016).

We have already explored the often conflicting and contradictory reasons given by members of our focus groups for believing that there are sufficient grounds for making an arrest. Yet, when suspects resist arrest further questions arise. Is it 'reasonable', in the minds of ordinary people, for the police to struggle with a suspect, or force them to the ground, or apply handcuffs? Does it matter how many officers are involved in making an arrest? What amounts to 'excessive' use of force in such circumstances? It is to these questions that we now turn.

Using Force

There were three video clips that involved officers using some measure of force, two of which we have already discussed: first, when officers pulled a car onto the hard shoulder of the motorway, suspecting that it was stolen, the police passenger jumped from the patrol car, opened the car door and attempted to pull a resisting driver from behind the steering wheel. Secondly, when one of the three young men suspected of breaking into a car in a supermarket car park resisted being arrested by an on-site police officer called to the scene by security personnel, there was a struggle and, with the assistance of the security staff, the young man was forced to the ground, handcuffed and confined in the rear of the officer's car. The third video clip was the last to be shown to the focus groups. It will be described in detail later, suffice to say that it depicted officers deployed as a group on board a personnel carrier arresting a man very forcibly outside a nightclub late at night.

Taken together, the video clips may be considered to form a crude hierarchy of force. During the motorway stop the police officer struggled to pull the driver from the suspected stolen car and to subdue him as the pair tussled alongside the car. However, whilst the driver was arrested on suspicion of stealing the car, he was not handcuffed, nor was he forced to the ground. In the superstore car park there was a similar struggle, but with the assistance of the security personnel, the young man was forced to the ground and handcuffed. The final video clip appears the most violent: punches were thrown by the suspect, who was roughly forced to the ground, turned onto his face, whereupon he fell into the gutter, had his face held on the ground, was handcuffed and pushed into a police van, all at the hands of several officers. What is important to bear in mind is that, apart from handcuffs, police officers in all three video clips used no weaponry[4] and no serious injury appeared to be inflicted on any of those involved. These are all examples of routine arrests accomplished more or less as they have been since the inception of professional civil policing (Emsley 1985). It is also worth mentioning that in the video clip that depicted the most serious criminal matter—the robbery of the elderly man in his own home—*no force* was used by officers investigating the allegation.

Arrest on the Motorway

We have already seen that the manner in which the young driver was arrested was one of the two issues of concern and dissension amongst our focus groups. That discussion only briefly touched on the issue of how force was used to arrest the driver. Here we will focus exclusively on *how* the driver was arrested, especially those features of the arrest that provoked the greatest discussion. Two themes could be detected in those discussions. The first concerned the *forcefulness* of the officer's approach, both verbally and physically; the second focused more upon the prudence of the officer's action and its *impact* on the unfolding scenario. There was a clear preponderance of adverse comment, but equally there were many dissenting voices to be heard as well.

Verbal Forcefulness

The 'motorway stop' video clip showed that as the two cars were pulling up on the hard shoulder of the motorway, the passenger in the police car leapt out, almost before the patrol car had halted, and ran back towards the car that the officers suspected had been stolen. The video camera caught up with the action to find the police officer standing outside the driver's open door, tussling with the driver who at first was behind the steering wheel and then emerged onto the hard shoulder, still tussling with the officer. As the camera approached this scene, the officer could be heard to say, 'Get out, before I drag you out'. These words, in whole or part, were recited by numerous participants, sometimes immediately after the video clip had concluded. For instance, a 'safer neighbourhood' group in a very deprived area reacted immediately: '"Get out the car." "Get out the car!"' (WS330043). Muslim émigré mothers erupted into a feverishly animated discussion punctuated by recitation of these words (WS330059). The way in which the officer spoke to the driver was regarded by many as 'arrogant' and peremptory, because they could not discern anything that the driver had *done* to merit it. In a neighbourhood watch group in an area of mixed housing and light industry the immediate response was to praise the officers for how they had vainly, but patiently, tried to muster help, but then continued:

---

[4] The status of 'handcuffing' is officially ambiguous. The Association of Chief Police Officers official guidance on the use of handcuffs reminds officers that the use of handcuffs would be an assault unless it can be justified (ACPO 2010). However, the IPCC expressly excludes the use of handcuffs as a 'weapon', preferring to regard it as a 'restraint' (IPCC 2016).

P1: ... when that first officer approached that lad, he was arrogant ...

P2: He just said, 'Get out the car' and pulled him ...

This was followed by a chorus of voices agreeing. (WS330095)

How did our participants expect the officer to approach the driver? Again, there was remarkable agreement that the officer should have politely *asked* the driver to alight from the car, preferably explaining why he had been pulled over. Students at a sixth form college serving the Black Country area drew an invidious comparison between how the officer did approach, as opposed to *should* have approached, the man: ' "Get out the car ..."! "Could you step out the car, *please?*"!' (WS330006). Race equality workers took a similar view:

P1: They should have asked him to get out car before they started 'Get out of this car before I drag you out'.

P2: 'We've pulled you over because of this. We need to ask you to get out the car so that we can discuss this with you because of that'. They didn't explain *why* they needed to get him out the car. (WS330075)

Physical Forcefulness: '... or I'll drag you out'

It was not only what the officer *said* that elicited disfavour amongst our participants, it was also what he *did*. A multi-ethnic group of young volunteers engaged in a regeneration project immediately observed: 'I think the copper came out of it "aggressive", like, because he tried to drag him out the car *at the start*' (WS330080, emphasis added). A consultative group of local authority 'service users' was another of the groups to raise this issue:

I think that because he *had pulled over* and he wasn't really ... he wasn't really ... or it didn't seem like he was being aggressive. Y'know, he wasn't trying to avoid them. I personally think the way they dragged him out the car—and he was shouting unnecessarily as well, he wasn't saying anything and they was shouting at him ...

[Someone intervened to say 'You don't know'.]

... I'm only going by what I saw. I thought he raised his voice a lot unnecessarily and I thought he was a bit too aggressive. (WS330082)

At a community kindergarten in a very deprived area of public housing parents were very voluble in their criticism. To a chorus of agreement it was said:

P1: Straightaway, first off, I have to say, there was no need to drag him out the car like that. He pulled up!

P2: He hasn't even gone, 'Will you get out the car?' He's gone, 'If you don't get out, I'll drag you out', but he's already dragging him!

P3: It's not like he drives off or does a runner! He just starts being disrespectful to him.

Res: What do other people think?

P4: I agree with that completely. Manhandling that driver is completely wrong. He should have asked him to get out, not forced him to get out.... If they'd simply said, 'Can you get out the car please?' and handle it better.... They walk straight in and start manhandling somebody and ordering them around, 'Get out before I drag you out'. What's going to happen? You're not going to get anywhere with anyone, treating them that way. Just not. I don't care what they think they've done. (WS330049)

For some participants it was both the physical and verbal aggression to which they objected. As soon as the video clip concluded, one participant amongst a support group for those who care for the elderly and infirm said, 'I think they were very, very arrogant. They didn't ask him to get out of the car, they dragged him … they tried dragging him out and that was bad, y'know. And they didn't say why they'd stopped him' (WS330090). Mid–career professionals living in a rural dormitory town, felt it was: 'ridiculous', 'very aggressive', 'very force-ful' (WS330083). This response is strikingly reminiscent of Weitzer's research in Washington DC (Weitzer 1999). One of his respondents expressed herself thus:

I've seen guys physically snatched out of cars, pushed face first onto the hood of the car when they're being handcuffed or detained …. I have respect for the police because it is an extremely tough job, dealing with the public, and [Spartanburg] is still a difficult area to work in every day. But if you're going to arrest someone and they're not [using] physical force against you, there is no reason to go in that car and snatch a person out of it. If you say, 'Okay, the car is stopped. Put your hands out the window' [and] the person is doing this, there's no reason for that. He should be able to get out of his car on his free will and then be handcuffed. It's not necessary to go in and physically and bodily pull someone out of a car. (Spartanburg woman, 38) (p 837)

As these extracts show, many believed that not only did the officer act peremp-torily, he did so *despite the compliance* of the driver with police instructions to pull over and stop. Community volunteers in an urban regeneration project took this view:

P1: But he didn't make any effort to get away though, did he?
P2: No, he wasn't aggressive at all. He'd pulled over. He cooperated. He probably was a bit startled as to what was going on. I don't know. I felt straightaway, y'know, he'd got his hands like this [makes a surrender gesture] 'Don't touch me'. (WS330080)

There was also a minority who felt that even if the driver had been non-compliant it still would not have justified the force used by the arresting officer. This view was voiced amongst race equality activists:

P1: They should have asked him to get out the car before they started 'Get out of this car before I drag you out'.
P2: 'We've pulled you over because of this. We need to ask you to get out the car so that we can discuss this with you because of that'. They didn't explain to you *why* they needed to get him out the car.

Another participant wondered whether something had transpired prior to the camera arriving.

> P1: Even if that lad had said, 'No', I think that that response is too aggressive … 'No, I'm not getting out the car'.
> P3: Because he wasn't physically aggressive. He kind of went limp in a sort of way, didn't he? He put his hands up, sort of … he wasn't sort of struggling with them. (WS330075)

What this wide array of groups are implicitly challenging is the 'reasonableness' of the officer's use of force, because they perceived it as peremptory, unnecessary and excessively aggressive.

Prudence and Impact

There was also a large measure of agreement that the way the officer arrested the driver soured the whole incident, which led to the hostile banter that was the focus of chapter three. A member of a youth club in a desirable rural dormitory village interpreted it as an assertion of dominance:

> They pulled him over. He'd cooperated with them and they just pulled him straight out the car and stuff. The bloke was getting out. That's immediately going to set things off on a bad foot. Acting aggressively towards him. He cooperated all the time, but he seemed constantly aggressive towards him. He seemed that … he was in a higher position and … (WS330089).

A local authority consultative group of tenants and residents felt it 'inflamed the situation'.

> P1: Exactly! That's all you've got to say. 'Would you mind getting out the car for a moment, I want to have a few words with you' […] Not, 'Get out the car!' situation. That inflamed the situation.[This was followed by indistinct animated crosstalk.]
> P2: Exactly! It inflamed it straightaway. (WS330043)

A member of another consultative group identified explicitly with the driver: 'If someone approached me like that, then obviously I'd have had the same attitude as that young lad. I'm sorry.' (WS330045)

Others sought to explain or excuse the police officer's intemperate behaviour, referring to the police officer one participant said:

> He seemed quite young … that police officer. And I just felt that when they're that young and they're doing such a high-speed chase, their adrenalin is pumping. So, he got out that car straightaway, you could still see the male testosterone levels going in him. Y'know, his approach was quite aggressive. And I think, the way in which he …… he reacted to that young lad … that's why, I think, things went so downhill. Because I think his mannerisms, his tone, everything about him was, like, about aggression. (WS330047)

In other words, these participants felt that not only was the forcefulness of the officer unnecessary, it had adverse consequences that could easily have been avoided.

Dissension and Debate

So far, we have drawn attention to the substantial measure of agreement amongst our focus groups that the officer was wrong and imprudent in the way he forcefully arrested the driver. However, in some groups there was dissension, leading to debate, which was sometimes quite strident.

Non-compliance

One issue that provoked debate was whether the driver of the car had displayed any resistance to the police, before being dragged from the car. One source of dispute was the driver's action in pulling over to the 'hard shoulder' of the motorway as soon as the police illuminated their blue lights. This debate is illustrated by the response of another contributor to the tenants and residents consultative group mentioned above:

> P1: How many times have you seen them pull a car up and the car drives off as soon as the police get out?
> [This is answered by an indistinct voice agreeing.]
> P1: And that is what he was worried about with that kid. That was a fast car, that was.
> P2: As soon as the copper flashed him with the blue lights, he pulled over.
> P1: Yeah, but how many times have you seen them pull up behind them ...
> P3: They drive off.
> P1: ... they're off like a shot. (WS330043)

Imagining the future

In the examples above, participants relied not only on what actually happened in the video clip, but imagined what *might* have happened, but this is inherently contestable since everyone is equally entitled to imagine different future courses of events. The issue was hotly debated in a consultation group for urban regeneration. After several contributions condemning the aggression of the police officer:

> You've got to understand though ... They're on a motorway; the police's stopped; there're only two of them; he's out the car, next to that one; the driver and keys are still in that car. What they've got to do is to get that person—the driver—physically away from that car, so he can't start the car and get in lane one ...
> [...] once that that car's going to swerve back on the motorway, or ... do y'know what I mean? It's like: 'There's a man down the road and it's [name]—who looks perfectly innocent, lovely chap—and he's got a gun and he's concealed it in his jacket pocket' and I walk up and say 'Hello Mr [name], I believe you've got a concealed gun!' It's not going to happen. It's a response to that situation and it's always to that individual situation. And I think the key point with this situation was that they believed the car was stolen when they stopped it. Because it did

appear to be on false plates ... If the officers who had of stopped the car before had had a bit of brain about them and said, 'The car's on mistaken plates and there's a notice been put on it to change the plates within fourteen days', they'd have probably stopped that car and said, 'You dozy so and so, you're still driving that car. Here's a thirty quid fine. Learn the lesson.' (WS330039)

The point that the first of these contributors is making is that the officer was using force preventatively: not in reaction to something the driver *had* done, but in anticipation of what he *may reasonably be expected to do*.

In some instances, perceptual processes led people to imagine features and events for which there is no evidence in the video itself. A student at an FE college who believed the officers' actions were justified, imagined the following exchange:

Yeah, well he did say to him, 'Could you just get out of the car?' and he just sat there. He said, 'What?' So, there you go, just disobedient. It's not complying with the law. So, it was right that he was grabbed out of the car. (WS330028)

Danger

These extracts touch upon another imagined scenario invoked both by critics *and* those who opposed them. This was the question of danger. We have already discussed (p 66) how participants considered the likelihood that the suspect might be armed. However, the most prominent danger in this case was that the suspects would drive off in an attempt to escape. Critics emphasised how the officer placed himself and also possibly the car driver, as well as passing traffic, in danger. On the other hand, defenders of the police officer's actions took the view that the presence of this and other dangers necessitated immediate and forceful intervention.

Amongst race equality activists there was general acknowledgement that many uncertainties surrounded the incident and they accepted that officers needed to be wary in case the car was suddenly driven off:

P1: In that situation they've got to presume the worst, haven't they?

P2: They've got to presume that he's going to drive off and potentially go into their car. That could have injured a lot of people. They've got to get him out the car and make the car secure so he can't use the car as a weapon ... That was probably their thinking behind it.
[...]

P3: I've watched the 'Police, Stop' things now and then, and there are people who stop and then drive off, don't they? (laugh) Being ... police officers they must have experienced this. So ... so they must make the decision sometimes about how quickly they want the person to get out the car. So there is that conflict there. Not everybody's nice are they (laugh).
[This elicited agreement from others.]
I suppose from his point of view, you know you're innocent and if someone wants you to get out the car, I suppose you want to know why they want you to get out the car (laugh). So, there's that conflict all the time between police officers and members of the public. (WS330075)

This too was something that was hotly debated: was the danger of a sufficient scale and likelihood of being realised that it justified the officer's actions, or were his actions unnecessary, even counterproductive (because it soured the encounter from the outset)?

Arrest in Superstore Car Park

In the previous chapter we discussed the video clip in which three young men were seen breaking into a car in a superstore car park. You will recall that there was very little doubt amongst our focus groups about the suspicious nature of them and their conduct, despite the fact that in due course it was revealed that they were doing a favour for one of their girlfriends who had locked her keys in the car. Breaking into a car (for whatever purpose) was regarded as such aberrant behaviour that most people felt that it was obviously suspicious and the security guards were entitled to involve the on-site police officer, who in turn was justified in detaining the men and seeking confirmation of their story. This section deals with a brief moment of this encounter, when one of the three men vociferously objected to being formally arrested and handcuffed, there followed a struggle between him and the police officer, who—with the aid of the security guards—forced the man to the ground and handcuffed him. There is one further detail to add: having confirmed the innocence of the three young men, the officer returned to his car, wherein sat the third young man, and de-arrested him in respect of suspicion of attempted theft. However, the young man continued to be abusive. So, the officer rearrested him under section 5 of the Public Order Act 1986, which makes it an offence to 'use threatening, abusive or insulting words or behaviour, ... within the hearing or sight of a person likely to be caused harassment, alarm or distress thereby'. It is worth noting that 'section 5' has become a controversial police power that the courts have sought to curtail[5] and various lobby groups have sought to repeal or reform this provision on the grounds that it unduly interferes with freedom of speech.

We have already seen that participants in our focus groups were divided over whether the arrest of the young man was necessary or justified. They were equally divided about *how* those arrests were executed. However, on the whole, negative opinions consistently claimed more attention in the discussion of our focus groups.

Aggressive Force

As in the previous case, it was the use of verbal and physical aggression that disturbed many of our participants. Two of the young men did not resist being arrested and handcuffed, but the third did and he was told to calm down,

---

[5] See *Harvey v DPP* [2011] EWHC 3992.

grabbed, wrestled to the floor, pinned to the ground and forcibly handcuffed. It was this use of aggressive physical force that divided opinions about the conduct of the officer most starkly.

Forced to the ground

It is common practice amongst police officers in many jurisdictions to force non-compliant and resisting arrestees to the ground. This has obvious attractions for the arresting officer: the arrestee will find escape much more difficult, and, if face down, will be limited in their capacity to spit at, hit, kick or bite the officer. The weight of the officer can be used to hold the person down, whilst the hands can be employed in securing handcuffs. Like any other use of force, however, such a manoeuvre must be justified in law and proportionate in its execution. In this case, the officer was assisted by the private security staff present at the scene, who have very similar powers to those of a police officer to use force: namely, only for a lawful purpose, when it is 'reasonable in the circumstances'. Also, private security personnel are usually in a 'master and servant' relationship with the owners of the car park, and someone who is breaking the terms of the implicit contract into which they have entered, might thereby become a trespasser against whom force might be used to eject (or, in this case arrest). However, it is worth keeping in mind, that there is nothing exceptional about this arrest: it is a common occurrence in policing (Waddington et al. 2006). Nevertheless, amongst many of our participants there was a strong negative reaction to this portion of the video that was visceral and amounted, in many cases, to revulsion. For instance, members of a community action project in a very deprived area took the following view:

P1: What I don't like is how the police dealt with it by putting him down on the floor. [To which, there were murmurs of general agreement by others in the group.]
P1: You see such a lot of that.
P2: Four of them just shoving him on the floor ...
P1: On his face ...
P3: I say, they going to see a policeman ... They see the police are not believing their story in the first place. So, obviously, they're giving attitude, to y'know, to prove what they're saying. And they're just too quick to, y'know, to pin him down and put the handcuffs on him.
P3: They should have waited.
[...]
P3: Well, they'd gone in aggressively, almost. I know they've gone pretty respectful in the beginning, but it didn't take long for them to get that lad on the floor.
P2: And how many it took to get the lad on the floor?
P4: 'Four'.
P2: There was about five, wasn't there? (WS330025)

For most people any use of force was regarded as an unpleasant aspect of arresting a resisting person. (In a survey of people who had experience of police use of force, being 'taken to the ground' was amongst those uses of force that aroused most concern. See IPCC 2016.) For some it was almost a revolting spectacle, such as these members of a support group for those caring for the elderly and infirm in a deprived area:

Res: What about the way he got him to the ground?

P1: Oh!

P2: I didn't like that.

P3: No, I don't approve of that sort of restraining at all.

P4: They do, though, don't they? Pull their arms behind their back.

P2: Why can't they just … They can hold him and handcuff his hands behind his back. That would be enough. Not to knock somebody down onto the ground and all of them sitting on top of him virtually.

P4: Then you got the thing that they're going to kick you; they're going to spit at you.

P2: Well, they don't know that …

P4: I watch all the police programmes, I do …

[…]

Res: Did anybody think it was justified. The way they got him to the ground?

P5: On a scale of … 30–70 perhaps. The guy was becoming more aggressive. He was, however, at that point restrained. He had his handcuffs on, hadn't he, at that stage? [This was greeted with murmurs of agreement.]

P4: They could do nothing else.

[…]

P2: He started swearing and was getting aggressive, but then started talking about solicitors and injuries. I think then the police officer might have thought, 'Well, actually I might have to do this properly and get him checked out and make sure there isn't any injuries, in case there's a case for solicitors and things.' That *maybe* his thinking. (WS330090)

It is worth noting that the young man was *not* handcuffed before being forced to the ground. Having taken hold of the young man, the officer began to lead him back towards his car, but the young man resisted. The officer applied an approved armlock, known as a 'goose neck', but the man resisted more strenuously, although non-violently. It was then that the officer tried to force him to the ground, but was unable to do so until the security personnel joined him. *None* of our focus groups appeared to recognise this, perhaps because these distinct moments were so brief that they were subsumed in a perception of the two men tussling.

Tripping or 'kicking'

What did not escape the attention of some participants was that the young man was tripped in order to make him fall to the ground. Several objected, whilst others took the view that it might be a suitable option. A group of young community action volunteers in a deprived multi-cultural area were divided on the issue. One of them said, 'It was a bit too much at times. He just kicked him. He just went flying. I was: "What?!"' On the other hand, another participant defended the tactic: 'I don't think it was a kick. I think it was, "That's how you get them down", that's part of a way to get them down. You put your foot out and as they walk forward they go down, but they don't hit the floor.' (WS330080)

Other groups debated whether, what they perceived to be, the young man's entirely *verbal* resistance necessitated such a use of force, or not. For instance,

106

mothers attending a community centre serving Middle Eastern émigrés gave a generally positive appraisal of how the officer dealt with the situation. However, the tone changed when asked about the manner of the arrest, which was greeted by general murmurs of discontent.

P1: Actually, I thought he was a bit too firm, to be honest. Probably that's what spoilt it. [...]

P2: But he wasn't attacking them or anything. [...] just shouting and all of sudden he had two guys getting him on the ground.

P3: If you see how many it took to hold him down. Just to get the handcuffs on. There was about five of them.

P2: Why did they get him down just to put the handcuffs on? [...] you don't need to physically throw him.

P1: You know what? I'm thinking of the police situation and the previous experiences the police have had in that situation to protect himself. I don't know what training they give them (laugh). Y'know, if somebody is becoming aggressive. I don't know what training they give them: whether they have to deal with it in that way. Yes, I do agree, I think it [...]

P3: I think, that the way that guy that was arrested, may be they had to, because he got very close to police officers. In his face.

P4: Quite threatening. Yeah!

P2: After what? After what? [...]

P3: He was shouting, but I don't think he touched him. I didn't see him touch him in any way. It was verbal, very in his face.

P1: Aggressive! (WS330059)

In some groups discussion became quite heated. Residents in a hostel for the homeless became so heated that portions of the audio recording were incapable of being transcribed:

P1: And when that security guy's come over, he's just kicked him 'Get him on the floor'. He's only done that because somebody else was jumping in. [...]

P2: This guy, the police asked him nicely. What he did was walking off and being aggressive. He had no choice. [...]

Res: You thought it was OK?

P2: Yes, it was OK. He just put him in the car.

Res: What about others? Did you think it was OK?

P3: I don't know, they've got to do their job, but that happens all the time.

Res: Did you think it was right?

P3: The police? Yeah!

P4: 'Do you think it was right?' No! [...]

P5: He done nothing wrong and the police are there.

P6: So why doesn't he keep his mouth shut? [...]

P4: If he was talking to me like that ... [...]

P7: He was pushing his badge, wasn't he? Out of order! [...]

P4: You get put on the floor, mate. So, what's he going to do you for? Know what I mean?

[Followed by a chorus of 'out of order' from others.]

P4: Invades your personal space, mate. Everyone's got their own personal space, haven't they?

P8: He was walking away [...] He was walking away.

P9: He was backing off when the coppers were pointing at him, 'Don't point at me! Don't point at me'. And he's gripped him and pulled him away. [...]

P9: It's the copper's attitude, man! The geezer's going to get defensive when he's done nothing wrong and the copper's pointing at him, y'know. Your back's going to get up. [...]

P7: There's enough of them there to hold them, without arresting them. (WS330079)

Only in one group was there uncontested endorsement for the officer's tactics. It came from members of a church youth group, one of whom cast the 'trip' in a quite unusual light: 'I thought the officers were really really good. And I liked the graceful kick of the man down. And I thought it happened really really nicely. And I thought he was fine.' To which another observed:

'I thought the cops did pretty cool. But I think they should have arrested the guy earlier, because they allowed him to cause a real public nuisance. As soon as they realised he was going to be a problem they should have arrested him earlier. Because they allowed it to escalate and it looks bad, especially when it takes four cops to bring down a kid.' The young people were then asked directly what they felt about how the police got the young lad down on the floor. Someone replied that it was 'good' and others agreed (WS330060).

With only this exception, the use of force was regarded as *at best* a necessary evil that needed clear and unequivocal justification.

Fairness and Responsibility

As mentioned in the previous chapter, the innocence of the three young men on the substantive matter of 'stealing the car' was regarded by some as explaining or excusing the hostility shown by the young man who was arrested. These focus group members reasoned that the young man was justified in feeling outrage and resisting arrest, for not only was he 'innocent', he had acted virtuously to help a friend! There was fierce controversy between those who took this view and others who believed that outrage was not the justifiable response of an innocent man wrongly accused and served only to confirm the officer's suspicions. Others felt that whilst he may have been innocent of the substantive accusation, he needlessly created a quite separate issue for the officer.

Young people debated the issue particularly vigorously, perhaps because they identified with the young man featured in the video clip. These animated discussions would be worth quoting quite fully, but limitations of space condemn us to use a single example. Young volunteers at a community regeneration scheme debated the fairness of the police action so exuberantly that it too was difficult to transcribe:

P1: He was being rude, yeah! There was just suspicion at first, yeah? And then he started being rude. So they bang him! (laugh)

Res: By 'bang him' I take it you mean arrest him?
[This was answered by indistinct confirmation.]

P2: If he had nothing to worry about, he'd not be making a fuss in the first place. I thought, 'fair enough' because at the end of the day, if he's telling the truth, the woman will come back in the end. So why's he making a big deal out of that?
[This was followed by indistinct criticism of the amount of force used, countered by various voices referring to the need to get the resistant youth into the police car.]

P3: But you don't need to get him in the car.
[This elicited more indistinct excitable argument.]

P3: They only want to get him in the car, there's no need to kick him.
[At this point the researcher intervened to ask for one person to speak at a time.]

P4: I think if somebody's arrested and they're struggling, I think the police have the right to take him down.

P3: I think that could have been used as abuse against the police, anyway, for kicking him to the floor.

P5: They could have just bent him over a car though.
[More indistinct chatter followed, leading the researcher to renew the plea for each speaker to be heard. Addressing one of the speakers, he asked: 'You'd have "Tasered him"?']

P4: Yeah!

Res: Yes, well, OK. Who else would have Tasered him? … I think you wanted to say something?

P6: I think he had the right to … he didn't actually kick him, he was just trying to get him to the floor. So I think that what he was trying to do is stop him before he became over-exaggerated.

P3: He was like, only shouting. He wasn't actually causing any harm was he? So, I don't think there was any point in it.
[Indistinct excited chatter resumed.]

P3: The chap was in the right by helping his girlfriend. So I just think he was telling the truth.

P5: He wasn't trying to get away from them or struggling to get in the car. He was just shouting.

P7: They didn't need to put him to the floor. […]

P1: […] If he'd been calm, it would have been like 'Calm down' [softly spoken], but next thing [sound of expelled air] […]
[The researcher asked whether the lads' behaviour around the car was suspicious to which there was general agreement.]

P4: General abuse …

P3: But they didn't need to put him to the floor though.
[Followed by indistinct interjection.]
… but he wasn't causing any problems, just shouting.
[Further indistinct interventions.]

P3: That's what I meant: give him a chance to explain himself.

P8: He overreacted …

Res: Do you mean that man overreacted or the police …?
[There was general indistinct agreement that it was the youth who overreacted.]

P8: The police reacted as well. (WS330084)

Amongst young people generally in our focus groups, this relatively modest use of force by the police officer evoked intense and divisive expressions of opinion. However, this differed only in degree from other groups who were also divided on the issue.

Proportionality

The question of 'fairness' overlaps with 'proportionality': whereas judgements of 'fairness' tend to focus on *desert*, 'proportion' focuses, more practically, upon *necessity*: how much force needs to be used to achieve the compliance of the suspect?

Groups comprising older people tended to be supportive of the police officer's action as being necessary in the circumstances. Perhaps more surprisingly, groups composed of young people tended to concur. Adolescent members of a youth club in a desirable rural dormitory town tended to regard the young man who was arrested as being responsible for his own misfortune:

P1: If he'd cooperated in the first place they wouldn't have had to.
P2: I thought it was a bit far. I mean kicking him on the floor, trying to trip him up, but I think trying to arrest him was justified.
P1: But it's easier to arrest him on the floor rather than standing up.
P2: Yeah, he wouldn't have gone …
    […]
P3: If he'd just cooperated it would have been easier for everyone.
Res: How about the number of people involved, though? Did it take all the officers … There was the officer and those Meadowhall security guards.
P3: He could have got violent, so …
P4: There were three guys trying to break into the car. (WS330089)

In assessing whether any use of force is proportionate to the threat posed by an adversary, police are empowered to use force to forestall threats that might reasonably be anticipated. We have already seen how many of our focus group members relied not only on what *had* occurred, but also used their imagination to anticipate what *might* occur. How did they use their imagination to evaluate the pre-emptive use of force? Imagination tended to surround two questions: first, was the suspect trying innocently to retreat from the aggressive demeanour of the officer, or was he creating space to facilitate an escape bid? Secondly, did the suspect actually or potentially pose a threat or danger that needed to be mitigated? Young offenders serving a community penalty interpreted the young man's actions as innocent:

P1: It wasn't like he was threatening them. So, there was no need for him to be grabbed up by these four people. If you're not threatening no one, there's no need. He weren't coming across as a threatening person. He was walking backwards, if anything.
P2: And he weren't even going to run, was he?
    […]
P3: And he give him clear instructions, yeah! 'Don't touch me!' and he keeps on touching him.
P4: It's antagonising him, isn't it? […] arrest him.
P5: That's what they do, man. The police.

[...]

Res: What about when they arrested that chap and took him to the police ...?

P1: They didn't have to take him down, because he was showing aggression, yeah, but that was verbally. He wasn't physically getting in his face. He was backing away.

P3: The reason for showing him verbal abuse was because of how he was treated too aggressive. And they ripped his clothes, as you heard him say. If they didn't rip his clothes, I think it would be too aggressive for him. That would have been a verbal ... (WS330055)

Members of a security firms' trade association who had experience of dealing with truculent young people emphasised the need for caution and bringing the situation under control.

P1: It was when he kicked off, really. That's when you know [...] You know, this could turn nasty. Especially when there's ... If he gets ... if it had got nasty, then that would have been it, then. It would be ...

P2: People who say [to the contrary] have probably never been in the situation ...

P3: As with anything, it starts to attract ... other people were starting to come around weren't they? So, I think it was already going to get all out of hand. I think also they could have legged it at any time. (WS330021)

Competent

A valued feature of professionalism is that of detachment: professionals are supposed to maintain emotional distance from those to whom they render a service, and do so calmly and dispassionately. Police officers are in a rather different situation. We will return to this issue later, but suffice to say that in dealing with suspects the police officer is hardly 'rendering a service' to the most immediate recipients of their actions and may be doing so not only without their consent, but in the face of their resistance. Keeping calm and detached in a conflictual encounter imposes tremendous strains on the emotions of the police officer. Engaging in a physical struggle triggers the so-called 'fight or flight' response that may impede judgement. This was recognised by many of our participants, but they also expected the officer to act professionally and not allow personal feelings to intrude. Some went further, believing that the officer had a *duty* to manage the encounter by keeping the suspects calm and doing nothing to arouse needless antagonism.

Sikh worshippers felt that the police officer's actions were motivated by feelings of superiority:

P1: I think they could have spoke for longer, calmed them down before ... kind of getting him down to the ground.

P2: 'I'm an officer. You shouldn't talk to me like that.' But they talk to people badly as well.

P1: Well, the police think of themselves as ... y'know ...

P3: 'Superior'! (laugh) They do! (WS310030)

Another component of professionalism is that the practitioner must be expert in dealing with situations encountered as part of their work. That expertise is most dramatically tested when the situation threatens to go awry. How did focus groups judge the officer's management of the encounter? The central issue was whether the officer controlled or exacerbated the agitation of the arrested youth in the car park. In many groups this occasioned deep and lengthy discussion which space precludes us from reproducing in full. Instead, we feel that the discussion amongst a multi-ethnic group of young professionals attending a college devoted to educating people for jobs in white collar and management positions best captures the array of views.

P1: The police officer was polite enough to ask them before, when he approached them, … [one suspect] would not do as he was told. That's why he took him in custody and I think he did the right thing.

P2: I differ.

Res: Yes, go on!

P2: I think the approach is wrong, because if they were carrying out a criminal act, then they wouldn't have stuck around when the security guards turned up. So, therefore, to arrest somebody before … that will agitate things. That's the first thing he actually did was arrest them. And then, what it was, was instead of de-escalating things, things just got escalated more. And that's what the outcome was.

Res: You think the police officer shouldn't …?

P2: There should have been a different approach.

P3: He was very rough.

P4: Another thing is that at times they are brazen enough to … y'know … 'It is my vehicle' or whatever. It can happen. I'm not saying it should. But they are brazen enough to do it. So, the police officer, he erred on the side of caution. I didn't see the point in arresting: *detaining*—I didn't see the point in arresting. Two of them didn't argue about it, but the one did, but to no avail really.

P2: The thing is, depending on your background. If you've been in a situation like that and you've been a victim before, then that's a trigger isn't it? 'I'm innocent here. Not breaking the law, but you're just using arrest first until I prove myself'—it's a trigger.

P4: That's why I say, 'detaining' not 'arrest'.

P5: It was a very difficult situation for the police.
[This was greeted with indistinct agreement.]

P1: If he had left him to walk away, then maybe he could just have run away. He wanted to make sure … he wanted to make sure … hold them back.
[Leading to further murmurs of agreement.]

P1 [continuing]: That's what he did with the other two …

P2: I understand that, but as a police officer your training also gives you that insight, how to handle things differently. So, if he's been agitated, rather than being in his face … Manhandling him. As soon as you start manhandling him you take it to next level as well. Grab somebody; that will really start things. He wasn't running away. Yeah? He may have been loud, but a police officer is used to having people loud. He wasn't being abusive to start off with. He was just loud. Yeah?

P6: I think he did his best to put him into that situation, but the guy wanted him to do it. And because they have some experience with situations like that. Making good action and quick action in that respect needed…. I've never been in this situation, I might simply say 'It's not me', but I might have good experience how to break the window and pretend in front of the police that that is my own car or my girlfriend's one. [...] But when you see that he's about to do something wrong, you have to just disable. So I think it was very good.

P2: I understand that, but the thing is, there was no crime being committed any further. As soon as they turned up, they stopped everything. They explained what they were doing there. And there was enough security guards to back up the police officer and there actually wasn't a tension. Normally, in a situation like that there's a face-off, and that wasn't happening until he started approaching. So, therefore ... Depending on what kind of liaisons you've had with police in the past, that is a trigger, that's your red rag, especially if you're innocent.

P3: I think that nowadays its [...] because there is so much crime, the police can't wait to question people sometimes. And they have to act quickly. However, the police officer's behaviour was very aggressive towards the person as well. [...]

P7: I think also, like, when the guy was trying to explain, the police officer wouldn't let him explain, which I thought ... I think that's wrong. [...]

P2: Did you see he wasn't actually going in his face, he was staying back and the police officer kept approaching him; he was staying back, but kept being approached.

P4: He was asked. He was asked.

P2: I know he was asked ...

P4: You should've back off.

P2: ... but when you're angry. If you've done nothing wrong and somebody's put something on you. And if you've used stuff like that in the past, then guess what?

P4: But he started it. He started it.

P2: That's an opinion. [...]

P2: But what's respectful about 'You're under arrest' for something you haven't done?

P1: He wasn't put under arrest the moment the police officer arrived.

P2: He arrested them first!

P1: No, he questioned all three of them together and two of them ...

P8: Calmly told him.

P1: Calmly told him. What he said was, 'Shall I call the woman?' and they agreed to that and that gentleman didn't agree to it. And that's why ... what happened to him.

P2: No, what he said was, 'Until the lady turns up, you're under arrest'. So far as I understand. So, ...

P1: He had no intention of handcuffing them until ...

P2: But telling someone, 'You're arrested' for something you haven't done!

Res 2: What about this lady over here?

P9: I thought he dealt with it very well. He stayed calm and telling them firmly, but I agree with this man, if you're innocent and you're being arrested, you get angry, but I still think the police dealt with it well.

Res 2: How about the point that he was taken to the ground? This was aggressive?

P 9: I think they have to do that sometimes. I think the police do that quickly so that it don't get out of hand.

P10: He was handcuffed. They were trying to hold him down. Then he's struggling and they're struggling ... They have to do ... A necessary evil.

Res 2: How about this gentleman on the end?

P11: For me [...] it was his fault. The aggressive reaction was effective for me. The guy was aggressive and he did overreact. So, even when the police tried to handcuff him [...] it was the only way they could control him.

P12: Actually, I agree, because he started to be aggressive and you don't know what he could ... after [...] I think they did a good thing.

Res: You're the only one who hasn't spoken, *yet!* (laugh)

P13: I think it could have been dealt with a bit better. I think if they had done something wrong, they'd have tried to get away, or cause a bit of a scene when the security guard approached them in the first place, instead of ... I don't think they'd have hung around for the security guard to get back, if they'd done something wrong. For me, it kind of looked like the police was kind of pushing him and unfortunately he reacted to that.

P14: I agree with that.
[...]

P6: He's not working in 'customer service'!
[Greeted with laughter.]
I'm sorry, I think sometimes he must act like that.

P3: Obviously, if you're innocent and the police approach you like that then you're going to get very angry.

P6: But you don't know whether innocent or not, just yet. Somebody says, 'Wait and we're going to find out'.

P3: If you were innocent and the police come and approach you would kick off wouldn't you.
[Greeted with murmurs of agreement.]
I would've kicked off straight away. [...]

P3: I think the fact that they stayed there in the first place ... I don't think there was any way for the police to act as they did. (WS330067)

What is so interesting about this and the other debates on this video clip is that it highlights a subtle distinction between the police having the *capacity* to use force and actually using it (Bittner 1970; 1985). The public might value the police as 'monopolists of force' who might cajole and coerce compliance, thereby achieving what others cannot, but recourse to the actual use of force is much more controversial. Here, we find the public deeply divided regarding their expectations of how officers can and should manage the opposition displayed by the youth, especially since this was a reasonably straightforward matter about the enforcement of the criminal law.

Violent Arrest at Nightclub

The final video shown to the focus groups and yet to be discussed here, was also the briefest with just one minute and three seconds of playing time. The opening scenes are of a police personnel carrier arriving in a busy night-time street and officers alighting from the van and running up the street. In a voice-over, the viewer was told that this was the 'public order van' and it has been called to a nightclub where a 'CS gas canister has been let off in someone's face'. It continued: 'No one can identify the person who did it. But now police have another problem on their hands: a bystander is behaving very aggressively towards them'. The camera then cut to a confused scene in which three police officers were struggling with a man who appeared to be throwing punches at them. A fourth officer joined the mêlée and grabbed the man from behind pulling him backwards resulting in several officers tumbling, along with the man, to the ground. There was then a struggle on the ground during which an officer was heard saying 'get a cuff on him'. Then an officer stood up and pulled the man's one arm out straight and with the assistance of the others, turned him facedown. In the process of doing this, the man toppled off the pavement and into the gutter. One officer then held his head against the ground, whilst others continued to handcuff the man with his hands to his rear. Officers could be heard telling the man to 'Stay calm' and a crowd of onlookers could easily be seen as they watched these events. He was then taken to the rear of a police personnel carrier by several officers and as he was bundled into the rear compartment, a voice told him to 'Watch your head, mate'. The doors of the personnel carrier were slammed shut and the video ended.

Violence

The level of violence in this video clip was obviously much greater than in the previous two videos and some members of our focus groups reacted with an equally strong sense of revulsion, but they didn't go entirely unchallenged. Exemplars of a horrified response were abundant, including a community consultation group in a deprived area, some of whom worried that the man might have suffered permanent injury:

P1: By the look of them, they seem about twenty stone, to me.
P2: That might be a bit heavy-handed.
P3: And the one who dragged the hand with a handcuff on it out in the street.
P4: My worry was the head near the curb. I have known people who have cracked their skulls on their …
P3: They already have him down, don't they?
P5: They already had him down on the floor, why drag him anywhere? Why not just put his hands behind his back and get [him] upright.
P1: If you noticed, two officers kicked the legs of the one who they had arrested. They kicked him very hard that could have left him with permanent injuries, for a start …
P3: And the language they use when they chuck him in the van.
P5: Well he […] that when they arrested him.
P3: Yeah, even when they put him in the van, they know he couldn't go anywhere, and the language that they used … Now I don't think they deserve to be in the force.
P5: I think it was a terrible overreaction.
P3: I think they want to go in the army (laugh).
P1: I think there was too much force used. In fact I've got to say, personally, I think it was violence, aggravated violence by the police officers. They were not conducting themselves as professional police officers, I'm sorry to say. And that's the way I feel about it. […]
P5: I think they went in expecting to find a lot of aggression. I think they went in like a riot squad, rather than … And I can understand, to some extent, because they had

been told that there had been a gas canister, or whatever, but that was one individual and it didn't warrant that amount of aggressive … attitude, or whatever you
want to call it. I think they went in looking for trouble. If that makes sense (laugh).

P4: I think it was a total overreaction and police officers don't need to swear and they
did swear straightaway when they were getting him down to the floor.

P3: I think police officers should be a profession, not because an arrested person or
cautioned person is easier to move …

P4: No! There's no excuse for it. […]

Res: Some people have said, in that clip, that the force used was appropriate. Does
anybody think …

[This was roundly and swiftly rejected.]

P1: Was that the guy with the canister? I don't know.

[Greeted with laughter from others.]

P5: We couldn't establish that.

P1: He could have been a danger to the public, and that's why they tried to get him
down and out the way.

P4: I think there needed to be some force, but it needed to be appropriate force and
the fact that they pulled that guy off the footpath into the gutter was unnecessary, there was too much aggressive force—aggression and force there.

P5: You know those five police officers were dropping on your back, that could do
you serious damage.

P1: They were big blokes. (WS330037)

In some other groups, however, revulsion at the force used was dismissed derisively as 'soft'. An exchange in a tenants and resident consultative group illustrates this tendency:

P1: I think they needed to restrain him, but I'm not too sure about smacking his face
against the curb.

P2: I don't personally think that an 'excuse me my friend would you please behave
yourself?' would suffice.

P3: They are not going to put a cushion down there, are they?

P1: I didn't mean that. I didn't mean that.

P4: I think that at the end of the day, if someone is acting in that way, you don't
know what is going to go off. And you have to resolve the situation as quickly as
possible. For the benefit of the public anyhow … (WS330043).

In another group criticism of police behaviour was ridiculed as equivalent to
the attacker sitting 'on the naughty step' (WS330090).

The dilemmas of using force were, in some groups, articulated in clashes
(sometimes heated) of perspective and opinion. Amongst members of a community arts centre youth club there was a striking clash of views.

P1: He swore.

P2: Yeah but it didn't take four of them though … And you just watched and saw
how they smashed his head off the road …

P1: That was cool, actually. […]

P3: How would you like it if it was you? […]

P4: Yeah but you wouldn't!

P2: Bashed off a gutter regardless?

P1: No, but I'd fight back [...]

P2: But he hardly had a dig at them ... [...]

P3: ... and they smash your head off the gutter. Would you like it?

P1: They lay him down nicely.

P3: What?! (WS330071)

Amongst a multi-ethnic group of young professionals it was felt, on the one hand, that the police officers had behaved no less aggressively than the man they were arresting, whilst, on the other it was felt that officers were making the arrest in a way least likely to cause injury.

P1: You don't need to drag him across the floor ... to put his arm back.

P2: Normal Saturday night isn't it.

P3: They're too aggressive.

P4: I think they are acting okay in response to the way he was acting towards them, but once they had him on the floor I don't understand why they need to drag him ...
[Murmured agreement from others.]
... there was no need for that.

P5: Yes well when we saw the man ... Was he trying to hit the policeman? The police officer was, like, reacting back ...

P6: Exactly!

P5: ... I was asking, which man is the aggressive man? I thought, is that the man in the high viz vest? [...] So I think it was all too aggressive.

P6: It was like the public to me, he was just fighting and shouting exactly like a guy to be arrested [...] So colleagues help him.

P7: ... Otherwise, so he didn't behave like police. He was fighting and just trying ... not to arrest him ... He was just trying to fight him and he kicked him even. (Laugh)

P5: And so shouldn't more of the officers have been going to deal with the CS gas (laugh) report, instead of [...] officers being on him? ...

P7: You've only got two arms two legs so four maybe (laugh)!

P8: No! You see what it is: if you're under the influence of something
[Greeted with murmurs in the background of 'drugs']
... your behaviour ... You're invincible. [...] And I think their primary aim is to arrest you without causing harm to themselves or you.

P1: Yeah, dragging him across the floor! [said derisively]

P8: Yeah, but when they got you and you're still ... I think that's called 'reasonable force'.

P1: I don't think that was reasonable

P7: I don't think that was reasonable force, I think there was aggressive force.

P9: They pinned him to the ground, then also pulling him like that ...

P7: Then pushing his face down into the floor.
[Greeted with murmurs of agreement from others.]

P10: They removed the threat of violent behaviour, or of anyone else starting off. And, as you said, when they had something to drink they are Superman—this strength multiplies and it does need a lot of them. I don't understand ... Okay, fair enough. I know he'd been drinking, but I do not understand why he had to struggle so much. I'm not suggesting that the police can be aggressive, but what I am saying is that they know it will take a lot of people ... And he was still struggling wasn't he? And they were still struggling with the fact that he was still.

[...]

P11: It was what they needed, especially on Friday nights—Saturday or Friday (laugh).

Res: So you think it was justified?

P11: Yes I think it was justified.

P8: I agree.

P12: If someone is aggressive, they have to stop him as soon as possible.

P8: It's like, the young lady there said, it was like ... Not only had five of them got their backs turned. Now, the need is to get this person out of the way so that they can deal with other things. You're right about the CS, but the CS has already happened, so you will have some officers ... There's enough of them there. So you're down to half strength. Now, if someone is kicking off, you're taking care ... One of the problems first, is to get it out of the way first so you can deal with the rest. So there was another guy who was going to get involved, yeah, he was coming straight at them. While the five of them had got their backs turned they have become vulnerable. (WS330067)

What these exchanges also highlight is that *how* behaviour is described affords or denies legitimacy. Critics use words like 'smash', 'bash', 'drag', 'fighting and shouting', whereas defenders of police action use neutral words like 'flip him' to mean turning the man onto his front. Mothers of children who had been in trouble with the police were highly critical of the police; accusing them of 'brutality ... it's just wrong' (WS330025).[6]

Proportionality

Is the use of violence unavoidably 'brutal', or can it be justified in given circumstances? If so, under what circumstances is it justified? Our focus groups implicitly accepted that if officers were *attacked*, then they were entitled to defend themselves. The problem arose when officers used force to achieve their purpose, even when the threat of attack has been neutralised? In this context, when does 'flipping' become 'dragging him across the floor'?

One justification has surfaced already, the intoxication—whether by alcohol or drugs—that the man was thought to be exhibiting.[7] A group of Sikh worshippers had little objection to the officers' actions on these grounds. One of them opined: 'There was nothing else they could do' and then he lapsed into Punjabi. Resuming in English he said, 'but when you're in a situation like this, right? That guy was a bit drunk'. A little later he returned to the issue:

No he wasn't nervous, the guy wasn't nervous. In this kind situation there is nothing else you can do. I've been ... Years ago ... I've been at a nightclub where I've helped a bouncer and people like that, there's nothing you can do. Because they've been drinking, they seem to think that they are stronger—and they are actually, I don't know where they get their strength from, and it takes that many to pull down. That's the only

---

[6] Incidentally, the original television broadcast explained that the man was in possession of 'a large quantity' of amphetamines, which it was said, explained his formidable strength.

[7] Our focus groups were not told that the arrested man was found to be in possession of 'a large quantity of amphetamines' upon arrival at the police station. So any mention of his behaviour being drug or alcohol fuelled was entirely supposition on the part of our participants.

thing you can do, the only thing you can do. There's nothing else you can do. You can't really … There's no other way you can put them down. That's the only way. (WS310027)

Whereas another group of Sikh worshippers were critical and explicitly dismissive of the man's drunkenness:

P1: It was just so heavy-handed wasn't it?
P2: I thought they overreacted.
P3: I think they batted him good and proper.
P1: How many coppers does it take to hold down one man?
P2: I know he's had a drink. I thought that was really violent. Dragging his face across the ground! (WS310031)

Such stark divisions of opinion were commonplace amongst our groups, often expressed as arguments within the group. Students at a further education college divided sharply:

P1: He could have hurt himself … the way they dragged him, it could have broken his arm. They should have been more careful about that. Yes, yes he's fighting, but there are three people there, enough to handle, because they should have been strong enough … They've been trained to. So why do they need six people? […] They could have restrained him, put him up against a wall or something like that, or against the car. But why on the floor? It could have hurt … […]
P1: I think three people would have been enough for him.
P2: Not for him!
P3: They wanted to make sure. I think they wanted to make sure. Once you put the fourth person on in that's it. Made sure he was down and out and away.
Res: So you think they were too aggressive?
P1: Too aggressive.
Res: Does anyone else think that?
P3: I don't think they were aggressive enough.[Greeted with murmurs of agreement.]… I think they should have stamped on his ankles […]
Res: Do you think the police could have done more?
P3: Yeah, stamp on his ankles. He wouldn't be getting up and walking off then! (Laughs) […]
P3: If he had made a fool out of the coppers. If three tried to get on him and they couldn't get him down, then he would have made a fool out of the coppers, then some other people may have started. Shouting 'wooofs!' Or something. Then that would increase the volatile situation. (WS330028/29)

So too did young offenders serving a community sentence:

P1: I think the police done their job.
P2: Yeah they didn't terrorise him … Taser or gas him … He's lucky, he is!
P1: At the end of the day, they were restraining him … There's no harm in restraining somebody is there? […]
P2: And then, like, he wouldn't put his arms behind his back. So obviously they dragged his arm over so that they could put it behind him.
Res: So you thought the police were justified in what they do?
P2: Yeah. They did on his face on the floor and that, yeah!
P3: That's what they have to do, really.

Res: You said he was lucky?

P2: Yeah?

P4: Yeah! You normally get sprayed up and [...] And shit like that. [...] You have some nice coppers! [...]

[Greeted with general laughter.]

[...] He was swinging punches wasn't he? Until you get the cuffs on, officers' best mate!

Res: So does anyone think the police were too aggressive with him?

P2: No!

P3: They were all right with him.

[...]

P4: ... I don't know what it's called, can't remember the name ...

P2: Just restrain him real quick.

P4: 'Harmful force', or something like that.

Res: How about that there were so many of them?

P3: I think that was better, yeah? If it was just one copper and that one geezer, that would be a fight, wouldn't it? A scrap. But when they all go, they are taking control quick, aren't they? They are in control then.

P4: It was outside club, wasn't it? So obviously, look at how many people there are in a club. Just one officer ... (WS330057)

Such divisions were not restricted to the young. Members of a neighbourhood watch group in an affluent area also disagreed markedly.

P1: It does beg the question, why was he aggressive in the first place? We didn't quite see what made them react to this man who was being quite aggressive ... That wasn't quite clear. [...] they were faced with this aggressive man and they reacted to that. It took about—I don't know how many ...

[Others suggest 'five', 'six'.]

... about two or three should have been enough with the proper police holds. Certainly, with wrist locks you can put on that restrain people quite easily—when they're put on properly, there's not much you can do about it. But there seemed to be too many of them

[Someone interjected 'jumping'.]

... getting in each other's way you know. They've got to arrest him if he was aggressive but why he was aggressive I don't know.

P2: Couldn't it have been the man who had gas in his face?

P3: It could have been the man who set it off!

P2: That's what I'm saying: we don't know, we didn't see all of it did we? I don't know how it affects somebody, you know, gas in their face.

P4: How many amongst us would say that the man they arrested was drunk?

P5: Actually he looked quite wild!

P2: I don't know. He was just wild. Waving his arms about and all.

P6: [...] dragged into the gutter?

P1: That wasn't a good idea was it?

P6: About five of them.

P2: I say there was too many of them.

P3: I'd say there was five of them.

P1: But when somebody is trying to kick you ... to hurt you, it's errr ... adrenaline ...

P3: But then they left him in the gutters didn't they? And he was injured.

P1: Yes I can understand ... Hear what you say, but I'm just saying that if you've been in the situation like that it does sort of tend to ... Y' know ... Because they are trying to hurt you. All you're trying to do is to restrain them, but they are intent on hurting you. So you go to protect yourself haven't you one way or another. In some ways you can say, 'well does it take four or five?' He takes four or five: somebody to stopping heading you; somebody stop him kicking you with both feet; and both legs and both arms, you know ...

P3: It didn't look like it on there, did it?

P1: He was up for it wasn't he?

Res: Who thought it was too heavy-handed?
[This suggestion was generally rejected.]

P3: Going back to him in the car was more heavy-handed than what they would ... Because, first of all, they were being *abused*—attacked by that lad. To start with, put him down, they got him out the way. Then they could deal with the problem they got in the first place.

Res: Who agrees with that view?

P4: Yes I do.

P3: Yes and me.

P6: Yes I agree with holding them. I'm just confused why they dragged him.
[Greeted with murmurs of agreement.]

P3: Again I think there was a bit of the clip missing, you don't tend to see all of it. Perhaps it went on a little longer than we had anticipated.

P4: They get into trouble no matter what they do!

P1: They were a little ... I daresay that the other side of that point is ... I say the main thing is to stop yourself getting ... Why should policemen get themselves hurt? You're no good to the job. You're no good to your family, are you? So, you know, you make sure you don't get yourself injured ... You're there to solve the situation, yeah! I see these things, you know policemen who suffer from trauma. You know, when you're going to be a policeman you expect to suffer from trauma. You expect to come across situations like that. As I say, I could never be doing with policeman like that, who weren't mindful ... Not going in thinking about things, 'I couldn't get hurt again'. You know self-preservation comes into it, doesn't it?

P3: The thing is, he might have been attacking another member of the public and then turned on. So ...?

P1: You don't know.
[Indistinct voices were raised.]

P3: They were pushing down, they got him into the van, and that's out of the way, and then dealt with whatever they needed to do.

P7: He might just have been panicking, because of the gas. Because with CS gas you get running eyes and whatever.
[Further murmurs of agreement.]
He might have thought he was going to die or whatever.

P8: He might have been a drug addict ...
[More indistinct voices.]

P7: ... Absolutely panicked, and wanted to get out of the way.

P1: It could be any situation. As I say, this man wants to attack you basically, so you have got to react ...

P7: ... because he did attack them, didn't he? He didn't push them out of the way so that he could get away? (WS330078)

These extracts eloquently testify to the confusion that reigns in such an intense violent eruption. People who witness it, draw selectively from what they have seen and heard to try and construct meanings; occasionally they confabulate in order to fill in gaps.

Dragging

As we have seen in other discussions quoted above, one aspect of the incident that occasioned considerable comment was when the officer pulled the arm of the now pinioned man in order to turn him over onto his face, whereupon the latter toppled into the gutter. This divided our groups strongly. For instance, race equality activists, some of whom felt it was gratuitous, whereas others could detect a legitimate purpose in the manoeuvre:

P1: At the start I felt, you know, they're doing their job, they are trying to detain some-one who is being aggressive. But once they had that gentleman on the ground, I just think that they were being just *too* aggressive. Yeah, I think …

P2: It seemed like a rugby scrum to me.

P3: I just think they nearly took that one man's arm off, out of its socket. I think there is what we class as 'just sufficient', you know, restraint and just, you know, going over the top.
[Greeted with murmurs of agreement.]

P4: Yeah, because they were four or more holding him down, they didn't need to pull his arm, because there were four police officers on him at that point, they didn't need to pull him. But otherwise I think they were doing well, until that bit. […]

P5: I think they did what they needed to do. He needed to be restrained and put in that van. […]

P6: They got him in one position and they all piled in on top of him. Fine. They managed to get him cuffed and whatever, or getting ready to cuff him, but I think it was just that one officer that seemed to do something, to me, that seemed to be acting out of his own aggression.
[Greeted with murmured disagreement.]

P6: Now I just think, it was just that one officer. I felt that they contained the situation and that was all good, but that one officer, I think there was too …

Res: But how should the police have dealt with that?
[One person asked to whom the question was referring?]

Res: The one who is being arrested.

P6: I felt right up until the point where they got him on the floor … Because I noticed in all the other scenes, they have to take them down first of all, which I noticed that officer did. All of them took him down, piled on top of him and were restraining him. Up to that point I felt, 'Yes, they should. He is being aggressive, putting other people risk.' But then it was that one officer, where I think his head was hanging over the pavement, as well, … Do you know! I don't know anybody's ever seen where if you're in such an awkward position they can break your neck, they can kill you at that point. I just felt that that one officer, you know, just acted on his own whim, so to speak.

P5: I just think it was so quick and such ... they just got to get it done and that's one of those things isn't it? [...]

P7: And then you got brutality and everything else that goes with it. (WS330047)

This was an issue that divided the young as well as adults. Students at a further education college were similarly divided.

P1: it started off reasonable ...

P2: You mean dragging someone by their arm? Off the curb?

P3: I guess they did that probably to loosen his arm and dragged him to stop him doing it.

P1: What if they created injury or his head [...] off the curb? Then what?

P4: Dead!

P1: It's like that thing outside the bank when they nicked that man and he had internal bleeding and all those things. Then what? (WS330006)

A member of the local security trade association empathised with the police in this situation: 'The only thing you're going to think is, "Gets him down. Get him in the van"'. You're oblivious to the traffic or anything what's going on. They don't intentionally want to put him into the road, but they've just got to get him down. The guy's off his head.' (WS330021)

Number of Officers

When discussing the arrest in the superstore car park, we discussed the question of the number of officers required to overpower someone resisting arrest. Needless to say this issue was considered to be even more acute in the context of this video clip. Ethnic minority groups tended to find it particularly troubling. Mothers of children who had been in trouble with the police (who were exclusively Black) saw little need for so many officers to be involved:

P4: ... it's when there is a great big group of them.

P5: One person and there's about six coppers.

P6: That's being the whole point, hasn't it in what we've seen? Too many officers on one ... well mainly young lads, we've seen, hasn't it. (WS330025)

Middle Eastern émigré mothers attending a community centre also thought it was a token of needless aggression:

P1: They were too aggressive.

P2: They were too aggressive.

Res: 'They were too aggressive' you thought? When were they too aggressive?

P3: It took six police officers.

[Which provoked an interjection: 'Four!']

... However many it was to take one person down. (WS330069)

Violence of the Arrestee

Whether a tactic was proportionate or not depends on the level of resistance that needs to be overcome. We have seen above that when assessing the arrests of the suspected stolen car driver and the volatile youth in the superstore car park, our focus groups drew attention to the fact that neither suspect was physically violent.

In the case of the aggressive man outside a nightclub there was a striking absence of comment about the level of violence that the police officers confronted. Some participants did draw attention to the possibility that the man might have been suffering the effects of the CS gas canister that had allegedly been discharged in the nightclub, or was perhaps distressed by the suffering of others. Yet, very few of our focus groups mentioned the obvious fact that this was a muscular young man who was being physically violent towards police officers. We have seen passing references to the man presumably being intoxicated and how this confers greater strength upon people. Quite why this was so, is a matter for speculation. What we can note now is that it was, at least, possible for our focus groups to have drawn conclusions about the scale of resistance with which officers were faced. A neighbourhood watch group in an area of mixed housing was one of the few to discuss the aggressive man in any detail and to weigh it in the balance of proportionality.

P1: He was aggressive.

P2: He was a big fellow.
[This met with general agreement.]

P1: You wanted a dozen there, didn't you? I felt as if I wanted to help them!
[This was greeted with general laughter.]

P3: He's a thug.

P1: He must have been abusive in the first place, for they wouldn't have gone at him like that.

P4: He was properly drunk.

Res: What do other people think? Was that force necessary?
[Two people agreed.]

P5: He was lashing out. He was already held by one arm and lashing out at officers with the other. There's only one thing to do ... There's only one thing that will happen if he starts doing that.
[...]

Res: Does anyone think the police were too aggressive?

P1: Well I think there were too many of them on him, but then again, you really don't know what it's like to be in that situation. It's one thing to sit here, looking at it, another for the policeman actually dealing with it. So, possibly, yeah, they were justified.

P2: Well he's got two arms two legs, so you need four just a holding him down!
[Which provoked general laughter.]

P3: And one on his stomach!
[Further general laughter.]

P1: No [name] I think if there's only been one policeman there, you had something to say, 'Why was there only one policeman?' To me, there ought to have been four, half a dozen? I think they did the right thing.

P6: Given the situation of what had happened, somebody had let off a CS gas canister, I think the police were well within their rights to turn up with those many officers. It's a public order offence, you don't know what you're going into. The last thing you need is to turn up with two officers in one car, with a gang or group of people outside the nightclub (or wherever it was like that). You know.

P1: I'm not saying there are too many people there altogether, but perhaps there were too many of them jumped on him ... I suppose they must be aware of these things, but he wouldn't be able to breathe if they all sat on him like that. [...]

P8: Bearing in mind that that fellow was tanked up with beer and his inhibitions just go anyway. I mean, that's like trying to get round a caged animal, isn't it? You need as many police officers, and it takes a lot more than four or five to deck somebody. And to get him cuffed. (WS330052)

Non–lethal Weapons

It may seem counter-intuitive, but one possibility fleetingly entertained by several of our focus groups, was for the police to have used alternative means of controlling the man that would not entail close quarter combat. Several mentioned CS spray and some even felt that an electro-stun weapon (such as a Taser) would have been preferable. This was the view advocated by representatives in a local authority 'youth forum' despite the opposition of the 'youth leader':

Res: Do you think they should have been more aggressive?
[There was general rejection of the suggestion.]
P1: Less! Use the Taser and just let him fall on the floor and when he gets back up then put him in the van.
Res: So do you think the Taser is less aggressive?
[Followed by a chorus of 'yes'.]
P1: Than five or four men coming on him and pushing him on the floor.
P2: It just gives him 1000 volts and he's down.
P1: He's out for the count, he couldn't care less!
[Greeted with general laughter.]
Res: So do other people think that is a better method?
P3: At the end of the day, I don't like Tasers. I don't like anything like it.
P4: Wouldn't that be a lot easier than five men jumping on him at once?
P3: But you don't know what effect it can have on the person.
P5: But if they didn't act so aggressive then they wouldn't have to …
P3: I just feel that …
P4: Well they just baton them. Whack him!
P3: No!
[Further general laughter.]
P3: [following an interlude]
I just don't agree with Tasers. I think that it's something we've imported from overseas. I think it is something that we follow other people. I think it is something we are becoming: a society where some of our police officers are too aggressive instead of able to sort the situation out.
P5: Do you think that is because people are becoming more aggressive that they've got to […] sorted it out?
P3: But I also think that there's a whole host of things … There's a perception of what the role of the police is. There is a perception of what you young people are. And people don't challenge any of this and look at the positive sides […] and we concentrate always on the negative. And I think police officers—there are some damn good police officers out there, but they all get labelled the same. And some of the behaviour we have seen today is absolutely disgusting.
P6: They don't do themselves any favours either, because that response of all four of them jumping on that individual. They could have been other young people or other adults that were intoxicated, they could have said, 'well let's have a […] let's have a nice fight' … (WS330050)

125

What is striking about the discussions reproduced above is not only the dissension that the use of force arouses, but also its intensity. It arouses passionate debate, at the centre of which is the very characteristic that many researchers believe distinguishes the police from other occupations—their monopoly of legitimate sovereign force. Controversy, debate, argument and rhetoric swirl around the police. Some respondents felt the use of force was 'unprofessional', 'unseemly' and perhaps at odds with the public service ethos that the police profess to uphold.

Conclusions

Hitherto, discussion of police use of force has concentrated, almost exclusively, on the use of potentially injurious, if not lethal, tactics and weaponry, or those episodes that erupt in the public domain, like the beating of Rodney King and the death of Ian Tomlinson. Here we have focused on *normal* use of force in everyday policing.

The first conclusion is that the public relies, as does the law itself, on whether any use of force is 'reasonable', but this is not a clear and fixed standard; on the contrary, it is highly controversial. What seems a reasonable response to one person, might be wholly exceptionable to another. This is one obvious respect in which the reasonable or unreasonable use of force depends upon perception: judging the reasonableness of a course of action involves imagining what the officer might know or fear, not only about the immediate circumstances, but how the situation might develop. Some people imagined that if the car being driven on the motorway *was* stolen, then the force used might have been prudent and justified. Others felt that the officer should not anticipate the counterfactual possibilities of what *might* occur, but rather react to the circumstances as they appeared at the time and possibly change. Hence, many felt that the young driver should have been approached in a less aggressive manner and the driver politely invited to alight from the car. Refusal might justify some measure of force, for this group, but could not be anticipated. Some felt that even the aggressive man outside the nightclub should have been asked why he was being so aggressive, before subduing him with overwhelming force of numbers.

Politeness also figures in the adverse judgements made about the way in which officers spoke to suspects. They expected the police to be civil, not least in what they did or did not say. This was not only prior to any physical contact, but also during struggles themselves. People expect police officers to 'keep their cool' even during heated verbal exchanges and physical combat.

Another conclusion that can be drawn from these focus groups is that physical grappling with suspects, especially when several officers engage in the task, is not regarded with equanimity. The notion, to be found in 'use of force hierarchies' employed by police in various jurisdictions, tacitly assumes that 'empty hand' techniques are the most acceptable tactics and officers receive precious little training in such techniques or in how to avoid becoming involved in grappling at all. Once officers are equipped with devices to quell resistance—incapacitant sprays, electro-stun devices, and firearms—then not only does training come to be seen (quite rightly) as necessary, but strict accountability procedures are instituted for reporting their use. Research in the USA has revealed the uncomfortable truth that such 'empty hand' techniques are second only to the use of dogs in the likelihood and severity of injury to all parties (Alpert et al. 2011; Amandus et al. 2011). It may also be that the use of incapacitant sprays or electro-stun devices may be more acceptable (although obviously unwelcome) than 'grappling' when members of the public are confronted with the realities of how force is used.

Further, there was a high expectation that officers should only use force in circumstances where the guilt of the individual could be assured, or at least where there were very good reasons to believe that guilt was assured. Using force to prevent escape whilst an allegation was investigated (as in the superstore car park) was regarded by many as peremptory.

Many people also felt that police use of force should be restricted to circumstances where officers were *physically* attacked. This had two implications: on the one hand, it was often thought to be unacceptable for officers to use force to overcome passive resistance—such as the refusal to vacate the driver's seat in the car pursued along the motorway, or using force against the argumentative youth suspected of attempting to steal a car in the superstore car park—because in neither instance was it thought that they posed a threat to officers or other innocent parties. The second implication seems to be that officers should only use force *in response to* significant violence being directed at them. To employ force in order to *prevent* attack (such as driving away at high speed) was perceived as peremptory; resting on assumptions rather than evidence. It was also sometimes felt that force would only be legitimate if used in cases of extreme jeopardy. In one group it was asserted, in the context of the arrest outside a nightclub, that 'If it was someone with a gun or something else, then yeah, I'd agree with any violence to bring them down, but that type of thing, no!'

Finally, only a few of those in our focus groups had or professed to having any direct experience of using force and had little or no appreciation of the physical realities that using force entailed. In the incidents concerning suspected theft of a car and the aggressive man outside a nightclub objections were voiced regarding the number of officers employed in forcing the suspect to the ground. This seemed to offend some latent ethic of 'equality of arms' or a 'fair fight'. Whereas those few who were retired police officers or door staff in pubs and clubs[8] could appreciate the necessity of wrestling a resistant suspect to the ground face down to prevent injury to arresting officers and their helpers, and also to the resistant person themselves, as well as the physical difficulty of doing so. This appears to represent a direct clash of reality and expectation.

---

[8] Participants were not asked for personal details; what they did or had done as a job sometimes emerged from conversation.

6

Police Culture

Introduction

In this chapter we redirect our gaze away from members of the public and instead towards various ranks of police officer. The police are sometimes, perhaps often, accused of being 'out of touch' with the public. Certainly, the police role is conducive to isolation (Niederhoffer 1967; Clark 1965): shift work does not facilitate a 'normal' social life and hence social activities tend to be conducted with other officers working similar hours. The law enforcement role of police officers may deter members of the public from developing friendships with them for fear that they might be revealed as inadvertent lawbreakers. Equally, police officers may be deterred from reciprocating the friendship of people beyond the police, for fear that their own minor peccadilloes may become known to people who might wish to harm them or take advantage of their frailties to further criminal enterprises. On the other hand, there is active encouragement to develop friendship networks *within* the police service. Policing is often portrayed as the kind of embattled occupation that fosters camaraderie and police officers may engage in sport and other pastimes through clubs and societies that represent the police. The malign expression of this solidarity is the way in which police officers allegedly 'close ranks' when they or any of their fellows are criticised (Ayling 1999; Bebbington 2006; Brodeur 1981; Hillsborough Independent Panel 2012; Westley 1956; Stoddard 1968; Skolnick and Fyfe 1993; Sedley 1985; Klockars et al. 2004; Holdaway 1995; Cockcroft 2013; Chan 1999; Holdaway 1983).

A rather different picture emerges from researchers who focus their gaze *within* the police and often draw attention to structural rifts between officers. It has long been acknowledged that there is mistrust between 'street cops' and 'management cops' (Reuss-Ianni 1983; Reuss-Ianni and Ianni 1983; Smith and Gray 1983) and police culture is fractured by loyalties to one's station and unit, as well as specialist responsibilities (see Waddington 1999; 2008; 2012).

Police Focus Groups

By comparing focus groups of police officers with those discussed in previous chapters (which, it should be repeated, did sometimes contain individual retired police officers), we were able to assess the extent to which the police differ from the public in appraising fellow officers.

During the research an opportunity arose to undertake focus groups within the West Midlands Police, using the same videos as the rest of the study. Focus groups were held with: a senior management team comprising ranks from Superintendent to Inspector, consisting of eleven people one of whom was a woman and all were white; two groups of experienced general duties (mainly patrol) officers (ten in one group and eight in the other, a total of six of whom were women and two were non-white); and, finally, a group of eleven recruits who had recently completed their police training (three of whom were women and one man was non-white). All these groups policed the same areas as those from which our general focus groups had been selected.[1] These police focus groups were asked to evaluate the officers depicted in the video clips in exactly the same way that non-police focus groups had been. In addition, they were *also asked* to imagine how *the public* would appraise police behaviour in each video clip.

So many interesting overlaps and gulfs appeared during this process that not all of them can be discussed here. So, we have selected four major issues—consensus and dissension, suspicion, management of situations and use of force—each of which will be discussed mainly in relation to one of the four video clips.

Consensus and Dissension

As we have been at pains to emphasise, the characteristic feature of our data is the diversity and intensity of opinion found amongst and between focus groups. One might imagine that such diversity of opinion would be less common amongst our police focus groups. Certainly, the long-running debate about the existence and characteristics of 'police culture' would strengthen the view that officers tend overwhelmingly to share common attitudes (Westley 1953; Bayley and Mendelsohn 1969; Cain 1973; Chan 1996; Cockcroft 2013; Fielding 1994; Holdaway 1983; Manning and Van Maanen 1978; McLaughlin 2006; Muir 1977; Smith and Gray 1983; Waddington 2012). Certainly, there were occasions when police focus groups exuded a stereotypical police response, but these were fleeting, often humorous and were more than eclipsed by the frequency and ferocity of disagreement within and between our police focus groups. The groups disagreed amongst themselves, very often in exactly the same terms as did the general public. So, allow us to begin on a note of agreement between

---

[1] The police focus groups were conducted under conditions of strict anonymity. Given the more restricted sample from which they were drawn this could not be assured if copies of the original recordings were made widely available. Hence, recordings of these focus groups are not available from the Economic and Social Data Archive. Transcripts are available from prof.p.a.j.waddington@gmail.uk.

police officers and members of the public regarding their criticisms of how the stopping of the suspected stolen car on the motorway was conducted.

Motorway Stop

It will be recalled that amongst the general public this video clip produced the least favourable appraisals from our focus groups. Our police focus groups very largely agreed with these critics; they deplored the descent into bickering exchanges in much the same terms as did the general public. There was an *additional* cause for criticism made by officers, namely the threat by one of the officers to arrest the young driver under 'section 5' of the Public Order Act. Some officers drew attention to the fact that it was highly improbable that such an offence *could* be committed within the confines of a police car and others considered it risible. A solitary senior officer expressed irritation with the courts,[2] for effectively removing from officers the protection of 'section 5' when they are sworn at and abused by members of the public. Others amongst the senior officers pointed out that it was the frequent abuse of this protection that had led the courts to effectively neuter this provision. The general mood is best captured by one experienced officer:

> Towards the end the officer goes, 'You've got an attitude problem', and he says, 'I ain't paying this'. It was a case of … like pantomime … like Christmas. I'd have just let him go off, and then say 'Here's your ticket, goodbye'. Of course, the eighteen year old … he's naïve, he's got an attitude problem, but you haven't got to go on the same level as him. You've got to, like, be professional. You've got to, like, 'I'm being professional. I'm doing my job. If you want to [have a] go, you're talking to yourself'. All I'm going to say is, 'Here's your ticket. Have a nice day. Pay it within whatever time it is.' It was just a case of, 'Let's just go straight to the kill. Get on his level and have a conversation with him' and I just thought, I wouldn't even have a conversation with him.

Just like members of the public, our focus groups with police officers found this video clip posed profound and problematic issues, over which there was considerable debate and disagreement that were discussed in much the same terms as our general focus groups. The debate was so intense amongst recruits that to reproduce it in full would consume too much space. Instead, allow us to present a brief extract in the recruits' own words:[3]

> I thought it was disgraceful how he approached him initially, I thought …
> Appalling.
> I thought he was very aggressive.
> I just think it was well out of order.
> I thought it was all terribly unlawful: he went to the passenger's side and used force when he shouldn't have, dragged him out. He wasn't cautioned […]
> He dragged him out of a car and then was having a dispute with him on the hard shoulder with all the oncoming traffic.

---

[2] Presumably referring obliquely to the case of *Harvey v Director of Public Prosecutions* [2011] EWCA Crim B1.

[3] Because of the intensity of the debate, no attempt has been made to label which participants said what.

There's no politeness. No, 'Would you mind stepping out the vehicle please, Sir?' He was 'Get out the vehicle!' [which was shouted] straightaway. [...]
When I was eighteen, if a police officer had done that to me, I'd have gone off ... [...]
It was a stolen vehicle; you've got to get him out the car in case he goes off. You've got to get the keys out or whatever. Get him out. Although if he'd pushed him back, he'd have been a couple of [...]
No, but that lad *did* have an awful attitude.
I don't think he did ...!
He's dragged out the car ...
Dragged out the car, for nothing!!!
Dragged out the car, arrested, de-arrested and y'know?
A fine on top!
You're fined for having a VDRS and you've been told to do something.
And in the meantime, you couldn't drive. Yeah! [...]
Because he got him out the car, it came to a health and safety issue, didn't it? He had to get him off ... into the back of the car ...
It was more a health and safety issue getting him out of that car! Wrestling with him virtually next to the motorway! [...]

The discussion continued in much the same vein for at least twice as long as this extract.

We noted earlier that members of the public in our focus groups felt that officers had a responsibility to *de-escalate* potentially volatile situations. The Senior Management Team agreed.

P1: ... if we'd approached him nicely, spoke to him nice, then the confrontation would probably not then have happened. If we'd explained why we pulled him over and why he was stopped, that kid might not have been so 'anti' [...] 99 per cent of our job is speaking to people: speak to them nicely, you get the results we want: that goes for dealing with prisoners to people we see on the front counter.

P2: The bottom line is, we've got to be professional. And *that* wasn't professional!

P3: We could have controlled that situation far better really [...]. Once you're getting into a tit-for-tat discussion with anybody of any age, then you've lost it!

P4: That was a 'parent–child': 'Right you're not having any supper!' 'And your pocket money's gone!' It really was, wasn't it?
[...]

P1: If you think of the complainants that come to the front office. Really, all they want is (1) an explanation and (2) apology for the way they've been treated, and then they go. And they don't expect to [...]. And I must see three or four of them every time I'm on duty. [...]

P5: This is the second scenario now—and I accept that it is probably biased in that way—where what we're faced with is that we react to how we allow that to influence our decision-making process. It's not what it ends up as! And I appreciate that probably that happens quite often. And we go in ... and hear what everybody says about taking control. Our greatest weapon is the use of speech and communication. You don't need to grab somebody to take control. And I think it is dangerous to grab them at the side of a motorway and get into, potentially, that tussle situation, than it is to go through the niceties of 'Can you turn the ignition off?', 'Can you ...?' There's lots of things there that fall outside training: why has he gone to the driver's side? Why not the passenger side? If the car drives off, the car drives off. So be it!

P4: Nobody dies that way, do they?!

P5: It stopped. If he doesn't get out of it and the car does drive off, then we carry on following it on the motorway until it […] at some point or it runs out of fuel or whatever else. But, what we're given as the scenario has influenced his decision-making and how he has approached that situation. And he hasn't, at any point, thought about … [Name] has just said it: 'How often do we deal with complaints because of the attitude of officers, instead of because of our lack of service and how we delivered to people.

P6: It's the same thing, why are we not delivering service to people? Because we're not speaking to them nicely. It's the same issue.

P4: There's something else. There are occasions—hard stops with firearms […]—where it seems entirely proper, in fact it's *necessary* to start right up at the high level of aggression. Conflict management model: we're going there, armed officers, weapons drawn, 'Get out of the car! Get on the ground', sort of thing, y'know. Most of us have seen that in action, certainly I have. *But* in situations like the three we've seen so far—this one's just like it—if you come in too high, you really haven't got too far to go … nowhere to go then, apart from losing face. And most officers, being human, don't like to lose face. [Name] is absolutely right: if you go in gently; perhaps in hindsight you will find that you went in too gently, you might even lose one. In my opinion that's a risk worth taking actually, because in the other 99 per cent of the time people will leave *or come into custody* thinking 'Actually, the officer dealt with me OK'. And I think that in each case, we've seen an officer goes in either too aggressively, or with the wrong attitude—y'know, they've prejudged it. And this was not one of these scenarios when you needn't to go in heavy. Y'know, the car's stopped, y'know. It could have been much more polite and it wouldn't have gone up. And certainly, grabbing somebody out of the car like that, you have no idea how they're going to react in the heat of the battle. The driver might not have thought, 'Actually, there's a lorry coming the other way. We're just a few feet from eternity'.

P7: All I was going to say about the arrest was that there was no problem with that, as far as I was concerned, in the initial period. Instead of entering into the argument then, questions could have been asked to either get more evidence of the offence or erase it, rather than what happened, 'I'm going to argue with my prisoner about it'. That time could have been far better used finding out what had happened and if you've got three innocent people you just let them go. That's all.

P1: […] detaining and then the grounds found afterwards.

P8: Well, you have to think on your feet. We've all dealt with things where you do […] prisoners and you are on your own and you need their cooperation really. 'So, it's about this vehicle that may be stolen and I must ask you to stay here so I can ascertain the circumstances.' If they start to play up, then yes I'm on the radio. Y'know, at the end of the day, you're not going to physically detain three people, you're just going to do your best to seek their cooperation, more than anything.

P4: That could have been catastrophic. (Senior Management Team)

Other experienced officers were critical of the lack of competence displayed by the officers in the video clip:

P1: I think they were right to arrest them, but I think that from the word go they were unprofessional. […] they shot past the car, which means that if they didn't know who was in it, that vehicle could have done anything. Then they should have cuffed him whilst he was still inside the vehicle, because he's got a duty of care to him. If he runs out into the middle of the traffic, who's going to cop it then? He let him get on his feet before he cuffed him—well even then he didn't cuff him—and got him back to the police vehicle. And then proceeded to argue with him! Y'see, I think he was completely unprofessional.

P2: He didn't take control of the situation to start with. I mean, realistically, you've got the car on the hard shoulder. If you're in a position to grab hold of the lad, I'm sure you're in a position to take hold of the keys in the ignition. Take the keys out of the car and cuff while he's in the vehicle, because it keeps control of the situation. He immediately grabbed him and told him, 'Get out of the car'. (Experienced officers)

Whilst our police focus groups were at least as critical of the officers' behaviour in this video clip as were members of the public in our general focus groups, nevertheless, they empathised with the officer in finding himself in a difficult situation:

... they seem to be victims of the worst set of circumstances ever: (a) a car with a report for bilking on it; (b) he's on false plates and he hasn't took the plates off the first time he was stopped. As a result of all that, their behaviour has been modified. They're thinking, as I would be thinking, as we all would be thinking, 'This car's been nicked from a "car key break"[4] and they're going to drive off and I'm going to get run over here'. That's what's in his mind as he's approaching that car.
[Background murmurs of agreement can be heard.]
And he deals with it really well, but *then*, once we are in the [...] seats and this guy is sitting in the back of the police car ...
[Other experienced officers criticised the failure of teamwork.]
I think they disadvantage themselves. One bobby did in the first place. When he got the keys out, why isn't the other out of that car? If that car is now not mobile and can't drive off, why leave your oppo having a set to—rightly or wrongly—in the doorway by the side of the motorway, with hands flailing everywhere. It could have been controlled a lot better. And then you get, because of that, why does he get thrown into the back of the car without cuffs on? When his oppo in the Civic, is sat there la–de–da, just never been fetched out, just sat there fine? (Experienced officer)

In sum, there is little evidence in our data of 'closing ranks'—something of which the police are often accused. Solidarity *is* evident, but is more subtly expressed in the frequency with which the focus groups use the collective pronoun 'we' and were empathetic. Yet, they also expressed some of the fiercest criticisms of this video clip that we heard. Indeed, it appeared that many of them were affronted that the officers depicted in the video clip had brought the police into public disrepute. They identify with the officers in the video clip as members of the same 'police family',[5] but feel that they have 'let the side down' by their lack of 'professionalism' (a concept to which we will return).

---

[4] This is police argot for burglaries where car keys are stolen and used to steal valuable vehicles, like that driven by the young driver in the video clip.

[5] Which is conspicuous at many police 'line of duty' funerals, where most, if not all, British police forces are represented by officers in uniform.

Suspicion

Not only did the officers share the many opinions expressed amongst our non-police focus groups about the motorway stop, they also shared many of the general public's suspicions about Chantelle's role in the robbery of the elderly man. 'Suspicion' is often regarded as a hallmark characteristic of police officers. The informal 'A, B, C' of policing is to 'Accept nothing. Believe no one. Check everything'. So, how did our police focus groups respond to the robbery of the elderly man?

Robbery of the Elderly Man in His Home

The police focus groups exhibited a remarkable pattern: recruits, senior management, and *one group* of experienced officers all reflected much the same view as the general public. They harboured strong suspicions about Chantelle's role and worried that the elderly man had not received sufficient medical care and social support. However, the *other* group of experienced officers took a very different (and, amongst themselves consensual) approach. Their discussion was peppered with remarks that distinguished the elderly man and young woman from 'genuine victims' and implied deep scepticism about what the officers in the video clip were being told:

> P1: We're saying, from a police perspective we saw straight through it, aren't we?
>
> P2: No, 'may be ...'
>
> P1: ... But from the general public watching the TV ...
>
> P2: ... At one point he said—didn't he? That there were no marks on her anyway. So he's twigged that and he's going down that road anyway. But if they're taking the story at face value and it's a genuine robbery then they've done OK anyway, haven't they?
>
> P1: Yeah.
>
> P3: The only thing I would have said is that I'd have separated them and get their stories.
> [This was followed by an indistinct ribald comment that provoked laughter from other members of the group.]
>
> P4: You can tell they don't because at the end he's very laissez-faire about it, whereas if you've got a genuine victim of a knifepoint robbery you'd do your customer care a bit better, whereas he says, 'I'm sure you've been through worse'. Y'know, he doesn't really believe that for a minute.
> [...]
>
> P3: From the public's point of view, they might not have the experience we've got in terms of straightaway we're suspicious of the whole situation. For them they might just see an elderly man who's been the victim of a robbery. (Experienced officers)

Interestingly, one of this group's members recalled having viewed the episode when it was originally broadcast and remembered the outcome (the conviction of Chantelle's boyfriend). He kept this to himself throughout the focus group discussion until its conclusion, when he was invited by the researcher to disclose it. He informed the others that, 'As far as I can remember it was genuine robbery; it was her boyfriend that did it.' There was a moment of stunned silence, broken in astonishment by the remark: 'Shock and horror!' The first officer continued, 'So, you see, he's a *genuine* victim'. This was followed by a jumble of indistinct but incredulous remarks, before someone reminds the group: 'She was altering the description wasn't she? He was saying "eighteen" and she was saying, "No, early twenties"'. Further astonishment followed until another voice asked, incredulously, 'It was a family relative?' The officer who recalled seeing the episode replied: 'I just know it was a genuine robbery by her boyfriend. He was a genuine robbery victim. And a prisoner of war. We should have treated him better'. The discussion concluded with a cry of 'Yeah!' from many of those present.[6]

There was little in the discussions to suggest that our focus group officers formed suspicions on any basis other than those heard voiced in the general focus groups. When presented with exactly the same information in the form of video clips—judging from what they said—the officers were neither blessed with privileged professional insight to recognise suspicious behaviour, nor were they encumbered by peculiar cynicism that led them to suspect what other members of the public did not.

Management of Situations

Attempted Theft of a Car in a Car Park

The second video clip that opened a rift between different police focus groups was the suspected theft of a car in a superstore car park. Interestingly, here the roles above were reversed: the experienced officers who had been so distinct in their views because they were suspicious of the elderly man and his young companion, now found themselves in the 'mainstream'. It was the other group of experienced officers who now became distinctively defensive about the officer's handling of the situation:

> P1: A difficult situation to control, I think. Looking at the information you've got: you've got two suspects. Is he going to start making loads of inquiries? Considering he's on his own; considering the information he'd got, I think he did reasonable.
>
> P2: I think it was great. [...] He got there and you'd got a broken-in car and two blokes who'd run off, y'know, and a description of both of them. But they didn't! They both remained at the scene ... Which might or might not have an effect on how you view that. Y'know, they're under no obligation to stay and daresay that the security people wouldn't have made any attempt to detain them if they had have done. [...]
>
> P3: The same really. I think it's very easy, isn't it, to criticise? And I'm sure we'll see other things, when you're in a situation like that and there's just you to deal with it ... I think he did really well, to be honest. Y'know ... because you don't know at the end of the day, y'know, ... what they've got on them; what they're going

---

[6] It is difficult to portray this in text, because some members of the group were so aghast that they sat with their mouths agape throughout.

to do; you've got no idea, have you? And I think it was definitely the right thing to detain them. They were safe; everyone else was safe … (Experienced officers)

The other group of experienced officers included participants who were far more critical of how the officer in the video clip handled the situation and debated the issue quite vigorously.

P1: I thought the officers aggravated the situation.
  […]
P2: I thought we became drawn into an argument with the suspects. I thought that was needless. We were making assumptions before we knew that an offence had been committed. I reckon what you've got to do is talk to them.
P3: He did it by the book!
Res: Sorry?
P3: He did it by the book: reasonable suspicion, he's acted correctly. He's arrested him. He's got suspicion. It's by the book.
P1: I disagree. They created a problem that didn't exist to start with. They've ended up arresting him when they shouldn't have. They were scruffy: 'What's the crack?' There was no ID. It was a shambles really.
P4: The situation was very difficult. You'd got security and a police officer, and they come up with a reason for why they're breaking into the car. A few more inquiries could have avoided that situation.
P5: I didn't see the harm in arresting them on suspicion. You've got your suspicion there and obviously detaining them was to make those inquiries […] that person there. I didn't see anything wrong with that personally. (Experienced officers)

Senior officers were even more critical, making many of the criticisms made by members of the general public:

P1: My first view, in terms of looking at that is that this officer has gone […] in terms of the stereotype of the people. If they had turned up and there had been an elderly couple trying to get into a car, there would have been more questions asked as to who's the car is and what has happened. […] Later on, they're asking questions of the woman who has locked her keys in the car […]
P2: Yeah. I think the PC came across to me as quite arrogant. There was an assumption here and he made very little effort to calm the situation or ask any questions. And of course, there was something of a […] later … Call me a legal pedant, but threatening to lock him up for a Public Order Act and then actually arresting him for theft of a motor vehicle might put him in a difficult situation when they turn up at the cell block. I think that would be quite interesting […] but that obviously, is not something the public see; that's the cop's head on, but it wouldn't have done a lot for me in my confidence in that officer if I was […] his commanding officer, to be honest. (Senior Management Team)

Apart from the stark disagreement, there was also considerable debate in all the police focus groups about the officer's general management of the situation, which reflected many of the same issues raised by members of the public in the general focus groups.

Several experienced officers objected to the way the officer in the video clip immediately threatened to arrest the obstreperous individual.

He said things like, 'I'll lock you up, because I'm the police', 'If you don't do this, I'll lock you up for public order', instead of trying to explain that 'This is the situation. Until we get it verified who the owner of the car is, you'll be detained'. And not get drawn into 'Well, I'm a police officer and I'm going to take your liberty away because I can'. Y'know. It wasn't very professional. (Experienced officer)

Another added, insistently, that this amounted to 'a prisoner we don't need'.

P1: I think there was a slight issue with him warning him about his manner and then locked him up for theft. And like it's been due to his manner and then the theft's negated and he's still left with an irate male. Whereas, if he'd explained all of that, as I said, in the first instance, he wouldn't be left with that situation: someone innocent of the theft, but he still wants to lock him up because he's wound up! Which probably doesn't look very good! (laugh)

P2: And then he can't afford to lose face and he'll take that prisoner to the block then, rather than maybe doing what's right and saying, 'Right, in view of what I know now, your behaviour was unreasonable, however in the situation I'm going to de-arrest you'. Y'know, it wouldn't have lost any face but it would probably have been the better thing to do.

P3: Yeah!

P4: What caused the reaction, that's the thing? What caused the reaction to police? [...] Was it the way he spoke to him?
[Others in the same group disagreed.]

P5: I think he had good rapport. Looking at those three offenders. You've got two there who are subdued. It's just one that he's got to weigh up: is he just making up excuses, because obviously he's backing away from the situation—a potential suspect trying to make an excuse to get out of it.

P6: He could be on his toes in two seconds flat.

P5: He's got to react to it. He's made a positive arrest. In the end, in the long [...] he's had to lock him up for section 5 for his conduct. I just think he could have been just a little bit more controlled in terms of response by the police. (Experienced officers)

There was also disagreement amongst the other group of experienced officers, one of whom said:

You go in at that level, they'll meet you there. Whereas, if you go in open-handed, open body language; 'This is what I need to do' and you try and get them to work with you, they're more likely to [...] Whereas, if you go in, 'I'm the police. I'm going to lock you up, blah, blah, blah', straightaway its [...]. Then it's 'My army's bigger than your army', 'We're bigger than you are' ... Oooohhh! It's all ego. It's all testosterone. (Experienced officer)

The Senior Management Team were equally divided about the officer's management of the situation.

P1: I think it's his unprofessional approach in the first place that made it uncontrollable. Because [...] the way he spoke to them, lack of clarity. He'd got security staff who were there before him without any volatile ... Yet, the police officer arrives with the anger [...] almost like, 'I'm going to try and be your mate, but I'm not really your mate ...' Really unprofessional.

P2: Wasn't there, 'Chill out!' or something ...? Patronising, yeah?

P1: Yeah, 'chill out'!

P3: Yeah, well, in terms of the original response, we've got the fact that three people are potentially breaking into a car. So there's an immediacy to that. Whereas, as has been said, security have actually held them or got them quite amicably at that point, which should change the officer's attitude, because if we've actually got people who are doing something or up to something they'd be more inclined to get away. I think a couple of things for me are always those ones that raise the situation: pointing, touching—'What are you pointing at?' 'Why are you touching me?' That creates something from nothing. And the question at that point is that threatens several times that he's going to arrest them, whereas he's already put his hands on them. So, if you've got your hands ... OK, what is he in relation to that? And that's what created everything thereafter.
[...]

P2: Yes, he could have actually made an ally rather than anything. (Senior Management Team)

Another senior officer was conflicted in trying to decide how to evaluate this video clip:

P1: I think, at the end of the day, you've got an officer whose trying to deal with an incident, etc. We *are* selected from society, so the people you have and are dealing with ... Yes, I appreciate what you're saying, we are professional [loud cough] but we all come from different walks of life and have different ways of dealing with situations. Rather than trying to [...] persons into a certain set mould—an expectation that they should behave in a set manner, but might have been comfortable to that officer, talking to that group [...]. I agree with [Name] about the laying on of hands: he made a decision to arrest, he should have done that. He should have arrested him. That would have resolved that. He was on his own—I appreciate that they're not doing a lot, there's a lot of standing around, but they're not actually assisting or helping with him, they're just hanging around. He's looking at the one lad: yes, he may have taken offence at the pointing [...]. Yes, he may have taken exception there. But once that has taken place, that officer has now taken over that situation, regarding everything that the inquiry is expecting him to do, he's now dealing with a confrontation. Whether it's created or not, he's now dealing with that confrontation and that's the issue that's distracting him away from the actual investigation. There's no support that's coming in from anybody else that's trained up to give him the support he needs, to calm the situation while he's dealing with it. As soon as he's made that decision to arrest him, he's taken out of the game. The annoying thing is, that having done all that, in real time, etc., once it's been identified as ... It's a [...] car and it isn't going to go any further, it's a genuine situation that's taken place. To me he hasn't gone back into calm that situation down. 'What about my [...]'. Simplistically, it wouldn't have changed the situation because realistically there was already conflict between that person that was arrested and that officer, which you always get when in any case when you deprive someone of their liberty. He should have spent more time just calming that down—'What about the ripped trousers? What about this, blah, blah'. If he'd apologised—not saying he would actually have been [...] — but if he'd actually apologised—and this is a culture we have, not being able to apologise, or not being given, perhaps, that perception a lot of the time and not being given the discretion—he may have been able to turn that back around. 'Yes, sorry, that's why I did this, blah, blah,

blah. Yes, I was out of order, I appreciate you're jeans have been ripped. This is what you need to do to resolve this issue' or 'Let me help you to resolve this while I'm here'. A bit of give and take. That could have done a lot to turn that around [...] once he'd calmed down the situation where he could have done that.

P2: The one thing for me, though, around this and around everything we've said, but still for me as a member of the public and a person, the reactions of that individual was still unacceptable. Whatever the officer's done, I think there's a grave danger of us getting into the realms of saying that the officer has created everything. That person didn't need to react in that way and they've created part of that situation and they've got to take some personal responsibility for that. Albeit that the officer was rude and didn't need to be; was arrogant as they were; that person still went way above what the response should have been. (Senior Management Team)

The debate was even more vigorous amongst recruits who rehearsed many of the same arguments made by their more senior and experienced colleagues, as well as, of course, the general public in our focus groups: failure to introduce himself as a police officer; the jovial 'What's the crack?'; pointing at and touching the agitated youth; his threat to arrest this same young man. Others pointed to the difficult circumstances with which the officer was faced: his being in plain clothes; the absence of other police officers; the ineffectual contribution made by the security personnel; and the unacceptable conduct of the young man who was arrested.

Force

Many officers were critical, not only of the way in which the officer misman-aged the situation in the superstore car park, but also felt that the officer's use of force was questionable. This was not necessarily because it was too aggressive or violent, but because it was not justified as necessary and may not have been legal. These issues were magnified hugely in the final video clip to which all focus groups were exposed: the arrest of an 'aggressive man' outside a nightclub.

Violent Arrest Outside Nightclub

The attitude of many officers was that whilst this was not a problematic arrest, given the resistance that the man was displaying, nonetheless they could empa-thise with members of the public who felt that it was distasteful: 'it doesn't look good, does it?' 'It does look terrible'; 'it was awful really'. Such remarks were never contested and seemed to be taken for granted by almost all the officers in our focus groups. Whilst some felt it was inevitable, everyone seemed to feel that it was a regrettable reality of routine police work that offends public perceptions.

I think that highlights the reality of the difference between rolling around the floor with somebody and basically what they get taught, because fighting with somebody ain't nothing like [...]. Perception-wise, I think it's terrible. (Experienced officer)
I think based on that short clip, the public perception of what we do, is that we're a bunch of yobs, to be honest. (Experienced officer)
It always looks bad. To members of the public, it would have looked like real hard [or 'harsh'] force (Recruit)

Officers were well aware of how the tactics used in the video clip could be misinterpreted by the public as: *'dragging* him into the middle of the road', *'rub his head in the tarmac*! Get his *face on the gravel* though, that'll sort it out (laugh)', *'his head over the kerb* as well (followed by a laugh and a cry of exasperation); *'kicked* him from the back!'.

Whilst they could empathise with the public's view, they felt that the public's limited understanding of such matters led them to false perceptions:

> To a member of the public, they … see an innocent member of the public being *dragged* across the floor by one arm, while three other officers are kneeling on him. Well, that isn't what's happening. I think we should educate the public to understand, we're not there to hurt someone. The old phrase, 'It took four of you to arrest me!' Well, in actual fact, it didn't. 'It took four of us to stop hurting you.' That's the truth of the matter. (Experienced officer)

How did our officers judge the proportionality of the arrest? To some, the prospect of resolving the situation without force had passed by the time officers arrived on the scene:

> P1: We passed the stage where we could negotiate with the chappy. He seemed at the point there when even members of the public in the background could see that he was being aggressive […] took positive action and got him into the van.
> P2: We didn't see all of it. […]
> P3: He was already scrapping, wasn't he? (Senior Management Team)

Moreover, the aggressive person may be well versed in how effectively to resist the police: 'These people have had […] holds put on them before, so they know how to … position himself and make it harder.' (Senior Management Team)

Some regretted that there was little opportunity to use less forceful methods of subduing the man:

> I think that from the split-second bit we could see, before there was any hands-on. I think, it was quite clear that there was no clear 'Calm down, sir, please', because he's already giving it loads, isn't he? Communication, with the whole techniques of getting somebody under control and restrained, there wasn't much because there's five or six people … (Experienced officer)

Also, officers in our focus groups recognised how the general chaos of events would handicap officers responding to a call for assistance:

> It was all a bit confused. It was almost the case that this bloke had launched himself at one of the bobbies and took everybody by surprise. Obviously, there's been a bit of a free–for–all to start with. And I think that with a camera crew around, I was quite surprised that there wasn't the […] communication that you'd get—'Stop fighting', 'Stop fighting', trying to get the handcuffs on, 'Calm down'. None of that seems to have been happening. Which, if you'd had that soundtrack to the same images, it would have been a different story, I think. (Experienced officer)

They were going to what they thought was one incident and clearly the officers at the front, when they got there … Whether this person has anything to do with the CS canister being released or not, this person is showing some sort of aggression towards the officers. Whether it's related to the incident or not is irrelevant, they had to deal with that fact that was in front of them. It looked untidy, it looked messy, but things like that always do. Ultimately, they achieved what they wanted to do: to restrain the person … well, to arrest him. Then when he was under arrest, to restrain him because he was problematic in being in custody, if you like, y'know. It wasn't a case of putting your hand on his shoulder and saying, 'Come with me, the Queen wants you' [laughter]. He's not going to go with you was he? Y'know, they set out to handcuff him […]. OK they handcuffed him and put him in the van. OK, he was still alive and breathing, nobody got hurt. (Experienced officer)

Others felt that officers tended to act too freely in the 'heat of the moment':

P1: There's someone cuffed to the rear there. They don't need five bobbies for some-one whose handcuffed to the rear, regardless of what he's doing. Unless he's 'man mountain'! And that looked terrible. You've got a man still restrained. You don't need all those people, yet we're all there, getting him in the van …

P2: It's that thing: we always rush to handcuff somebody […] instead of taking it slowly and handcuff them. I know it's hard to do … (Experienced officers)

Others were more censorious and felt that the use of force, indeed the arrest itself, may have been unnecessary, even gratuitous:

P1: He's been arrested for something. A prisoner has been arrested because he's pissed or something. He's […] his gob […]. He hasn't assaulted anybody? He hasn't stolen anything. He hasn't committed any …
    […]

P2: It's that old Friday/Saturday night thing […]. They thought, 'I don't like him' and jumped on him! (Experienced officers)

It's nonsense, isn't it? Because there's ten of us here and someone's been sprayed with CS […] We aren't bothered about that. We're bother about the chap whose pissed us off, because we don't like him. So, there's someone whose been assaulted and there might be someone whose going to be assaulted because somebody's going around with a weapon. We ain't bothered about that because […] we can all jump on him. Someone says, 'Where's the guy with the CS?' 'I don't know about that […]? (Experienced officers)

This view was endorsed by the other group of experienced officers, who felt even if the man who was arrested *was* the person who released CS gas:

P1: Even then, we shouldn't be jumping all over him.
P2: You do get people who just want to knock your head off.
P3: And you do get bobbies who go in with that attitude, 'This is how it's going to be' and that's exactly what they get. They get aggression and their colleagues get hurt when we roll around the floor with them. There was one bobby there who put his hand on that person, but we don't know what was said beforehand.
P4: And it starts a chain reaction, doesn't it?
P1: With all our training and equipment and stuff like that we shouldn't have to […] We shouldn't be doing that. We should be all professional: we should get out of

the van and stand in a line; then someone tells you what's happened. We should be more professional.

[...]

P4: When you watch G20 and stuff like that on the TV from the sky, because they're filming it from a camera. You see the line, because they're in a line with everyone holding a shield, there's always a couple of bobbies that get a bit pissed off [...] And we laugh, because we all know people who've got shorter fuses than others. They're the people who sometimes put their hands on before assessing the situation. (Experienced officers)

The specific issue around which much of the discussion centred was whether the number of officers involved was excessive. The majority view was that it *did* require several officers to subdue a single individual, but the public fail to understand this:

P1: [...] It takes that number of people to control some people. You don't know how strong he is, what background he's got. Nothing about him.

P2: He was quite a big lad.

P3: That one lad who literally went up to him. He threw him with one arm! Pushed him away.

P4: The first officer that did ... was the first to have hold of him. He was struggling to contain him. He shrugged a second officer off like that ... That's when it got ...

P5: But the public don't understand: they think that to take one person to the floor you need one or two bobbies, they don't realise it takes five or six. We never publicise that. We never show that that's what it's really like.

It's always going to be four–onto–one. Obviously there's good reasons why that's done—more for the person who is under arrest than for anyone else. (Experienced officers)

However, there were dissenters:

P1: I actually take the view, coming back to that debate, for me—seeing it as a police officer and a member of the public—did it really take that many officers to take him down? People will say, 'Does it take five of them to get him down?'

P2: But it does! It does!! (Senior Management Team)

Others believed that the stress of combat may cloud the judgement of officers and give an unfortunate impression to the public with little or no experience of such matters:

We always take them to the deck, flatten them. Why? (Experienced officer)

It does look terrible ... And there's no need for it. Every Friday and Saturday night you all have your 'red mist', you all want to join in. You don't want your mate to get injured. You want to get the bloke under control, but nine times out of ten two or three bobbies could control a person better than five or six bobbies can, but it's [...] And it will happen again Friday night in town. (Experienced officer)

The only thing I'd say is that members of the public and everyone ... until you're in a stressful situation ... We're back to the conflict management model: you learn about stress and how you do things that you normally wouldn't do, because you lose control of different things that you would normally do. And I think it's really hard ... it's really easy to criticise in a situation like that when you're under stress and perhaps your body isn't doing what it would normally do under normal circumstances. But until people put themselves in those situations when they feel that stress they'll never understand … what it does. (Experienced officer)

This is it though isn't it? When you've got your 'red mist' and your heart rate rises you're gross motor skills kick in. All the fine tuning stuff—y'know your pressure points, holds and kicks—you just go for the hands on stuff you're trying to gain control. (Experienced officer)

Given, then, that struggling with people who are seeking to avoid or escape from arrest is seen to be so conducive to the use of excessive force, what did our officers imagine could be done to mitigate or even eliminate such a spectacle with its adverse effect on public perceptions? Most reliance was placed on *communication* with the person under arrest, witnesses and bystanders, and the general public:

I've just put 'communication' that's all. It was all over so quick. I don't know whether he'd swung at a bobby or they'd just arrest him […], I don't know. But even when he's offering resistance on the floor. To communicate to him that he isn't going anywhere, to calm down, whatever. But also to communicate amongst the officers. I heard one of the officers saying, 'No, no, no! This way!' They were arguing about which way to put the cuffs on! Just talk to each other; take two seconds; he's on the floor, make sure he's still breathing (laughter); put the cuffs on; y'know. But *talk* to each other. It just shows a bit more air of control to the public: 'OK, the police have got someone on the floor, there's not much I can do about it, but they are doing their job', y'know? I think use of force is always contentious amongst members of the public because, y'know, they don't necessarily understand the use of force we can have and what we can decide to do, and just how severe, sometimes, that use of force can be. And it's up to the individual officers to justify the takedown and they're just going to have to write that up and it's their business. But communication, both between themselves and the chap—and the crowd … (Experienced officer)

A variant of this emphasis on communication was to advocate that one of the officers present should have taken command:

They got out of the van positively: there was a sense of urgency and hats were going on. In fact, I … there was obviously recognition of CS […] because you hear somebody shout, 'Don't rub your eyes'. So obviously somebody's trying to get a grip somewhere … (Senior Management Team)

That's what we don't do. We jump on somebody. Somebody needs to step back and take control of it and then it's fine then. They're on the floor, they're all handcuffed; no issues. But we all jump on someone and start fighting. And I do it as much as anyone else, don't get me wrong! But if you've got a sergeant with them, he needs to step back and start supervising … and it works! Trust me, I've tried it! (Experienced officer)

A minority view was to rely on technology: low lethality weapons like CS spray or electro-stun devices like the 'Taser':

That's where we really let ourselves down when it comes to violence. The public don't understand how many people it takes to restrain somebody who's playing up—safely, without injuring them. Because how many people do we realistically injure? Very very few in comparison. We're all reluctant to use CS—I don't know why. We're reluctant to see Taser coming in—[…] afraid of it. But we'll be quite happily roll on the floor punching each other. (Experienced officer)

You've said already 'Why don't we use the gas?' Push them away, get it out the way, spray them, let him have it for a few minutes, then get the cuffs on. Don't we all feel the need to go [accompanied by a growling sound] (Experienced officer)

If my mom saw that, I think she'd say, 'Well, he shouldn't have been playing up in the first place'.

[This was greeted with general agreement.]

You could have possibly gone for CS. There had already been CS used in the area … (Recruits)

I thought he should have 'CS-ed' him … because it's all about public perception isn't it? (Experienced officer)

It'll be good, when these programmes start getting shown with Taser being used. (Experienced officer)

Apart from their effectiveness in disabling an adversary, such weaponry promises to do so without inflicting permanent injury.

I think the irony of it is that initial control skills are lower with CS. To step back and fill the space with CS. I think more people would have more to say about that. And that's how, in theory, you're supposed to use force to begin with. But I think it's all very British, isn't it? We don't like rolling around with people and dragging people to the floor. The takedown was […] but the irony is that if one bobby had just gone (gestures pressing a spray button) we have not much to say about that compared to a takedown. (Senior Management Team)

Yet, experienced officers could see the drawbacks:

We're reluctant to use it, we're worried about public perception, but it's not advertised as being low level of force. That one in Nottingham, it was done by the book, 100 per cent by the book, without any question whatsoever. But it looked terrible on camera, because when Taser hits them, it doesn't look nice. But we didn't defend ourselves, we just said, 'Yeah, right …' (Experienced officer)

Conclusions

How can we summarise how focus groups of police officers of different ranks compared to the public and to each other? First, when presented with exactly the same information about an encounter there was considerable similarity between the views of the video clips expressed by the police focus groups and those drawn from the general public. Secondly, that similarity lay not in agreement on a common appraisal of each video clip, but in the extent and vigour of *disagreements* about how they should be appraised. There was little or no evidence that officers adopted a defensive 'police cultural' stance when responding to any of the focus groups. They did identify with the officers depicted in the video clips, as reflected in the frequent use of the pronoun 'we'. They also empathised with the officers, appreciating the difficulties of dealing with volatile situations and people. At the same time, they could emphasise with how the public might perceive the video clip and, to judge from our focus groups, they were pretty accurate. They could be critical, often fiercely so, especially of conduct they felt betrayed their sense of professionalism—being impartial, refusing to be provoked, maintaining emotional distance.

There was little evidence of the kind of gulf that other researchers have found between 'management cops' and 'street cops' (Reuss-Ianni 1983). On the whole, there was much agreement between groups, albeit in their divergent views. The greatest difference arose in connection with the robbery at the home of the elderly man, which most officers appraised in much the same terms as the public; but one group of experienced officers disagreed fundamentally, believing that the elderly man had connived with his young female companion to fabricate a fictional account of what happened. How police should conduct themselves during encounters with members of the public was controversial and police argued just as fiercely as the public did about what officers did, why they did it, and were they justified?

7

Legitimacy and Dissension

Introduction

The data that has occupied Chapters 3 to 6 supports our contention that there is remarkable dissension, complexity and volatility in public appraisals of how police officers use their powers, particularly the use of force. Members of the public were able to approve of specific moments or aspects of the brief video clips that they were shown, whilst disapproving with equal vigour of other moments and aspects of it. Indeed, the very same moments and aspects provoked both approval and disapproval from various contributors to our focus groups. There appeared to be consensus only about which moments or aspects of the video clips were controversial, two of which stood out: suspicion and force. Whether the police officers were correct in suspecting others in the video clip of wrongdoing often relied on stereotypes of age, gender and appearance. There was also a general distaste for anything resembling aggression and violence, its acceptability as an instrument of police work depended heavily on inferences about what the suspect had done, was doing and might do in an imagined future. Surprisingly, focus groups comprising only police officers revealed many of the same characteristics: they were obviously more phlegmatic about the use of force, but readily imagined how such force might not 'look good' to the wider public. What are the wider implications of our research? This is the focus of this chapter, which will consider both the methodological and theoretical implications of dissension for our understanding of the police and policing; how suspicion is constructed; and how police use of force can be made palatable. These are issues of relevance to academics who view the police as an interesting object of analysis, but also to the police themselves and to policymakers, campaigners and others with normative and practical interests in reforming policing. With all these viewpoints in mind, let us turn to the issues arising from this research.

Dissension?

Our research is not the first to discover that people's attitudes to the police are fluid. The academic research literature, taken as a whole, shows a bewildering array of research results obtained from different samples using a variety of scales. In their 2002 exhaustive review of the literature on public attitudes to the police, Brown and Benedict conclude: 'There is still no consensus about the effects of education, gender, socioeconomic status, victimization or fear of victimization on perceptions of the police.' (Brown and Benedict 2002: 567; see also Scaglion and Condon 1980; Dean 1980; Brandl and Horvath 1991.) Cullen et al. (1996) found that none of the demographic factors, whether considered separately or together influenced attitudes to police use of force. Demographic factors fare equally poorly in explaining how people respond to contact with the police. For instance, Ekblom and Heal (1982) found that demographic factors had no discernible influence on how people felt about the police response to their call for assistance. Finally, White and Menke (1982) complain that surveys of the 'public mood' regarding policing have produced results that are 'contradictory and thus lack convergent validity' (p 211). They continue, 'findings indicate that the mood of the public is very different depending *on the level of specificity* of the items used to tap that mood' (p 211). There are two conclusions one might draw from this cacophony of confused results: on the one hand, it could reflect abject failure on the part of a generation of researchers to find the elusive key to enlightenment; or, on the other, perhaps it reflects the reality that there may be no settled patterns of influence. The public attitude may be fluid, because the police are not of vital interest to them. Weisburd and his colleagues (2011) found that even those living in crime-ridden housing areas where police were actively targeting wrongdoers, had little awareness of the police presence in their neighbourhood. Rosenbaum et al. (2005) also cast doubt on the influence of contact with the police, noting that most people had had no recent contact with officers, but nevertheless had views about policing, which they attribute to 'vicarious contact'. Rosenbaum et al. also draws attention to another persistent weakness in quantitative understanding of public attitudes to the police, namely the apparent gulf—even contradiction—between views about specific events and generalised avowals of approval or satisfaction (see also Frank et al. 2005). They conclude that specific attitudes are much more volatile than general (or 'diffuse') attitudes because they each belong to distinct 'universes of meaning' (see also White and Menke 1982). How an officer deals with a routine matter may create an impression on those who witnessed it, but that may not translate into a distinctive 'universe of meaning' such as that explored by Loader and Mulcahy (2003), which was extremely broad, reflecting competing all-embracing visions of the police officer as a symbol of contemporary English society.

The imperative in quantitative research is to find a limited number of influences that explain as much of the aggregate differences between individuals as is possible. The dispersion of individual attitudes is often likened to the 'noise' that obscures the 'signal'. However, this metaphor is quite instructive, because having defined the mean average, or some other statistical parameter, as the 'signal', this tends to dominate theoretical attention and deflects it from the dispersion of individual data points around it. We suggest a radically different perspective, one that embraces dispersion. We suggest that individual divergences in perceptions of and attitudes towards police behaviour is the norm. Different individuals can view exactly the same episode of police–public contact and arrive at wholly contradictory conclusions. Our position is that such apparent contradiction tells us something extremely significant about policing. Police–public encounters are deeply controversial occasions, even amongst passive onlookers. People disagree—some approving of police action and others not—and they do so fervently. Such disagreement is not an indicator of *disinterestedness*, or some failure of understanding, but of genuinely, often passionately, held views about such matters. That is the reality.

Legitimacy

The 'Head' and 'Tail'

Can this be explained? We think it can. The explanation lies in the research of David Easton and Jack Dennis (1969, especially chs 10–11) into the *political* socialisation of American children in the 1960s; research that is often cited by Tyler and his disciples for distinguishing between 'specific' and 'diffuse' support. What is largely, if not wholly, ignored is that Easton and Dennis explained the child's political socialisation as a product of what they called the 'head and tail' of the political system. The figure that looms largest in the American political system is the President of the USA, who is adorned in the trappings of power. Any Presidential appearance is heralded by the anthem, *Hail to the Chief*; Presidential speeches are given from lecterns prominently displaying the Presidential Crest; the Presidential limousine is surrounded by a convoy of security vehicles with red and blue flashing lights, and often accompanied by police outriders; military personnel salute as the President passes by; and so forth. These are ample reasons for an American child who witnesses the public appearances of the President on television to conclude that the President is an extraordinarily potent figure of authority. If the President is the 'head', who is the 'tail'? Easton and Dennis answer that it is 'the cop'! Why? Because a police officer is an equally potent figure of authority in the *immediate* vicinity of the child. When that other figure of authority—the parent—is looking to park the family car, they do not park in a 'no waiting' zone, no matter how inconvenient it is to avoid doing so. The inquisitive child who asks why, is likely to be told that if the car is parked in the wrong place, a police officer will give the parent a ticket. The child thus learns that even the mighty parent defers to the power of a police officer. From the perspective of political science, the humble cop ticketing motorists for parking offences is a linchpin of state authority! Like the President, the cop possesses the trappings of power: when the sirens wail, law-abiding motorists make way for the patrol car to hurry past; when a cop, standing in the middle of a junction, raises a hand motorists halt as bidden; when cops ask members of the public questions, they expect—and often receive—answers (Sykes and Brent 1983); they carry weaponry forbidden to other citizens and do so openly, and wear a badge of office prominently on their chest.

Socialisation goes beyond recognising power relations. What these children were exhibiting was their absorption of the *legitimacy* of political power. 'Legitimacy' has recently surfaced as a focus of interest for procedural justice analysts, but tends to be equated (and thereby diminished) as merely a felt obligation to obey the police during future encounters. However, a recent contribution to the discussion has elevated not only the importance, but also the theoretical dynamism, of the concept as a reciprocating 'dialogic' exchange between an authority figure and those over whom authoritative power is wielded (Bottoms and Tankebe 2012). In this view, legitimacy is not a *possession* of an authority figure, but the response of one party of a *claim to legitimacy* made by the other.[1] To accept the claim to legitimacy is to cast oneself in the role of *subordinate* in a power relationship. Once legitimacy is conferred the authority figure can influence the subordinate without resistance, because the subordinate willingly defers to the authority. The parent avoids parking in the no parking zone, even if there is no cop in the vicinity because the cop is an agent of law and Americans like to think of themselves as law-abiding. Accepting claimed legitimacy is not a one-off event, however: authority must be perpetually reaffirmed with each transaction. Hence, authority is always and everywhere contingent on the continued acceptance of the claim on which it, often tacitly, rests. If the claim has or acquires a 'hollow ring', then legitimacy is likely to be resisted.

This is the context in which controversy can erupt: authority may not be clearly and unambiguously accepted or rejected by those over whom the authority figure seeks to wield power. Those putative subordinates may dispute amongst themselves whether the claims to legitimacy should be accepted or not. At the level of the Presidential 'head' of the political system this is hardly exceptional: after all, Easton and Dennis were writing in the aftermath of the assassination of President Kennedy; amid the turmoil aroused by the Vietnam War; when university campuses were sites of rioting; civil rights protesters were marching; Watergate was about to deluge the body politic in acrimony and a sitting President resign rather than face impeachment. When Martin Luther King gave his famous 'I have a dream' speech from the steps of the Lincoln Memorial, he was not merely criticising racial segregation in the South, but

---

[1] For our purposes, the claimant for legitimacy will be called the 'authority' and those to whom those claims are addressed, 'subordinates' (but, of course, they are only truly 'subordinate' once they accept the claim).

challenging the very foundations of a political system that avowed the value of equal rights and yet tolerated segregation. However, the cop/'tail' of the political system is no less a controversial figure: cops were deeply implicated in the enforcement of segregationist laws and violently opposed the Civil Rights Movement; it was cops who campus opponents of the Vietnam War confronted; cops too were at the forefront of the ghetto riots, often targets of accusations of provocative actions and excessive force; it was a time when radicals referred to the police as 'pigs'. Controversy swirled around the police in America almost with as much vigour as it swirled around the Presidency. Once legitimacy is successfully challenged, authority is lost and political power must rely increasingly on naked coercion. Rioting is not important just because of the threat to life and property it entails, but because it is a repudiation of the legitimacy of 'law and order' and a demonstration of the fragility of state power once legitimacy is denied (Dahrendorf 1985). We should also not be surprised that controversy swirls around the President and the cop, because they are the 'head' and 'tail' of a system the lifeblood of which is controversy. Interestingly, where controversy is mute, it is often described as a 'police state'.

Implicit Legitimacy

If anyone doubts the legitimacy of the President, then they can be referred to the US Constitution and Supreme Court. If anyone challenges police power, they will normally be referred to 'the law' under whose auspices the police claim to exercise their powers. However, the legitimacy of authority is not confined to overt confirmation of explicit claims, such as laws, doctrines or declarations. Rituals also play a potent role in legitimation, not only through what is enunciated, but what is also *enacted*. Police funerals are not simply occasions to mourn the death of a public official, but are public displays that evoke sympathy and emphasise the 'sacrifice' of police officers in the public interest (Manning 1997). This 'silent' expression of legitimacy very often merges with the exercise of power itself. Silent expressions of legitimacy abound in policing: for instance, when police 'close' a road by the mere expedient of placing a flimsy signboard on the carriageway, or by stretching plastic tape between lamp posts; if motorists and pedestrians do not encroach, they engage in a dialogic process that simultaneously involves the exercise of power *and*, by so doing, the reaffirmation of the legitimacy of the police to 'close' roads and inconvenience those who wish to travel along them. Where legitimacy is successfully taken for granted, it is at its most powerful. The English 'bobby' was 'sacred' (Reiner 1995) when police officers were almost invisible public figures, but as they became more prominent so their authority became 'profane' and more readily challenged.

We go further: explicit claims for legitimacy are more vulnerable to rejection than taken-for-granted legitimacy. Why? Because explicit claims for legitimacy invite challenge. First, most, if not all, claims for legitimacy contain a strong moral imperative: the authorities claim the *right* to exercise authority, which, if accepted, imposes a reciprocal *obligation* on subordinates to obey (Tankebe 2013; see also Gouldner 1960 for a discussion of the 'norm of reciprocity'). That moral imperative invariably is presented as derived from unquestionable ideals, but those ideals themselves might, in fact, be questioned. For example, in the name of 'fairness' suspects are cautioned about what they say, whereas some people might reject fairness in favour of 'cracking down' on wrongdoers. Secondly, explicit avowals of rectitude are open to rational and empirical refutation. Ideals do not depict the world as it is, but how it *should* be. For instance, the British police have long cherished their image as uniquely *unarmed*, yet they have never been entirely 'unarmed': since their inception, officers have routinely patrolled carrying 'truncheons' and firearms were often available at the police station if needed.[2] This invites challenge on semantic grounds, but also principles of legality: wherein lies the legal authority for officers to carry such a weapon? Likewise, what is the *political* authority for police to obtain and use more fearsome weaponry when decision-making is shrouded in the principle of 'constabulary independence'? Moreover, this example illustrates not only how hitching police authority to the ideal of being an 'unarmed' force can also demonstrate how the exercise of authority *in the real world* can be invidiously compared to legitimating *ideals*. For instance, when police 'baton charge' a disorderly gathering, not only do images of police striking members of the crowd with batons and arrestees exhibiting bleeding head injuries populate the news media, they also invite invidious comparison with the ideal of 'minimum force'. Thus, in the midst of the 1984–85 coalminers' strike, the photograph of a mounted officer, with baton raised aloft, bearing down upon a woman fleeing, shielding her head from the onrushing horse, adorned the rostrum during the Labour Party Conference debate on the strike, with remarkable rhetorical effect (Waddington 1991).[3]

Not all ideals are equal. Some enjoy overarching influence, what are sometimes referred to as 'master frames' (Snow and Benford 1992). Amongst the ideals that legitimate policing, the most fundamental of them is undoubtedly 'justice'. It is in pursuit of justice that police claim to use their powers. They are agents, not of government, but of the criminal *justice* system. However, it is precisely in the gap between ideals and practice that the legitimacy of the police proves problematical.

The Dilemmas of Legitimacy

This raises the issue of the *content* of legitimating claims. Overwhelmingly, academic attention tends to engage this issue from a normative perspective.

---

[2] This rather decorous name for what in any other context would be considered a 'cosh' or 'cudgel'.

[3] Oddly, perhaps, this can constrain authorities to 'walk the talk': that is, to abide by the highest expressions of the ideals rather than do what they consider instrumentally rational. For instance, police have restrained themselves from using armed tactics and equipment that might have appeared to renege on their 'unarmed' image (P. A. J. Waddington and Hamilton (1997)).

Political theorists usually ask whether claims to legitimacy are *or should be* normatively compelling. Criminologists tend to challenge whether particular practices such as antiterrorism laws are compatible with the high-flown rhetoric of 'the rule of law' (see, for example, Hodgson 2013). Our approach is more modest: we focus simply on the conflicts, inconsistencies and contradictions that afflict the legitimating claims of the English police, and to the dilemmas that these create for officers in the execution of their duties.[4] In doing so, we are following McBarnett's (1978) distinction between the 'rhetoric' of law and its 'practice': the rhetoric of law consists of legitimating ideology, from which practice departs significantly. However, such mystification has implications not only for those (like suspects) who might suffer from such departures, but also for practitioners whose routine actions may be exposed as violations of legitimacy.

What has happened, is happening or will happen?

The character, Sergeant Joe Friday, in the popular 1950s television 'cop show', *Dragnet*, became famous for intoning: 'The facts, ma'am. Just give me the facts.' But what are 'the facts'? In reality, 'the facts' are endlessly contestable. We saw something of this in our focus groups' reactions to the 'aggressive man' outside a nightclub. What the video displayed was a young, muscular man, struggling with someone in a high-visibility jacket and throwing punches. The encounter lasted seconds and took place in a whirl of flaying arms and legs. The viewer was told that police had not been called to deal with such a man; they had arrived at the nightclub to deal with an alleged incident in which CS gas had been discharged into someone's face. Our focus groups often expressed disquiet at their own confusion about what had happened; the relationship of this 'aggressive man' to the CS gas incident; the identity of the person in the 'high-visibility' jacket; the spark that had ignited the fight; and much else besides. What they did not know, and of which they remained ignorant, was that according to the original programme, on his later arrival at the 'custody suite' the man was found to be in possession of a 'large quantity of amphetamines', of which he had consumed a significant dose himself, and it is surmised by the commentator that this explained his agitation and aggression towards the police. Had focus groups been aware of this, it might have altered their expectations of how the police officers should have dealt with him: would it be appropriate to try and reason with someone under the influence of amphetamines? As it was, and without prompting, some of our focus group members speculated that intoxication conferred 'superhuman' strength, which explained the vigour with which

---

[4] It is important to note that issues of legitimacy may arise outside the scope of 'the execution of their duties'. Officers who steal money from a social club of which they are a member; or commit serious crimes like murder and rape; or who egregiously flout the most basic standards of propriety, such as bribery and corruption, are likely to bring discredit on the institution, as well as themselves, and thereby undermine its legitimacy. However, our data allows us only to focus on officers performing their duties in ways that are considered broadcastable by broadcasters and this is unlikely to include egregious, legitimacy-threatening behaviour.

officers arrested the man. Some participants claimed to have experienced such men, who, they insisted, sought deliberately to fight the police as part of their 'Friday night' recreation. Those who attributed the man's behaviour to intoxicants or wilful recreational aggression tended also to be more accepting of the aggression displayed by the police, which they interpreted as necessary. However, this entails going beyond 'the facts' to inferences that inevitably involve stereotypes. However, no one involved in the incident itself could have been aware of what would be revealed later when the man was searched. This is symptomatic of the chaotic and confused factual circumstances in which officers are frequently obliged to act.

Where there is no chaos, the facts of the case may be obscured by malicious deception. This was, at least, the feeling of many members of our focus groups when considering the robbery at the home of the elderly man. The confidence with which so many of our focus groups asserted Chantelle's culpability on such slender evidence was remarkable testimony to the power of stereotyping. They were not alone, as one of the two focus groups, consisting of 'frontline' experienced officers, tended to agree with them and attributed this to their superior experience and powers of perception. When the Sergeant amongst that group (who could remember viewing the original programme) eventually disclosed that Chantelle's boyfriend was convicted of the robbery and no action was taken against Chantelle, there was stunned silence amongst the focus group. Officers commonly claim to be blessed with greater powers of insight as the result of their experience. Whilst it is true that officers do acquire esoteric knowledge about some aspects of offending (such as countersurveillance tactics employed by pickpockets) and are supplied with additional information (such as the validity of car registration plates), there is little evidence to support the claim that police officers (even specialists) are distinctively astute in recognising wrongdoers.

Not only might ill-intentioned people seek to obscure the truth of what has happened, but also impeccable sources of information might unwittingly mislead. This is what occurred at the outset of the video clip depicting the stopping of the suspected stolen car. Officers were told, in good faith, that a car with a given registration number had been reported as having driven away from a petrol filling station without paying for fuel. As they followed the car for some distance on the motorway, the officers were informed that the number displayed on the registration plates did not correspond to the official database—the number was false. What the officers did not know was that the car was subject to a notice under the VDRS. Whether this was because they did not ask, or control room operatives did not pass the information to them, or the information was unavailable, the viewer was not told. Instead, the officers drew what they considered to be the conclusion—thought to be obvious to most of the focus group participants—that the car was stolen and the occupants had driven off without paying for fuel. If the car had been stolen, would the driver still have pulled over without being chased? This was debated in some focus groups and it was correctly observed that similar video clips are common on television showing pursued cars pulling over and then, when the driver considers it most opportune, speeding away.[5] What appeared to be solid evidence of wrongdoing, simply evaporated with the petrol station's withdrawal of the allegation of theft and the revelation that the driver had been issued with a VDRS notice.

All these problems arose in connection with what had happened or was happening, but the fallibility of 'the facts' escalate enormously when imagining any future course of events. Would the suspected stolen car speed away? Would the young man who had broken into the car in the superstore car park and was now protesting his innocence suddenly run off? Would the elderly victim of a knifepoint robbery collapse overnight from some delayed reaction to the trauma? However, the police are mandated to *prevent* any *anticipated* breach of the 'peace' and empowered to make arrests to prevent future offences being committed. There are also counterfactuals to be considered: if the police officer had not pulled the driver from behind the steering wheel of the suspected stolen car, would he have taken the opportunity to speed away? Some of our participants entertained quite florid fears concerning the likely presence of weapons that were entirely speculative and yet were used to justify actions that some other participants considered unjustifiable.

Finally, 'facts' change, even within a specific brief encounter. Apart from the violent arrest, the viewer of the video clips had only a glimpse of incidents that may have lasted considerably longer than the five or so minutes that could be viewed. Suppose that only the initial period of the motorway stop of a suspected stolen car had been shown; to what conclusion would our focus groups have come? Suppose, equally, only the struggle between the police officer and the young driver had been shown; would that provoke entirely different assessments about police behaviour? We cannot say, but unprompted discussion suggests that there would have been very different opinions expressed. However, in reality, bystanders witness only the merest glimpse of unfolding police–public contacts, whilst those with comprehensive knowledge (police officers, victims and witnesses) would be likely to have vested interests in interpreting events.

In short, the ambiguities and uncertainties that accompany policing are mirrored in the interpretative search for meaning that is required in order to form an assessment of how well, or poorly, police officers acquit themselves. If police policymakers succeed in changing how officers actually behave in the course of contacts with the public, it is far from certain that this would alter how officers were assessed, because interpretative licence would remain.

Suspicion

We have already discussed how claims for legitimacy tend to include a strong moral element. In the case of the police, that moral element is the pursuit of

---

[5] It is normal practice for police to pull up behind the suspected vehicle. Had this patrol car done so, the officers would have been able to see whether the engine was turned off from the cessation of exhaust gases.

justice. One of the restraints imposed upon all those who act within the criminal justice system is that suspects enjoy the 'presumption of innocence'. This was a notion that was frequently invoked by our focus groups, especially when the person who was the object of police attention was revealed to be innocent of any offence: the owner of the car in the car park confirmed that the three youths who broke into it were acting with her consent, and therefore were innocent of theft; and the driver of the suspected stolen car was the legitimate owner. The fact of their innocence weighed heavily on the minds of some of our participants, who felt that the way in which they were treated was not compatible with their innocence. In the minds of our focus groups, the police should not handcuff, still less grab and force to the ground, someone who is innocent; they certainly should not pull an innocent driver from behind the wheel of his car and struggle with him on the side of the motorway. This view collides with both legal and operational imperatives, for legally the police are arbiters not of 'guilt' or 'innocence', but instead are empowered to use their powers on the much less certain basis of 'reasonable *suspicion*',[6] subject to the principles of necessity and proportionality. Operationally, as we have seen, the 'facts' of a situation are often unavoidably confused, ambiguous and contestable. Together, these imperatives mean that error is the abiding companion of policing. *None* of our participants disputed that officers were entitled to conclude that the car being driven on false plates was stolen, yet it was not stolen and this gap between 'suspicion' and 'proof' is common in the criminal justice process. Eye witnesses are notoriously fallible: they report something in good faith, but reality turns out to be very different (Waddington 1993). No doubt the staff at the filling station on the motorway believed that the young driver *had* failed to pay for his fuel, but they were mistaken. Information from official sources, such as the Police National Computer (PNC) is as vulnerable to human error and technical glitches as any other database. And 'things' are not always 'as they seem': there was no doubt that the three young men in the superstore car park *had* broken a passenger door window to gain access to the locked car. What was not apparent was that they had been asked to do so by the absent young woman owner who had locked her keys inside the car. Furthermore, such uncertainty can create both positive and negative errors. The positive errors occur when police act assuming that suspicions will prove to be valid. However, if the police abstain from taking action because the situation is ambiguous, then they can be censured for failing to act with sufficient expedition to prevent wrongdoing (Jay 2014).

The problem of error is not a solitary problem of legitimacy lurking within the criminal justice system. Another highly contestable notion is that of 'credibility' of evidence. Although there will be some allegations that are inherently incredible—abduction by aliens—many issues of credibility are in some way linked to the personal attributes of the source. The most frequently contested

---

[6] In the USA this is known as 'probable cause', but is essentially identical with 'reasonable suspicion'.

source are people. It is not just police officers that have to make such judgements, as Rock's meticulous ethnography of an English Crown Court notes (Rock 1993), barristers routinely cross-examine *not* forensically to analyse the evidence, but instead to attack the credibility of witnesses: to *insist* that, at least, they are or could be mistaken; *question* their sobriety at the time of the offence; *challenge* their emotionality and sanity (both at the time of the offence and when making a criminal allegation); *allege* that they suffer from some personal character flaw that casts doubt on their veracity, such as a criminal record, especially for dishonesty; or that they possess a vested interest in the conviction of the defendant; and so forth. The list is extensive, but it all undermines the notion that criminal justice is dispensed solely on the weight of evidence alone. A similar process of assessment affects which cases reach court in the first place. Official sources estimate that in 2013–14 there were in the region of seven million crimes committed in England and Wales (Office for National Statistics 2015), and this excludes a large swathe of offences such as those committed against corporate entities from shoplifting to vandalism of public property, or illegal voluntary transactions (e.g. for drugs). One might add to this the unknown array of situations that arouse suspicion, but prove upon investigation to be entirely innocent. There is simply no way that any criminal justice system could cope with that level of demand without prioritising cases. Most cases are discontinued by the police, who simply decline to arrest about three-quarters of those whom they have legal power to arrest; they can also and often do take 'no further action' in many cases, or issue formal warnings. Beyond the police there are the prosecuting authorities, like the Crown Prosecution Service, who are mandated to 'discontinue' cases that are unlikely to lead to conviction (Her Majesty's Crown Prosecution Service Inspectorate and Her Majesty's Inspectorate of Constabulary 2007). Notionally, discontinuance depends on an objective assessment, but that assessment entails calculating how juries will evaluate the evidence. Research on 'mock juries' in sex offence cases by Munro and her colleagues (Ellison and Munro 2009a; 2009c; 2009b; Finch and Munro 2005; 2006; 2007) shows that in relation to sex offences, lay people tend to import 'common-sense' prejudices into the assessment of evidence. In other words, jurors evaluate the credibility of the putative 'victim' as much as, if not more than, the evidence they have given. It follows that CPS lawyers and investigating police officers, who are tasked with assessing objectively the likelihood of conviction, are obliged to also pay attention to the credibility of the 'victim' as seen through the eyes of such imagined juries. Such assessments were illustrated by our focus groups. They were not, for example, at all reticent about assessing the lack of credibility of 'Chantelle'. Indeed, she was not regarded as a credible victim by almost all our focus group participants. Her reliability being undermined, not by anything related directly to the robbery, but by the fact that her presence in the elderly man's home, drinking beer and watching television was regarded as anomalous; her confusion, or lack of it; and by critical features which suggested that her account was scripted.

The robbery of the elderly man illustrates another contestable component of the criminal justice system's claim to legitimacy—'victimhood'. Chantelle ostensibly was a 'victim' of a horrific robbery, yet this afforded her no protection from the withering appraisal of her character by many amongst our focus groups. Should 'victims' be believed? Recently, the *politics* of victimhood surrounding cases of so-called 'historic child sexual exploitation' have brought questions of suspicion/credibility to the fore of public debate. Why is it that some victims are invested with credibility where others are not? Leaving aside the more egregious failings of police officers, our research seems to suggest that routine suspicion by police officers involves judgements that differ little from those ordinary members of the public might make faced with similar situations. Drunken drivers who crash their cars are sometimes tempted to escape the scene on foot and call the police as soon as possible to allege that their car has been stolen. Allegations of theft might follow a relationship breakup if the parties dispute each other's claims to property rights in household items, such as televisions. Violence is often accompanied by accusation and counter-accusation that the other person 'started it'. There is not only the danger that innocent people will be wrongly investigated and tried, but also that the true offender will escape justice (Higgins 2016).[7]

The phrase, 'the police are to [the state],[8] as the edge is to the knife' (David Bayley, quoted by Chevigny 1995) is applied to the use of force, but this is misleading. The real 'edge of the knife' is the professional reliance on *suspicion* as a basis for action. If an officer's suspicions are confirmed by the proven guilt of the accused, then all well and good, but if suspicion is found to be baseless then it is wrongful—not just a mistake, but a slur. This is a positive error, but negative errors can prove even more damaging, because the accused might escape justice and continue to harm victims. However, suspicion only comes to light when officers intervene into the lives of ordinary citizens and the most problematic form of intervention entails the use of force.

Force

The use of force played an important role in generating controversy. It was not only that officers depicted in the video clips used physical restraint that antagonised so many of our participants, but because they displayed *aggression*, for example, by making threats—'Get out, before I drag you out'! Police officers who were shown the same video clips agreed that from the perspective of an external observer the use of force by officers did not 'look good'. Yet there was nothing exceptional about the way officers used force in any of the video

---

[7] The issue has, of course, arisen most acutely with regard to sexual offences, especially rape, where the consent of the complainant is often the focus of a contested trial (see Rt Hon Dame Elish Angiolini (2015)).

[8] Bayley is quoted as referring to the 'government', whereas police in Britain (and elsewhere) have traditionally guarded jealously their independence from 'government' and their oath of office obliges them to swear loyalty to the Crown.

clips. No weapons, other than handcuffs, were used, and no one appeared to be injured. Struggling and grappling with suspects has been a feature of policing, probably since its inception. Indeed, the police in previous eras were probably far more violent in their treatment of suspects than are their contemporary counterparts (Emsley 1985; Brogden 1991; Weinberger 1995). So, what is force and why is its use so problematic?

Intervention

First, let us continue the preceding discussion to consider how an officer should *act* on the basis of accusations made and information that becomes available at the scene of an alleged offence. It is not only the fact that police harbour suspicions on grounds that are inevitably error-prone that proves so controversial, but that they then *intrude* into the lives of citizens to: *investigate* whether an offence has been committed, and/or *stop or disrupt* an offence that is being committed, and/or *prevent* an offence that they believe is about to be committed. These are tremendous powers that are exercised on the slender thread of suspicion alone, and because suspicion is not only error-prone, but is also necessarily acted upon in fairly peremptory fashion, controversy is seldom far away. As soon as officers have only 'reasonable suspicion' that an offence has been, is being or is about to be committed, they can lawfully arrest the person, provided it is necessary and proportionate for them to do so (Police and Criminal Evidence Act 1984, section 24). The threshold at which this power can be exercised is justifiable because (a) failing to take control of a suspected person might impede the interests of justice, for example, the suspect might escape and/or destroy evidence; and (b) having arrested someone confers additional rights on the suspect that are ironically designed to protect those who police genuinely believe have committed an offence, for instance, they must be told why they are being arrested and cautioned in the prescribed terms. Strangely, full investigation of suspected offences is often delayed until after arrest, because the evidence necessary for 'reasonable suspicion' is much weaker than that necessary for conviction in court. Often, investigation results in a person being 'de-arrested', or charges revised and rescinded, and the 'suspect' being released. It is almost inevitable that many of those arrested will be released, not necessarily because officers become convinced of their innocence, but simply because there is a grudging recognition that evidence is insufficient to convict. Whether or not arrest leads to charge and prosecution, the potential disruption to the life of those suspected may be significant. Evidence may need to be seized, which would normally entail searching people and property. If evidence can easily be destroyed, it may be necessary for police to arrive unannounced and even to force entry probably at an early hour when least expected—literally a 'rude awakening'. Stopping or disrupting an offence that is occurring may be achieved with little more than the appearance of an officer, but it is likely to involve more direct action: accosting people who are thought likely to have committed an offence and detaining them whilst preliminary investigation can illuminate often confused circumstances, such as those in the superstore car park. If a suspect(s) is escaping or attempting to escape, then the officer will feel obliged to give chase and physically apprehend the escapee, as did officers who stopped the suspected stolen car on the motorway.

The problems that confront the police are not unique; any emergency service faces comparable problems of taking action in conditions of uncertainty with potentially serious adverse consequences for fellow citizens. Emergency medical staff need to diagnose and begin treatment with only limited information available about a patient. They too make many mistakes as a result of which patients die or suffer prolonged disability. Firefighters must seek to extinguish a blaze without adequate knowledge of the materials that are aflame and rescue endangered people without full information about their whereabouts. Coastguards, lifeboat crews and mountain rescue teams might seek to save people in distress without necessarily having accurate information about where they might be found and the peril they face. What distinguishes the police when they suspect wrongdoing? *Being suspected* of a criminal offence is rarely greeted with equanimity by 'suspects'. On the contrary, the accused (and sometimes their relatives and associates) will feel indignant and likely resist the accusation, either verbally or physically. If that resistance obstructs officers in using their powers of arrest,[9] officers are empowered to 'use reasonable force, if necessary'. The issue, however, is not its legality, but the public acceptability of the police using force. The very appearance of a police car outside residential premises might spark community attention, as might an officer accosting someone in a public place to talk to them. Often police investigation is quite intrusive. Police officers stop and search people in public places on thousands of occasions each year, only a small proportion of these stops resulting in any serious offences being disclosed. Sometimes, the person's hostile reaction to such a public degradation leads to minor offences being deemed to have been committed and the person arrested. Not surprisingly, stop and search is deeply resented by those who experience it (Bradford et al. 2009a). Perhaps surprisingly, those who have been stopped and searched do not doubt the need for the police to have this power, nor to exercising it in their case, but they *do strongly object* to how stop and search was conducted by officers in their case. In sum, most people find this procedure to be humiliating (Bland et al. 2000; Miller et al. 2000b; Miller et al. 2001; Miller et al. 2000a; Quinton 2011; Quinton 2014; Quinton et al. 2000).

To a large extent police spend much of their time 'triaging' incidents. When their suspicions are aroused, they act to confirm or dismiss those suspicions, and much, if not most, of their suspicions will be revealed as unfounded. However, 'triage' in policing is not a morally neutral process done for the benefit of the person receiving attention. On the contrary, it is shaming: it implies

---

[9] It is important to appreciate that this power is not restricted to self-defence by an officer against attack. Passive resistance that obstructs an arrest or other legal power can be overcome by the application of physical force. Neither is it restricted to the use of force against an accused. Those who might obstruct an arrest by passively blocking necessary access can be pushed aside.

that a person in authority had good reason to believe that the suspected person is involved in criminality; even if nothing incriminating emerges from the stop, the taint of suspicion tends to linger—the person stopped *must* have been acting suspiciously! If the suspicion is well founded, then it becomes prudent for an officer to anticipate how a guilty suspect might react and take preventative measures to minimise risk of harm to others, the officer and the suspect themselves. When the officer in one of our video clips heard the explanation of the young men in the car park—that they were breaking into the car to retrieve the ignition key—he formally arrested all three of them until their explanation could be verified. His concern, presumably, was that if it was a fabrication then an unsecured group might have taken advantage of a moment of inattention to make their escape. Whenever the error-prone process of forming suspicion and acting on it concludes with suspicion evaporating (as is commonly the case), then its lasting legacy is one of resentment, not only on the part of those suspected, but as our data shows, on the part of disinterested onlookers as well. The taint of stereotyping might now adhere to the officer who intruded into the life of his or her fellow citizens on the basis of slender suspicions that have proven baseless.

Physical force

Any intrusive intervention curtails liberty: being asked to identify oneself and explain one's actions, even if entirely innocent, compels a person to do what they might otherwise not want to do. Using overt *physical* force makes all this more acute, because physical force (even passive restraint in handcuffs) is often seen as not only injurious, but also to treat someone not as a rational agent—a mere object (rather than subject). Sometimes it is used as a *de facto* punishment (Westley 1953; 1970; Choongh 1997; 1998); but on the other hand, if someone is resistant and the offence is serious, then it may be appropriate to use significant force.

What is force? Research into workplace violence (Waddington et al. 2006) found that victims used a very inclusive definition of 'violence': incidents in which people who became angry and verbally aggressive, even in writing or comments made during a telephone call, might be considered 'violent, or threatening, or intimidating'. Our focus groups displayed the same inclusivity in how participants viewed police use of force. It involved interventions in which officers raised their voice, threatened suspects with arrest, encroached into 'personal space', all of which qualified, in the minds of some of our participants, as 'aggression', 'threatening' and 'violent'. Physical force used for any purpose other than self-defence—such as arresting a passively resisting suspect, or to prevent escape or minimise risk—was deeply controversial. Forcing suspects to the ground face down and handcuffing them was often seen as quite an extremely violent act. (In surveys for the Independent Police Complaints Commission it emerged as one of the top three causes for complaint and concern: IPCC 2016.) Displays of such violence were often accompanied by non-verbal expressions of disgust, revulsion and horror on the part of some in our focus groups.

If the use of force is unavoidable, then officers normally take hold of the suspect and if there is resistance they tussle with them. The use of 'empty hand' tactics and techniques receive only passing attention in the literature on use of force, but is worthy of more. Arresting a resisting suspect is inevitably physically arduous, even if the suspect's goal is simply trying to escape. An officer who remained calm under such circumstances would be unlikely to arouse their own sympathetic nervous system (the so-called 'fight or flight' response), and therefore not acquire the physical capacity to prevail in such a struggle. Activation of the sympathetic nervous system results in the infusion of adrenalin, increases blood pressure, diverts blood from non-essential organs to the muscles and is accompanied by the release of endorphins in the brain that serves as an analgesic, and is also associated with perceptual distortions and so forth. None of this is conducive to restraint and exercising good judgement. An activated sympathetic nervous system more often finds expression in displacement displays of aggression, such as swearing, using demeaning epithets and the like. What the onlooker witnesses is, to all intent and purposes, *a fight*, and, 'it doesn't look good'! Police officers might be seen to descend in moral stature to the equal of a 'thug in uniform'.

There is a further twist to this moral element: in order to arrest someone officers need to *genuinely* believe that the suspect is guilty of an offence, otherwise, the arrest would be based on surmise, hypothesis or speculation and be 'unreasonable'. This, however, is effectively a presumption of guilt, which militates against the supposed 'presumption of innocence'. If someone is thought genuinely to be guilty of an offence, overcoming any resistance they might show becomes all the more imperative—it would be a moral outrage if the guilty escaped justice. If they are guilty, their resistance becomes all the more reprehensible—the suspect with whom the officer is struggling hardly deserves the benefit of restraint; they are 'outlaws', 'desperados' and 'villains' who deserve all they get. Thus, officers, almost inevitably, believe right is on their side—a recognised stimulant to aggression and violence (Collins 2008).

Force can be used more 'surgically', for instance, the trip used by the officer in the car park, is commonplace on the judo mat. However, relatively simple manoeuvres, such as these, require training and continuous rehearsal, because using them is not an everyday occurrence even for police officers. The same objection applies to the use of batons, which in the hands of a competent (and physically fit) user can disable someone and bring them under control. However, police organisations in most countries find it impossible to release officers from their duties to keep fit and practice such unarmed (or lightly armed) combat techniques with sufficient regularity to maintain skills. The result is that officers make recourse to the force of numbers and tend to 'pile in' as they did when the man became aggressive outside the nightclub. However, this offends the implicit criteria of a 'fair fight' and has the appearance of a 'gang' or a 'mob' attacking a single individual.

Evaluating the use of force

The discussion so far has focused on the three video clips when officers did use physical force to arrest resisting suspects. We should also consider the one video clip in which they used no physical force at all—the robbery of the elderly man. What our focus groups praised about that video clip was that officers were 'calm' in dealing with this incident. What many of our focus group participants complained about in the video clip of the suspected theft of the car in the car park was that the officer *escalated* the situation, rather than *de-escalate* it. In this view, the officer began escalating the situation prior to the arrest of the truculent youth, when the officer intervened in a dispute between that youth and one of the private security staff who attended the scene. As the officer approached the two men, he called out to the youth in a loud voice, 'Oi! Watch your language! Watch your language, NOW!' Standing face-to-face and very close to the youth, he said, 'I'm a police officer' and in reply to the youth's interruption he added 'I'm warning you, now ...'. The youth again interrupted and the officer replied, 'Because you're committing an offence', which was followed by a dispute regarding the offence that he may have been committing. At this stage neither the officer nor the youth had made physical contact of any sort, but this did not prevent our focus groups objecting strongly to the forcefulness of the officer's intervention. What they objected to was the *incivility* and lack of professional *detachment* shown by the officer towards the youth, who was in their view perfectly entitled to dispute the actions of the private security guards. They also felt, like respondents to the IPCC surveys, that the officer had failed to communicate effectively and moved too quickly to threatening arrest. This illustrates what Sherman highlights in his discussion of *defiance* (Sherman 1993).

What seems to set the 'calmness' of the officer's handling of the robbery of the elderly man apart from how police dealt with the suspected car theft and suspected stolen car on the motorway, was that officers *did not impose themselves* on Chantelle and the elderly man. When the officer reached the door to the elderly man's bungalow, he knocked and Chantelle asked who it was. He replied that he was a police officer and when she unlocked the door, he asked, 'Hello. Has somebody rung us?' It was not until Chantelle confirmed that she had done so, that the officer stepped over the threshold and asked, 'What's gone on?' Many of the police officers who viewed this video, especially senior officers, were very critical of this, because they considered the officer to be 'sloppy' and 'casual'. Those officers who praised the handling of the suspected car theft, tended to appreciate the officer's need to take control of the situation, which involved three suspects who might at any moment suddenly 'bomb burst' and escape. This highlights the fundamental dilemma of police authority: police intervene in situations as figures of authority to which they expect others to defer (Sykes and Clark 1975). As Bittner (1970) famously remarked: they 'brook no opposition'. Such authority rests upon the capacity to compel, by force if necessary. However, to those who witness it, the manner and degree to which the officer exerts this authority is likely to be justified or not by the extent to which the person they are dealing with is thought to *deserve* it. Officers tread a perilous path between being authoritative and becoming officious. The officer in the superstore car park had, it was widely accepted by our focus groups, ample grounds to suspect that the three youths were stealing the car. However, they had made no attempt to flee the scene and offered a more or less plausible exculpation that could readily be confirmed. The officer arrested and hand-cuffed two of them without resistance, explaining that if the owner returned and confirmed their story, he would release them all. This was perfectly within his powers as a constable. When the third man resisted attempts by the officer to arrest him, the officer was empowered to use 'such force as is reasonable in the circumstances' to arrest him.[10] What else might the officer have done? Well, some focus group members felt that 'arrest' and intoning the caution was too formal. Instead, the officer should merely have 'detained' the men. Here, we encounter another legal nicety that the officer is duty-bound to obey. In the case of *Holgate-Mohammed v Duke*,[11] Lord Chief Justice Diplock defined 'arrest' as: '... a continuing act; it starts with the arrester taking a person into his custody, (sc. *by action or words* restraining him from moving anywhere beyond the arrester's control)'. Merely 'detaining' the three youths would not have altered the fact that they were under the arrester's control and having arrested them the officer was duty-bound to tell them on what grounds and to caution them. So, were our focus groups misguided in objecting to the arrest of the three young men? No, for whilst the officer can argue that he acted wholly within his powers, he did so in such a *manner* as to expose himself to criticism. It was his *mismanagement* of the encounter with the truculent youth to which critics in our focus groups objected. As we noted in Chapter 4, many of our focus group members complained about the casual attire and demeanour of the officer, captured by his greeting to the suspects and security personnel—'What's the crack?' So too, did many police officers. Some focus group members thought it inappropriate that an officer in plain clothes should become involved in a situation like this and many of them doubted whether he had made it clear to the youths that he was a police officer.[12] Acting with the authority of a constable was equated by many of our focus group members with presenting oneself (Goffman 1958) as a figure of authority, not just 'one of the boys' or 'a thug in uniform' [or, in this case, a 'thug in plain clothes'). By engaging in badinage the officer was thought by many (including fellow officers) to demean his office and its authority.

A view expressed by some members of our police focus groups was that the police organisation should be more honest about the use of force. Certainly,

---

[10] Which is not to say that the officer exercised his powers lawfully throughout the entire incident.

[11] *Holgate-Mohammed v Duke* [1984] AC 437, [1984] 1 All ER 1054.

[12] Although careful viewing of the video clip does confirm that he did announce who he was as soon as he approached the truculent youth.

television documentaries that focus on use of force (see, for example, Turner 2009) depict rather stylised training sessions with which footage of actual behaviour (for instance, at the G20 protests in 2009) is invidiously compared. Officers felt that the difficulties of arresting a resistant suspect and the need for more than one officer to do so by force, should be frankly admitted. Hopefully, they felt that then they would not be expected to achieve the unattainable. We consider this to be mistaken: what officers require are the skills to better manage volatile situations. To some extent this expertise exists in small pockets of the police organisation, such as 'hostage negotiators', 'family liaison officers' and elsewhere. Perhaps it is time that the police recognised the value of such skills for routine street policing.

'Specific' and 'Diffuse' Legitimacy

This research was deliberately designed to focus attention at the most *specific* level at which attitudes to the police might be formed and expressed—the encounter between officer(s) and members of the public in which officers use or could use their legal powers. Nevertheless, we believe that this helps to address the issue of the connection between 'specific' and 'diffuse' attitudes. The simple model is that each specific encounter makes a small cumulative impact at the diffuse level. However, this simple model is, in our view, flawed: first, conceptually, if 'specific' and 'diffuse' attitudes exist in distinct 'universes of meaning' then we need some explanation of why accumulated experiences leap from the one 'universe of meaning' to another; from the tangibility of experience to the insubstantial realm of the symbolic. Secondly, the quantitative accumulation of experience is not a satisfactory explanation for a qualitative shift. Thirdly, the evidence suggests that low-frequency, yet repeated, contact with the police does not accumulate, but those with high-frequency contact hold attitudes qualitatively more hostile to the police (Rosenbaum et al. 2005).

What explains the relationship between 'specific' and 'diffuse' attitudes? We can offer only informed speculation, but what was evident to us was that when discussing the particulars of each video clip, our participants overwhelmingly addressed their remarks to the specific individual(s) in the video clip. Comments such as, '*Those two* deserve to be thrown out of the force!', or '*He* was so patient'. This was so ubiquitous that it could easily pass unrecognised, but there were also (quite jarring) occasions when remarks were made about 'the police', such as 'Give them a uniform and they think they can do what they like!'; where the behaviour of officers was seen as symptomatic of a wider occupational propensity; or, more rarely, the officers in the video clip were seen as failing to conform to the standards of policing, for instance, 'He was young and inexperienced', 'They got themselves hyped up, they did'. The bias that we detected was to regard officers as individuals and not as representatives of 'the police' as a whole. We suspect that this is asymmetric: experiences that are *congruent* with diffuse attitudes (whether normatively positive or negative) will tend to be self-reinforcing—they are symptomatic of a general propensity. Experiences that are at variance with established diffuse attitudes will be regarded as aberrations arising from individual characteristics. In this way 'diffuse' attitudes are relatively insulated from disconfirming experience. However, this insulation of 'diffuse' attitudes cannot be endlessly sustained, for those with high-frequency contact specific experiences are unlikely to be with different individual police officers. If one officer is repeatedly brusque and heavy-handed, then this could be attributed to some personal flaw in that officer; if, however, different officers, performing similar functions, are brusque and heavy-handed, then it invites a more general level of descriptive and normative assessment. '*He* (or she) is brusque and heavy-handed' becomes '*They* are brusque and heavy-handed'. In addition, some specific encounters can have a devastating impact on the reputation of the police, perhaps because the event implicates not only the officer(s) most directly involved. For example, the Macpherson Inquiry and Report (1999) into the murder of Stephen Lawrence and its investigation did enormous damage by its conclusion that the Metropolitan Police and the police service generally was infected with 'institutional racism'. Interestingly, many officers throughout the country seemed to invoke a technique of insulation very similar to that employed by our focus groups, for they claimed that what was revealed by Macpherson was peculiar to the Metropolitan Police and, therefore, did not apply to them (Foster 2008). We imagine that the BBC documentary *The Secret Policeman* (Sculthorp 2003) would have been a greater embarrassment to many officers since the police recruits who expressed virulently racist ideas were not from just one force.

The Task for the Police

We do not claim that our results make the policing task any easier. It would be pleasing to be able to prescribe a clear course of action that the police should follow, but given the controversy that swirls around routine police contacts with the public, this would be misleading. However, if our conclusions are sound, we think they are valuable for the police, because if controversy is the norm then police and politicians will come to learn the limits of reform. Let us make some suggestions about how policing might adapt.

First and foremost, neither the police nor others should imagine that this is a simple issue: it is genuinely problematic and fundamental. It cannot be addressed by a 'training' course, because the public's view of police practice is often contradictory, reflecting contradictions deeply ingrained in the legitimation of police authority. The only way to cope with such genuine uncertainties and dilemmas is to appreciate them and attempt to negotiate them whilst recognising the inevitably of error. This conflicts with how police officers see public expectations: that officers should be decisive and authoritative (Holdaway 1983). However, neither of these expectations need be jeopardised by humility, a willingness to negotiate or to recognise that it may be necessary to change courses of action and even to apologise when it appears the initial approach was a mistake. The danger, of course, in admitting mistakes is that any failing is likely to be exploited in court proceedings by the defence. The implication of our research is that the making of mistakes is not some simple indicator of personal failing—as is now so generally assumed—but, rather, an inevitable accompaniment of an officer doing their duty. The same reservations surround the use of debriefs to review events, admit failures and seek improvements. However, one alternative is to devise fictional scenarios that contain realistic depictions of problematic policing situations for discussion, both among the police but also with members of the public (see, for example, Waddington et al. 2013). If nothing else, discussion of scenarios may encourage self-awareness and appreciation of other views that officers would be wise to take into consideration. Since these scenarios are fictional, there is no reason why members of the public should not be invited to give their views on how they might be resolved. After all, the best way of dealing with problematic police–public encounters is for them to be avoided, and research into very serious use of force incidents suggests that officers could have avoided using force had earlier courses of action been different (Bayley and Garofalo 1989; Uniform Crime Reports Section 1993). Finally, perhaps the police should recognise that violence is their 'business' and officers should be properly educated about violence, including its prevalence (Pinker 2012) and characteristic features (Collins 2008).

On the other hand, a greater willingness to admit error is likely to yield the great reward of cultivating 'motive-based trust' and a greater willingness to comply. Tyler has rightly emphasised the importance of the *quality* of how police officers treat members of the public rather than the goals they achieve through such encounters. However, this theory is ambivalent about the influence of subjectivity in interpreting the behaviour of officers and methodologically reliant on the perceptions of only one of the parties. In this volume we have presented evidence from the perspective of onlookers with no vested interest in the encounter, its participants or the outcome—focus groups watching a video clip. What they clearly exhibited was the diverse and often contradictory perceptions and interpretations of the behaviour of police officers dealing with a real-life routine situation captured in a video clip.

Tyler sees 'motive-based trust' as a valuable product of 'procedural justice' that is likely to facilitate policing purposes in future encounters. We agree: our data suggest that if trust is present then even mistaken actions will be tolerated. Indeed, we cite evidence that some of the participants were willing to *imagine* quite fanciful possibilities as justifying police actions that were clearly problematic—such as the presence of weapons in the suspected stolen car. There is also a dark side to this hypothesis, for where trust is *absent* quite the opposite applies (Tankebe 2008; Roberts and Herrington 2013): the police officer is not simply mistaken in believing that the car is stolen and the driver needs to be arrested, the officer's actions might be interpreted as a symptom of arrogance: 'It's the uniform, y'know, "We've got the uniform, we can do what we want"'. Such is the extent and intensity of disagreement that there is little prospect that if the officers had acted differently they would have secured greater approval. It seems as if almost any conceivable course of action would have possibly offended someone. This poses enormous practical implications for those who seek to develop police practices that foster trust and confidence amongst those individuals and groups who view the police with 'motive-based *distrust*'. Those implications will persist long into the future.

Cultivating trust relies on an ability to discern what others think and feel. Our research should encourage the police to develop empathy as a vital operational resource (Tyler 2011b). There is no behavioural formula that will enable officers to execute their duties free of interpretative licence. In which case, it is vital to understand how others view policing, not at the diffuse level of generalities, but in specific situations replete with ambiguities and conflicts. Since there must now be an enormous archive of broadcast police 'reality' programmes, the Home Office should negotiate with broadcasters to make this archive available to police educators (including those delivering courses beyond the precincts of police organisations). Perhaps officers could also develop skills in communicating with onlookers and other interested parties when performing some function that is controversial, especially when using or having used force. If there are onlookers, officers might remain at the scene and be willing to explain why a suspect was dealt with as he was. This would influence the way in which interpretative licence was exercised, but officers should be prepared to be honest and not proffer only self-justificatory reasons for acting as they did.

A persistent source of reputational damage lies in the police use of force. Here, there is official reluctance to confront the issues and thereby allow scenes of unseemly struggling to recur, sometimes with tragic results. Training seems to rely on a flawed understanding of how and when force is most commonly used—not to repel attacks, but to prevent escape (Waddington et al. 2006). When police are seeking to make the case for new technology, tactics and strategy then there is often a vibrant (albeit sometimes hysterical) criticism and debate. However, this often tacitly rests on the assumption that current methods of overcoming resistance are less injurious than competing technological innovations, which they are not. If this was frankly recognised, then training would likely be fundamentally revised. For instance, as we have seen with our video clips, one consequence of preventing escape is that officers tend to have both hands full, hanging onto the suspect. This precludes reaching for handcuffs, baton or CS spray. However, more appropriate training in how to use the hip and legs to trip an adversary may be very much more effective. Equally, there is official reluctance, it would seem, for senior officers to acknowledge the unavoidable corollary of struggling with suspects, which is stimulation of the sympathetic nervous system, which liberates much needed resources of energy, but is often accompanied by perceptual distortion and other decision-making deficits.

We have concentrated on use of force, because this was the issue that ignited most controversy within and between our focus groups. However, it is likely that other aspects of routine policing would also arouse controversy and they too should not be ignored in the hope that they will disappear—they won't. What can be done about these realities of policing? Yet, again, it seems that the ethos of 'community policing' is broadly correct: it is essential for police officers to engage as much as possible with those whom they police. This is best done, not in formal meetings, when police presentations are—perhaps inevitably—didactic exercises in self-justification, but instead in numerous one-to-one conversations with members of the public. Those conversations should not be divorced from the kind of specific incidents depicted in our video clips. Explaining why one took the action one did is not only a vital component of 'procedural justice'; it is also an excellent opportunity to educate the public in the necessarily inevitable fallibility of policing.

Bibliography

Allen, J. (2006), *Worry about Crime in England and Wales: Findings from the 2003/ 04 and 2004/05 British Crime Survey* [online text], Research, Development and Statistics Directorate, Home Office.

Allen, J., Edmonds, S., Patterson, A., and Smith, D. (2006), *Policing and the Criminal Justice System—Public Confidence and Perceptions: Findings from the 2004/05 British Crime Survey* [online text] (Home Office).

Alpert, G. P. and Noble, J. J. (2008), 'Lies, True Lies, and Conscious Deception: Police Officers and the Truth', *Police Quarterly*, 12 (2), 237–54.

Alpert, G. P., Smith, M. R., Kaminski, R. J., Fridell, L. A., MacDonald, J., and Kubu, B. (2011), 'Police Use of Force, Tasers and Other Less-Lethal Weapons', *NIJ Research in Brief* (US Department of Justice, Office of Justice Programs, National Institute of Justice).

Alvazzi del Frate, A. and Van Kesteren, J. (2004), 'Key Findings of the 2000 International Crime Victim Surveys' (Turin: UNICRI), available at <http:// www.unicri.it/services/library_documentation/publications/icvs/publications/ CriminalVictimisationUrbanEurope.pdf>.

Amandus, H., Bozeman, W. P., Caplan, Y. H., Clark, S. C., Denton, J. S., Flomenbaum, M., Gleason, L., Gunther, W. M., Hanzlick, R., Hunsaker III, J. C., Morgan, J., Prahlow, J. A., Oliver, W., and Sathyavagiswaran, L. (2011), 'Study of Deaths Following Electro Muscular Disruption', *NIJ Special Report* (Washington: US Department of Justice, Office of Justice Programs, National Institutes of Justice).

Amendola, K. L. (1996), *Officer Behavior in Police–Citizen Encounters: A Descriptive Model and Implications for Less-Than-Lethal Alternatives* (Washington, DC: Police Foundation) 8.

Ames, W. (1981), *Police and Community in Japan* (Berkeley: University of California Press) 247.

Angiolini, R. H. D. E. (2015), 'Report of the Independent Review into the Investigation and Prosecution of Rape in London' (London: Metropolitan Police).

Angle, H., Malam, S., and Care, C. (2003) *Witness Satisfaction: Findings from the Witness Satisfaction Survey 2002* [online text] (Home Office).

Applegate, B. K., Cullen, F. T., and Fisher, B. S. (2002), 'Public Views Toward Crime and Correctional Policies. Is There a Gender Gap?', *Journal of Criminal Justice*, 30 (2), 89–100.

Aye Maung, N. (1995), *Young People, Victimisation and the Police: British Crime Survey Findings on Experiences and Attitudes of 12 to 15 Year Olds* (London: HMSO).

Ayling, R. (1999), 'Fair Hearing?', *Policing Today*, 5 (1), 18–21.

Bayley, D. H. (1976), *Forces of Order: Police Behaviour in Japan and the United States* (Berkeley: University of California Press) 201.

Bayley, D. H. (1996), 'Police Brutality Abroad', in W. A. Geller and H. Toch (eds.), *Police Violence: Understanding and Controlling Police Abuse of Force* (New Haven, Conn.: Yale University Press) 273–91.

Bayley, D. H. and Mendelsohn, H. (1969), *Minorities and the Police* (New York: Free Press).

Bayley, D. H. and Garofalo, J. (1989), 'The Management of Violence by Police Patrol Officers', *Criminology*, 27 (1), 1–23.

Bebbington, S. (2006), 'Police Federation Annual Conference—Chairman Questions IPCC's Independence', *Police Review*, 7.

Belson, W. A. (1975), *The Public and the Police* (London: Harper and Row).

Belur, J. (2009), 'Police Use of Deadly Force: Police Perceptions of a Culture of Approval', *Journal of Contemporary Criminal Justice*, 25 (2), 237–52.

Belur, J. (2010a), 'Police "Encounters" in Mumbai, India', in J. B. Kuhns and J. Knutsson (eds.), *Police Use of Force* (Santa Barbara, CA: Praeger) 52–62.

Belur, J. (2010b), *Permission to Shoot? Police Use of Deadly Force in Democracies* (London: Springer).

Belur, J. (2010c), 'Why Do The Police Use Deadly Force?', *British Journal of Criminology*, 50 (2), 320–41.

Bittner, E. (1970), *The Functions of the Police in a Modern Society* (Washington, DC: US Government Printing Office).

Bittner, E. (1985), 'The Capacity of Use Force as the Core of the Police Role', in F. Elliston and M. Feldberg (eds.), *Moral Issues in Police Work* (Totowa, N.J.: Rowman and Allanheld) 15–26.

Bland, N., Miller, J., and Quinton, P. (2000), *Upping the PACE? An Evaluation of the Recommendations of the Stephen Lawrence Inquiry on Stops and Searches* (Police Research Series; London: Home Office, Policing and Reducing Crime Unit).

Bluder, S. and Tyler, T. R. (2003), 'A Four-Components Model of Procedural Justice: Defining the Meaning of a "Fair" Process', *Personality and Social Psychology Bulletin*, 29, 747–58.

Bolton, C. (1972), 'Alienation and Action: A Study of Peace Group Members', *American Journal of Sociology*, 78 (3), 537–61.

Bottoms, A. and Tankebe, J. (2012), 'Beyond Procedural Justice: A Dialogic Approach to Legitimacy in Criminal Justice', *Criminology*, 102 (1), 119–70.

Bradford, B. (2011), 'Convergence, not Divergence? Trends and Trajectories in Public Contact and Confidence in the Police', *British Journal of Criminology*, 51 (1), 179–200.

Bradford, B., Jackson, J., Hough, M., and Farrall, S. (2008), 'Trust and Confidence in Criminal Justice: A Review of the British Research Literature', *7th Framework Programme, 'JUSTIS: Scientific Indicators of Confidence in Justice'* (European Commission) 1–20.

Bradford, B., Jackson, J., and Stanko, E. (2009a), 'Contact and Confidence: Revisiting the Impact of Public Encounters with the Police', *Policing And Society*, 19 (1), 20–46.

Bradford, B., Stanko, E. A., and Jackson, J. (2009b), 'Using Research to Inform Policy: The Role of Public Attitude Surveys in Understanding Public Confidence and Police Contact', *Policing: A Journal of Policy and Practice*, 3 (2), 139–48.

Bradford, B., Murphy, K., and Jackson, J. (2014), 'Policing, Procedural Justice and the (Re)production of Social Identity', *British Journal of Criminology*, 54 (4), 527–50.

Bradley, R. (1998), *Public Expectations and Perceptions of Policing* (Police Research Series; London: Policing and Reducing Crime Unit, Home Office) 24.

Brandl, S. G. and Horvath, F. (1991), 'Crime–Victim Evaluation of Police Investigative Performance', *Journal of Criminal Justice*, 19 (2), 109–21.

Brandl, S. G., Frank, J., Worden, R., and Bynum, T. S. (1994), 'Global and Specific Attitudes Toward the Police', *Justice Quarterly*, 11 (1), 119–34.

Bridenball, B. and Jesilow, P. (2008), 'What Matters: The Formation of Attitudes Toward the Police', *Police Quarterly*, 11, 151–81.

Brodeur, J-P. (1981), 'Legitimizing Police Deviance', in C. Shearing (ed.), *Organisational Police Deviance* (Toronto: Butterworths) 127–60.

Brogden, M. (1983), 'The Myth of Policing by Consent', *Police Review*, XLI, 760–1.

Brogden, M. (1991), *On the Mersey Beat* (Oxford: Oxford University Press) 184.

Brown, B. and Benedict, W. R. (2002), 'Perceptions of the Police: Past Findings, Methodological Issues, Conceptual Issues and Policy Implications', *Policing: An International Journal of Police Strategies and Management*, 25 (3), 50–8.

Brown, D. (1987), 'The Police Complaints Procedure: A Survey of Complainants' Views', *Home Office Research Study* (London: HMSO) 91.

Brown, G. R. (2016), 'The Blue Line on Thin Ice: Police Use of Force Modifications in the Era of Cameraphones and *YouTube*', *British Journal of Criminology*, 56 (2), 293–312.

Brunson, R. K. and Weitzer, R. (2009), 'Police Relations with Black and White Youths in Different Urban Neighborhoods', *Urban Affairs Review*, 44 (6), 858–85.

Bucke, T. (1997), *Ethnicity and Contacts with the Police: Latest Findings from the British Crime Survey* (136: Home Office Research, Development and Statistics Directorate).

Burrows, J. (1986), 'Burglary: Police Actions and Victims' Views', *Research and Planning Unit Paper* (37: Home Office).

Cain, M. (1973), *Society and the Policeman's Role* (London: Routledge & Kegan Paul).

Campbell, A. and Schuman, H. (1971), 'A Comparison of Black and White Attitudes and Experience in the City', in C. M. Haar (ed.), *The End of Innocence: A Suburban Reader* (Glencoe, IL: Scott Foresman) 97–110.

Cao, L., Frank, J., and Cullen, F. T. (1996), 'Race, Community Context, and Confidence in the Police', *American Journal of Police Science*, 15 (Cambridge) 3–22.

Carr, P. J., Napolitano, L., and Keating, J. (2007), 'We Never Call the Cops and Here is Why: A Qualitative Examination of Legal Cynicism in three Philadelphia Neighborhoods', *Criminology and Criminal Justice*, 45, 445–80.

Carter, D. (1985), 'Hispanic Perception of Police Performance: An Empirical Assessment', *Journal of Criminal Justice*, 13 (6), 487–500.

Chakraborti, N., Garland, J., and Spalek, B. (2004), 'Out of Sight, Out of Mind? Towards Developing an Understanding of the Needs of "Hidden" Minority Ethnic Communities', *Criminal Justice Matters*, 57, Autumn, 34–5.

Chan, J. (1996), 'Changing Police Culture', *British Journal of Criminology*, 36 (1), 109–34.

Chan, J. (1999), 'Police Culture', in D. Dixon (ed.), *A Culture of Corruption* (Annadale, NSW: Hawkins Press) 98–137.

Chatterton, M. R. (1976), 'Police Arrest Powers as Resources in Peace-keeping', *Social Work*, 7, 234–7.

Cheurprakobkit, S. (2000), 'Police–Citizen Contact and Police Performance: Attitude Differences Between Hispanics and Non–Hispanics', *Journal of Criminal Justice*, 28, 325–36.

Chevigny, P. (1995), *Edge of the Knife: Police Violence in the Americas* (New York: New Press) 319.

Chibnall, S. (1975a), 'The Police and the Press', in J. Brown and G. Howes (eds.), *The Police and the Community* (Farnborough: Saxon House) 67–82.

Chibnall, S. (1975b), 'The Crime Reporter: A Study in the Production of Commercial Knowledge', *Sociology*, 9 (1), 49–66.

Chibnall, S. (1979), 'The Metropolitan Police and the News Media', in S. Holdaway (ed.), *The British Police* (London: Edward Arnold) 135–49.

Chivite-Matthews, N. and Maggs, P. (2002), *Crime, Policing and Justice: The Experience of Older People: Findings from the British Crime Survey, England and Wales* 08/02 (London: Research, Development and Statistics Directorate, Home Office).

Choongh, S. (1997), *Policing as Social Discipline*, ed. R. Hood (Clarendon Studies in Criminology; Oxford: Clarendon) 262.

Choongh, S. (1998), 'Policing the Dross: A Social Disciplinary Model of Policing', *British Journal of Criminology*, 38 (4), 623–34.

Chow, H. (2010), 'Police–Public Relations: Perceptions of the Police Among University Students in a Western Canadian City', *International Journal of Criminology and Sociological Theory*, 3 (2), 496–511.

Christie, N. (1977), 'Conflicts as Property', *British Journal of Criminology*, 17 (1), 1–15.

Clancy, A., Hough, M., Aust, R., and Kershaw, C. (2001), *Crime, Policing and Justice: The Experience of Ethnic Minorities. Findings from the 2000 British Crime Survey*, ed. D. Moxon (Home Office Research Study 223; London: Home Office Research, Development and Statistics Directorate).

Clark, J. P. (1965), 'Isolation of the Police: A Comparison of the British and American Situations', *Journal of Criminal Law, Criminology and Police Science*, 56 (3), 307–19.

Cockcroft, T. (2013), *Police Culture: Themes and Concepts* (London: Routledge).

Cohen, S. (1972), *Folk Devils and Moral Panics* (Oxford: Martin Robertson).

Collins, R. (2008), *Violence: A Micro-Sociological Theory* (Princeton: Princeton University Press).

Correia, M. E., Reisig, M. D., and Lovrich, N. P. (1996), 'Public Perceptions of State Police: An Analysis of Individual-level and Contextual Variables', *Journal of Criminal Justice*, 24 (1), 17–28.

Cox, T. C. and Falkenberg, S. D. (1987), 'Adolescent's Attitudes Toward Police: An Emphasis on Interactions Between the Delinquency Measures of Alcohol and Marijuana, Police Contacts and Attitudes', *American Journal of Police*, 6 (2), 45–62.

Crank, J. P. and Giacomazzi, A. L. (2007), 'Real Policing and Public Perceptions in a Non-urban Setting: One Size Fits One', *Policing*, 30 (1), 108–31.

Crawford, A., Lea, J., Woodhouse, T., and Young, J. (1990), *The Second Islington Crime Survey* (Middlesex: Centre for Criminology).

Cullen, F. T., Cao, L., Frank, J., Langworthy, R. H., Browning, S. L., Kopache, R., and Stevenson, T. (1996), 'Stop or I'll Shoot: Racial Differences in Support for Police Use of Deadly Force', *American Behavioral Scientist*, 39, 449–60.

Dahrendorf, R. (1985), *Law and Order, The Hamlyn Lectures*, 37th series (London: Stevens).

Darley, J. M. and Batson, C. D. (1984), ' "From Jerusalem to Jericho": A Study of Situational and Dispositional Variables in Helping Behaviour', in E. Aronson (ed.), *Readings About the Social Animal* (New York: W.H. Freeman) 37–51.

Dean, D. (1980), 'Citizen Ratings of the Police: The Difference Police Contact Makes', *Law and Policy Quarterly*, 2, 445–71.

Decker, S. (1981), 'Citizen Attitudes Toward the Police: A Review of Past Findings and Suggestions for Future Policy', *Journal of Police Science & Administration*, 9, 80–7.

Department for Communities and Local Government (2012), *The English Indices of Deprivation 2010* (London: Department for Communities and Local Government).

Dirikx, A. and van den Bulck, J. (2014), 'Media Use and the Process–Based Model for Police Cooperation: An Integrative Approach Towards Explaining Adolescents' Intentions to Cooperate with the Police', *British Journal of Criminology*, 54 (3), 344–65.

Dixon, B. and Gadd, D. (2006), 'Getting the Message? "New" Labour and the Criminalization of "Hate"', *Criminology and Criminal Justice*, 6 (3), 309–28.

Dixon, D. and Maher, L. (2002), 'Anh Hai: Policing, Culture and Social Exclusion in a Street Heroin Market', *Policing and Society*, 12 (2), 93–110.

Dowler, K. and Zawilski, V. (2007), 'Public Perceptions of Police Misconduct and Discrimination: Examining the Impact of Media Consumption', *Journal Of Criminal Justice*, 35 (2), 193–203.

Doyle, A. C. S. (2011), *The Memoirs of Sherlock Holmes* (London: Penguin).

Durose, M. R. and Langton, L. (2013), *Contacts Between Police and the Public, 2008* (Washington, DC: US Department of Justice, Office of Justice Programs, Bureau of Justice Statistics).

Easton, D. and Dennis, J. (1969), *Children in the Political System: Origins of Political Legitimacy* (New York: McGraw-Hill).

Eith, C. and Durose, M. R. (2011), *Contacts Between Police and the Public, 2008* (Washington, DC: US Department of Justice, Office of Justice Programs, Bureau of Justice Statistics).

Ekblom, P. and Heal, K. (1982), 'The Police Response to Calls from the Public', *Research and Planning Unit Paper* (London: Home Office).

Ellison, L. and Munro, V. E. (2009a), 'Turning Mirrors into Windows? Assessing the Impact of (Mock) Juror Education in Rape Trials', *British Journal of Criminology*, 49 (3), 363–83.

Ellison, L. and Munro, V. E. (2009b), 'Of "Normal Sex" and "Real Rape": Exploring the Use of Socio-Sexual Scripts in (Mock) Jury Deliberation', *Social and Legal Studies*, 18 (3), 291–312.

Ellison, L. and Munro, V. E. (2009c), 'Reacting to Rape: Exploring Mock Jurors' Assessments of Complainant Credibility', *British Journal of Criminology*, 49 (2), 202–19.

Emsley, C. (1985), "The Thump of Wood on a Swede Turnip": Police Violence in Nineteenth-Century England', *Criminal Justice History*, 6, 125–49.

Engel, R. S. (2005), 'Citizens' Perceptions of Distributive and Procedural Injustice During Traffic Stops With Police', *Journal of Research in Crime and Delinquency*, 42 (4), 445–81.

Ericson, R. V. (1982), *Reproducing Order* (Toronto: University of Toronto Press).

Ericson, R. V. (1989), 'Patrolling the Facts: Secrecy and Publicity in Police Work', *British Journal of Sociology*, 40, 205–26.

Eschholz, S., Blackwell, B. S., Gertz, M., and Chiricos, T. (2002), 'Race and Attitudes Toward the Police', *Journal of Criminal Justice*, 30 (4), 327–41.

Festinger, L. (1962), *A Theory of Cognitive Dissonance* (London: Tavistock Publications).

Fielding, N. (1994), 'Cop Canteen Culture', in T. Newburn and E. Stanko (eds.), *Just Boys Doing Business: Men, Masculinity and Crime* (London: Routledge) 46–63.

Fielding, N. (1995), *Community Policing*, ed. R. Hood (Clarendon Studies in Criminology; Oxford: Clarendon) 229.

Finch, E. and Munro, V. E. (2005), 'Juror Stereotypes and Blame Attribution in Rape Cases Involving Intoxicants', *British Journal of Criminology*, 45 (1), 25–38.

Finch, E. and Munro, V. E. (2006), 'Breaking Boundaries? Sexual Consent in the Jury Room', *Legal Studies*, 26 (3), 303–20.

Finch, E. and Munro, V. E. (2007), 'The Demon Drink and the Demonized Woman: Socio-Sexual Stereotypes and Responsibility Attribution in Rape Trials Involving Intoxicants', *Social and Legal Studies*, 16 (4), 591–614.

FitzGerald, M., Hough, M., Joseph, I., and Qureshi, T. (2002), *Policing for London* (Cullompton, Devon: Willan).

Flatley, J., Kershaw, C., Smith, K., Chaplin, R., and Moon, D. (2010), 'Crime in England and Wales 2009/10: Findings from the British Crime Survey and Police Recorded Crime', *Home Office Statistical Bulletin* (London: Home Office).

Fleming, J. and McLaughlin, E. (2012), 'Through a Different Lens: Researching the Rise and Fall of New Labour's "Public Confidence Agenda"', *Policing and Society*, 22 (3), 280–94.

Flood-Page, C. and Taylor, J. (eds.) (2003), *Crime in England and Wales 2001/ 2002: Supplementary Volume* (Home Office Statistical Bulletin, London: Research, Development and Statistics Directorate, Home Office).

Foster, J. (2008), '"It Might Have Been Incompetent, but It Wasn't Racist": Murder Detectives' Perceptions of the Lawrence Inquiry and Its Impact on Homicide Investigation in London', *Policing and Society*, 18 (2), 89–112.

Foster, J., Newburn, T., and Souhami, A. (2005), 'Assessing the Impact of the Stephen Lawrence Inquiry', *Home Office Research Study* (Home Office Research Study 294 edn.; London: Home Office Research, Development and Statistics Directorate).

Frank, J., Smith, B. W., and Novak, K. J. (2005), 'Exploring the Basis of Citizens' Attitudes Toward the Police', *Police Quarterly*, 8, 206–28.

Gabbidon, S. L. and Higgins, G. E. (2009), 'The Role of Race/Ethnicity and Race Relations on Public Opinion Related to the Treatment of Blacks by the Police', *Police Quarterly*, 12 (1), 102–15.

Gabbidon, S. L., Penn, E. B., Jordan, K. L., and Higgins, G. E. (2009), 'The Influence of Race/Ethnicity on the Perceived Prevalence and Support for Racial Profiling at Airports', *Criminal Justice Policy Review*, 20 (3), 344–58.

Gallagher, C., Maguire, E. R., Mastrofski, S. D., and Reisig, M. D. (2001), 'The Public Image of Police: Final Report to the International Association of Chiefs of Police', <http://www.theiacp.org/The-Public-Image-of-the-Police>, accessed 8 July.

Gamson, W. A. (1992), *Talking Politics* (Cambridge: Cambridge University Press).

Gibson, C. L., Walker, S., Jennings, W. G., and Miller, J. M. (2010), 'The Impact of Traffic Stops on Calling the Police for Help', *Criminal Justice Policy Review*, 21 (2), 139–59.

Goffman, E. (1958), *The Presentation of Self in Everyday Life* (Edinburgh: University of Edinburgh, Social Sciences Research Centre) 161.

Goffman, E. (1971), *Relations in Public: Microstudies of the Public Order* (London: Allen Lane) xix, 396.

Goldsmith, A. J. (1991), *Complaints Against the Police* (Oxford: Clarendon) 331.

Goldsmith, A. J. (1996), 'What's Wrong with Complaint Investigations? Dealing with Difference Differently in Complaints Against the Police', *Criminal Justice Ethics*, 15 (1) 36–55.

Goldsmith, A. J. (2010), 'Policing's New Visibility', *British Journal of Criminology*, 50 (5), 914–34.

Gouldner, A. W. (1960), 'The Norm of Reciprocity', *American Sociological Review*, 25, 161–78.

Haas, N. E., de Keijser, J. W., and Bruinsma, G. J. N. (2014), 'Public Support for Vigilantism, Confidence in Police and Police Responsiveness', *Policing and Society*, 24 (2), 224–41.

Haas, N. E., Van Craen, M., Skogan, W. G., and Fleitas, D. M. (2015), 'Explaining Officer Compliance: The Importance of Procedural Justice and Trust Inside a Police Organisation', *Criminology and Criminal Justice*, 15 (4), 442–63.

Harris Research Centre (1987), *Crime in Newham: Report of a Survey of Crime and Racial Harassment in Newham* (Richmond, Surrey: Harris Research Centre).

Havis, S. and Best, D. (2004), 'Stop and Search Complaints (2000–2001): A Police Complaints Authority Study: Summary Report' (London: Police Complaints Authority).

Hawdon, J. and Ryan, J. (2003), 'Police-Resident Interactions and Satisfaction with Police: An Empirical Test of Community Policing Assertions', *Criminal Justice Policy Review*, 14 (1), 55–74.

Henderson, M., Cullen, F. T., Cao, L., Browning, S., and Kopache, R. (1997), 'The Impact of Race on Perceptions of Criminal Injustice', *Journal of Crime and Justice*, 25, 447–62.

Hepburn, J. R. (1978), 'Race and the Decision to Arrest', *Journal of Research in Crime and Delinquency*, 15, 54–73.

Her Majesty's Crown Prosecution Service Inspectorate and Her Majesty's Inspectorate of Constabulary (2007), *Discontinuance: HMCPSI Thematic Review of the Decision-making and Management in Discontinued Cases and Discharged Committals Summative Report Based on the Rolling Programme of Casework Quality Assessment Undertaken in Eight CPS Areas* (London: Her Majesty's Crown Prosecution Service Inspectorate).

Her Majesty's Inspector of Constabulary (2014), *Everyone's Business: Improving the Police Response to Domestic Abuse* (London: Her Majesty's Inspectorate of Constabulary).

Higgins, A. (2016), 'Shoring Up the Foundations: Victim Belief Revisited', *Police Foundation blog* (The Police Foundation).

Higgins, G. E., Gabbidon, S. L., and Jordan, K. L. (2008), 'Examining the Generality of Citizens' Views on Racial Profiling in Diverse Situational Contexts', *Criminal Justice and Behavior*, 35 (12), 1527–41.

Hillsborough Independent Panel (2012), 'Hillsborough: The Report of the Hillsborough Independent Panel' (London: The Stationery Office).

Hinds, L. and Murphy, K. (2007), 'Public Satisfaction with Police: Using Procedural Justice to Improve Police Legitimacy', *Australian And New Zealand Journal of Criminology*, 40 (1), 27–42.

Hodgson, J. (2013), 'Legitimacy and State Responses to Terrorism: The UK and France', in J. Tankebe and A. Liebling (eds.), *Legitimacy and Criminal Justice: An International Exploration* (Oxford: Oxford University Press) 178–205.

Hohl, K., Bradford, B., and Stanko, B. (2010), 'Influencing Trust and Confidence in the London Metropolitan Police: Results from an Experiment Testing the

Effect of Leaflet Drops on Public Opinion', *British Journal of Criminology*, 50 (3), 491–513.

Hohl, K., Stanko, B., and Newburn, T. (2013), 'The Effect of the 2011 London Disorder on Public Opinion of Police and Attitudes Towards Crime, Disorder, and Sentencing', *Policing*, 7 (1), 12–20.

Holdaway, S. (1983), *Inside the British Police* (Oxford: Blackwell).

Holdaway, S. (1995), 'Culture, Race and Policy: Some Themes of the Sociology of the Police', *Policing and Society*, 5 (2), 109–20.

Holdaway, S. (1996), *The Racialisation of British Policing* (Basingstoke, Hants.: Macmillan) 226.

Home Affairs Committee (2009), 'Police and the Media', *Second Report of Session 2008–2009* (London: House of Commons, Home Affairs Committee).

Home Office/College of Policing (2014), *Best Use of Stop and Search Scheme* (London: Home Office).

Hood, R. and Cordovil, G. (1992), *Race and Sentencing: A Study in the Crown Court: A Report for the Commission of Racial Equality* (Oxford: Oxford University Press) xiv, 343p.

Hough, M. (2007), 'Policing London, 20 Years On', in A. Henry and D. J. Smith (eds.), *Transformations of Policing* (Aldershot: Ashgate), 191–212.

Hough, M., Jackson, J., Bradford, B., Myhill, A., and Quinton, P. (2010), 'Procedural Justice, Trust and Institutional Legitimacy', *Policing: A Journal of Policy and Practice*, 4 (3), 203–10.

Hough, M. and Mayhew, P. (1983), *The British Crime Survey: First Report* (Home Office Research Study; London: HMSO).

Hough, M. and Roberts, J. V. (2004), 'Confidence in Justice: An International Review', *Findings* (London: Home Office, Research, Development and Statistics Directorate).

Huebner, B. M., Schafer, J. A., and Bynum, T. S. (2004), 'African American and White Perceptions of Police Services: Within—and Between—Group Variation', *Journal of Criminal Justice*, 32 (2), 123–35.

Hurst, Y. G. and Frank, J. (2000), 'How Kids View Cops: The Nature of Juvenile Attitudes Toward the Police', *Journal of Criminal Justice*, 28, 189–202.

Hwang, E. G., McGarrell, E. F., and Benson, B. L. (2005), 'Public Satisfaction with the South Korean Police: The Effect of Residential Location in a Rapidly Industrializing Nation', *Journal of Criminal Justice*, 33 (6), 585–99.

Inglis, G. and Shepherd, S. (2007), *Confidence in the Police Complaints System: A Second Survey of the General Population in 2007* (IPCC Research and Statistics Series; London: Independent Police Complaints Commission).

Innes, M. (2004a), 'Signal Crimes and Signal Disorder: Notes on Deviance as Communicative Action', *British Journal of Sociology*, 55, 17–34.

Innes, M. (2004b), 'Reinventing Tradition? Reassurance, Neighbourhood Security and Policing', *Criminal Justice*, 4, 151–71.

Innes, M., Lowe, T., MacKenzie, H., Murray, P., Roberts, C., and Twyman, L. (2004), *The Signal Crimes Perspective: Interim Findings* (Guildford: University of Surrey).

IPCC (2016), *Police Use of Force: Evidence from Complaints, Investigations and Public Perception* (London: Independent Police Complaints Commission).

Ivkovic, S. K. (2008), 'A Comparative Study of Public Support for the Police', *International Criminal Justice Review*, 18 (4), 406–34.

Jackson, J. and Bradford, B. (2009), 'Crime, Policing and Social Order: On the Expressive Nature of Public Confidence in Policing', *British Journal of Sociology*, 60 (3), 493–521.

Jackson, J., Bradford, B., Hough, M., Myhill, A., Quinton, P., and Tyler, T. R. (2012b), 'Why Do People Comply with the Law? Legitimacy and Influence of Legal Institutions', *British Journal of Criminology*, 52 (6), 1051–71.

Jackson, J., Bradford, B., Stanko, B., and Hohl, K. (2012a), *Just Authority? Trust in the Police in England and Wales* (London: Routledge).

Jackson, J., Bradford, B., Hough, M., Myhill, A., Quinton, P., and Tyler, T. (2012c), 'On the Justification and Recognition of Police Power: Broadening the Concept of Police Legitimacy', Yale Law School, Public Law Working Paper No 251, Oxford Legal Studies Research Paper No 32/2012, available at <https://papers.ssrn.com/sol3/papers.cfm?abstract_id=2084428##>.

Jansson, K. (2006a), *British Crime Survey—Measuring Crime for 25 years* (London: Home Office).

Jansson, K. (2006b), *Black and Minority Ethnic Groups' Experiences and Perceptions of Crime, Racially Motivated Crime and the Police: Findings from the 2004/05 British Crime Survey* [online text], Research, Development and Statistics Directorate, Home Office.

Jay, A., OBE (2014), *Independent Inquiry into Child Sexual Exploitation in Rotherham 1997–2013* (Rotherham: Rotherham Metropolitan Borough Council).

Jefferis, E. S., Kaminski, R. J., Holmes, S., and Hanley, D. E. (1997), 'The Effect of a Videotaped Arrest on Public Perceptions of Police Use of Force', *Journal of Criminal Justice*, 25 (5), 381–95.

Jenkins, P. (2009), 'Failure to Launch', *British Journal of Criminology*, 49 (1), 35–47.

Johnson, D. and Kuhns, J. B. (2009), 'Striking Out: Race and Support for Police Use of Force', *Justice Quarterly*, 26 (3), 592–623.

Jones, T., MacLean, B., and Young, J. (1986), *The Islington Crime Survey* (Aldershot: Gower).

Jones, T., Newburn, T., and Smith, D. J. (1994), *Democracy and Policing* (London: Policy Studies Institute) 333.

Kaminski, R. J. and Jefferis, E. S. (1998), 'The Effect of a Violent Televised Arrest on Public Perceptions of the Police: A Partial Test of Easton's Theoretical Framework', *Policing: An International Journal of Police Strategies and Management*, 21 (4), 683–706.

Karstedt, S. (2009), *Trust in Justice—How Much Do We Need? A Short History of Trust and Its Present Condition* (University of Cambridge: Institute of Criminology, University of Cambridge).

Kautt, P. (2011), 'Public Confidence in the British Police: Negotiating the Signals From Anglo-American Research', *International Criminal Justice Review*, 21 (4), 353–82.

Kelling, G. L. and Coles, C. M. (1996), *Fixing Broken Windows: Restoring Order and Reducing Crime in Our Communities* (New York: Free Press) 319.

Kershaw, C., Nicholas, S., and Walker, A. (2008), 'Crime in England and Wales: Findings from the British Crime Survey and Police Recorded Crime', *Home Office Statistical Bulletin* (London: Home Office).

Kleinig, J. (2009), 'Ethical Policing', in A. Wakefield and J. Flemming (eds.), *The Sage Dictionary of Policing* (London: Sage) 107–9.

Klockars, C. B. (1985), 'The Dirty Harry Problem', in F. Elliston and M. Feldberg (eds.), *Moral Issues in Police Work* (Totowa, N.J.: Rowman and Allanheld) 55–71.

Klockars, C. B., Ivkovich, S. K., and Haberfeld, M. R. (2004), *The Contours of Police Integrity* (Thousand Oaks, CA: Sage Publications) 305.

Kohlberg, L. (1968), 'The Child as a Moral Philosopher', *Psychology Today*, 2, 25–30.

Lambert, J. R. (1970), *Crime, Police and Race Relations: A Study in Birmingham* (London: Oxford University Press).

Lasley, J. R. (1994), 'The Impact of the Rodney King Incident on Citizen Attitudes Towards the Police', *Policing and Society*, 3 (4) 245–55.

Lawrence, R. G. (2000), *The Politics of Force: Media and the Construction of Police Brutality* (Berkeley and Los Angeles: University of California Press) 254.

Lee, M. and McGovern, A. (2013), 'Force to Sell: Policing the Image and Manufacturing Public Confidence', *Policing & Society*, 23 (2), 103–24.

Leiber, M., Naila, M., and Farnworth, M. (1998), 'Explaining Juveniles' Attitudes Toward the Police', *Justice Quarterly*, 15 (1), 277–306.

Leveson, R. H. L. J. (2012), *An Inquiry into the Culture, Practices and Ethics of the Press* (1–4 November London: The Leveson Inquiry).

Lloyd, K. and Foster, J. (2009), 'Citizen Focus and Community Engagement: A Review of the Literature' (London: The Police Foundation).

Loader, I. (2006), 'Fall of the "Platonic Guardians"', *British Journal of Criminology*, 46 (4), 561–86.

Loader, I. and Mulcahy, A. (2003), *Policing and the Condition of England: Memory, Politics and Culture* (Clarendon Studies in Criminology; Oxford: Oxford University Press) 381.

Lowe, T. and Innes, M. (2012), 'Can We Speak in Confidence? Community Intelligence and Neighbourhood Policing', *Policing and Society*, 22 (3), 295–316.

Macpherson of Cluny, S. W., advised by Cook, T, Sentamu, T. R. R. D. J., and Stone, R. (1999), *The Stephen Lawrence Inquiry* (London: HMSO).

Maguire, M. (1982), *Burglary in a Dwelling* (London: Heinemann).

Manning, P. (1997), *Police Work: The Social Organization of Policing* (2nd edn.; Prospect Heights, Ill.: Waveland) 372.

Manning, P. K. and Van Maanen, J. (eds.) (1978), *Policing: A View from the Street* (New York: Random House).

Mastrofski, S., Snipes, J., and Supina, A. (1996), 'Compliance on Demand: The Public's Response to Specific Police Requests', *Journal of Research in Crime and Delinquency*, 33, 269–305.

Mawby, R. C. (2002), *Policing Images: Policing, Communication and Legitimacy* (Cullompton: Willan).

Mawby, R. C. (2003), 'Completing the "Half-Formed Picture"? Media Images of Policing', in P. Mason (ed.), *Criminal Visions: Media Representations of Crime and Justice* (Cullompton: Willan) 214–37.

Mayhew, P., Elliot, D., and Dowds, L. (1989), *The 1988 British Crime Survey* (Home Office Research Studies; London: HMSO).

Mayhew, P., Muang, N. A., and Mirrlees-Black, C. (1993), *The 1992 British Crime Survey* (Home Office Research Study; London: HMSO) 195.

Mazerolle, L., Bennett, S., Antrobus, E., and Eggins, E. (2012), 'Procedural Justice, Routine Encounters and Citizen Perceptions of Police: Main Findings from the Queensland Community Engagement Trial (QCST)', *Journal of Experimental Criminology*, 8 (4), 343–67.

Mazerolle, L., Antrobus, E., Bennett, S., and Tyler, T. R. (2013a), 'Shaping Citizen Perceptions of Police Legitimacy: A Randomized Field Trial of Procedural Justice', *Criminology*, 51 (1), 33–63.

Mazerolle, L., Bennett, S., Davis, J., Sargeant, E., and Manning, M. (2013b), *Legitimacy in Policing: A Systematic Review* (Campbell Systematic Review; CA: Campbell).

McBarnett, D. J. (1978), 'False Dichotomies in Criminal Justice Research', in J. Baldwin and A. K. Bottomley (eds.), *Criminal Justice: Selected Readings* (London: Martin Robertson) 23–34.

McCluskey, J. D. (2003), *Police Requests for Compliance—Coercive and Procedurally Just Tactics* (New York: LFB).

McCluskey, J., Mastrofski, S., and Parks, R. (1999), 'To Acquiesce or Rebel: Predicting Citizen Compliance with Police Requests', *Police Quarterly*, 2, 389–416.

McLaughlin, E. (2006), *The New Policing* (London: Sage).

Mead, G. H. and Morris, C. W. (1934), *Mind, Self & Society from the Standpoint of a Social Behaviorist* (Chicago, Ill.: University of Chicago Press).

Medland, A. (2012), 'Portrait of the West Midlands', *Regional Trends* (London: Office for National Statistics).

Meredyth, D., McKernan, H., and Evans, R. (2010), 'Police and Vietnamese–Australian Communities in Multi-Ethnic Melbourne', *Policing: A Journal of Policy and Practice*, 4 (3), 233–40.

Merry, S., Power, N., McManus, M., and Alison, L. (2012), 'Drivers of Public Trust and Confidence in Police in the UK', *International Journal of Police Science and Management*, 14 (2), 118–35.

Miller, J., Bland, N., and Quinton, P. (2000b), *The Impact of Stops and Searches on Crime and the Community* (Police Research Series; London: Home Office, Policing and Reducing Crime Unit).

Miller, J. and D'Souza, A. (2015), 'Indirect Effects of Police Searches on Community Attitudes to the Police: Resentment or Reassurance', *British Journal of Criminology*, 56 (3), 456–78.

Miller, J., Quinton, P., and Bland, N. (2000a), 'Police Stops and Searches: Lessons from a Programme of Research', *Home Office, Briefing Note* (London: Home Office) 1–6.

Miller, J., Quinton, P., and Bland, N. (2001), 'A Challenge for Police–Community Relations: Rethinking Stop and Search in England and Wales', *European Journal on Criminal Policy and Research*, 9, 71–93.

Millings, M. (2013), 'Policing British Asian Identities: The Enduring Role of the Police in Young British Asian Men's Situated Negotiations of Identity and Belonging', *British Journal of Criminology*, 53, 1075–93.

Moxon, D. and Jones, P. (1984), 'Public Reactions to Police Behaviour: Some Findings from the British Crime Survey', *Policing*, 1 (1), 49–56.

Muir, W. K. (1977), *Police: Streetcorner Politicians* (Chicago: Chicago University Press).

Murphy, K. (2004), 'The Role of Trust in Nurturing Compliance: A Study of Accused Tax Avoiders', *Law and Human Behavior*, 28 (2), 187–209.

Murphy, K. (2009), 'Public Satisfaction with Police: The Importance of Procedural Justice and Police Performance in Police–Citizen Encounters', *Australian and New Zealand Journal of Criminology*, 42 (2), 159–78.

Murphy, K. (2013), 'Policing at the Margins: Fostering Trust and Cooperation Among Ethnic Minority Groups', *Journal of Policing, Intelligence and Counter Terrorism*, 8 (2), 184–99.

Murphy, K. (2015), 'Does Procedural Justice Matter to Youth? Comparing Adults and Youths' Willingness to Collaborate with Police', *Policing and Society*, 25 (1), 53–76.

Murphy, K. and Cherney, A. (2012), 'Understanding Cooperation with Police in a Diverse Society', *British Journal of Criminology*, 52 (1), 181–201.

Murphy, K., Mazerolle, L., and Bennett, S. (2014), 'Promoting Trust in Police: Findings from a Randomised Experimental Field Trial of Procedural Justice Policing', *Policing and Society*, 24 (4), 405–24.

Myhill, A. and Allen, J. (2002), *Rape and Sexual Assault of Women: The Extent and Nature of the Problem. Findings from the British Crime Survey* (Home Office Research Study 237; London: Home Office Research, Development and Statistics Directorate) 118.

Myhill, A. and Bradford, B. (2012), 'Can Police Enhance Public Confidence by Improving Quality of Service? Results from Two Surveys in England and Wales', *Policing And Society*, 22 (4), 397–425.

Myhill, A. and Quinton, P. (2010), 'Confidence, Neighbourhood Policing, and Contact: Drawing Together the Evidence', *Policing: A Journal of Policy and Practice*, 4 (3), 271–83.

Nicholas, S., Flatley, J., Hoare, J., Patterson, A., Southcott, C., Moley, S., and Jansson, K. (2008), 'Circumstances of Crime, Neighbourhood Watch Membership and Perceptions of Policing: Supplementary Volume 3 to Crime in England and Wales 2006-07. Findings from the British Crime Survey', *Home Office Statistical Bulletin* (London: Home Office) 99.

Niederhoffer, A. (1967), *Behind the Shield: The Police in Urban Society* (Garden City: Doubleday).

Office for National Statistics (2015), 'Crime in England and Wales, Year Ending September 2014', *Statistical Bulletin* (London: Office for National Statistics).

Page, B., Wake, R., and Ames, A. (2004), 'Public Confidence in the Criminal Justice System', *Findings* (London: Home Office. Research, Development and Statistics Directorate).

Painter, K., Lea, J., Woodhouse, T., and Young, J. (1988), *Hammersmith and Fulham Crime and Policing Survey* (London: Centre for Criminology, Middlesex Polytechnic).

Park, R. E., Burgess, E., and McKenzie, R. (1925), *The City* (Chicago: University of Chicago Press).

Parker, K. D., Onyekwuluje, A. B., and Komanduri, S. M. (1995), 'African Americans' Attitudes Toward the Local Police: A Multivariate Analysis', *Journal of Black Studies*, 25, 396–409.

Peak, K., Bradshaw, R. V., and Glensor, R. W. (1992), 'Improving Citizen Perceptions of the Police: "Back to the Basics" with a Community Policing Strategy', *Journal of Criminal Justice*, 20 (1), 25–40.

Pearson, G. (1983), *Hooligan: A History of Respectable Fears* (London: Macmillan) 283.

Pease, K. (1988), *Judgements of Crime Seriousness: Evidence from the 1984 British Crime Survey* (London: Home Office).

Piaget, J. (1932), *The Moral Judgement of the Child* (Harmondsworth: Penguin, 1977).

Pinker, S. (1995), *The Language Instinct: A New Science of Language and Mind* (Harmondsworth: Penguin) 478.

Pinker, S. (2012), *The Better Angels of Our Nature: A History of Violence and Humanity* (London: Penguin).

Powell, M. B., Skouteris, H., and Murfett, R. (2008), 'Children's Perceptions of the Role of Police: A Qualitative Study', *International Journal of Police Science and Management*, 10 (4), 464–73.

Punch, M. (1979), *Policing the Inner City* (London: Macmillan).

Queensland Crime and Misconduct Commission (2006), *Public Perceptions of the Queensland Police Service: Findings from the 2005 Public Attitudes Survey* (Public Perceptions Series; Brisbane: Crime and Misconduct Commission) 34.

Quinton, P. (2011), 'The Formation of Suspicions: Police Stop and Search Practices in England and Wales', *Policing and Society: Special Issue: Stop and Search in Global Context*, 21 (4), 357–68.

Quinton, P. (2014), 'Police–Public Interaction During Stops and Searches: A Qualitative Exploration from England and Wales' (unpublished manuscript).

Quinton, P., Bland, N., and Miller, J. (2000), *Police Stops, Decision-making and Practice* (Police Research Series; London: Home Office, Policing and Reducing Crime Unit).

Redner-Vera, E. and Galeste, M-A. (2015), 'Attitudes and Marginalization: Examining American Indian Perceptions of Law Enforcement Among Adolescents', *Journal of Ethnicity in Criminal Justice*, 13 (4), 283–308.

Reiner, R. (1995), 'From Sacred to Profane: The Thirty Years' War of the British Police', *Policing and Society*, 5 (2), 121–8.

Reiner, R. (2003), 'Policing and the Media', in T. Newburn (ed.), *Handbook of Policing* (Cullompton: Willan) 259–81.

Reiner, R., Livingstone, S., and Allen, J. (2003), 'From Law and Order to Lynch Mobs: Crime News Since the Second World War', in P. Mason (ed.), *Criminal Visions* (Cullompton: Willan) 13–32.

Reisig, M. D. and Chandek, M. S. (2001), 'The Effects of Expectancy Disconfirmation on Outcome Satisfaction in Police–Citizen Encounters', *Policing*, 24 (1), 88–99.

Reisig, M. D. and Correia, M. E. (1997), 'Public Evaluations of Police Performance: An Analysis Across Three Levels of Policing', *Policing: An International Journal of Police Strategies and Management*, 20, 311–25.

Reisig, M. D. and Lloyd, C. (2009), 'Procedural Justice, Police Legitimacy, and Helping the Police Fight Crime: Results from a Survey of Jamaican Adolescents', *Police Quarterly*, 12 (1), 42–62.

Reisig, M. D., McCluskey, J. D., Mastrofski, S. D., and Terrill, W. (2004), 'Suspect Disrespect toward the Police', *Justice Quarterly*, 21, 241–68.

Reisig, M. D. and Parks, R. B. (2000), 'Experience, Quality of Life, and Neighborhood Context: A Hierarchical Analysis of Satisfaction with Police', *Justice Quarterly*, 17 (3), 607–30.

Reisig, M. D. and Parks, R. B. (2002), *Satisfaction with Police: What Matters?* (Washington, DC: National Institute of Justice, US Department of Justice).

Ren, L., Cao, L., Lovrich, N., and Gaffney, M. (2005), 'Linking Confidence in the Police with the Performance of the Police: Community Policing can Make a Difference', *Journal of Criminal Justice*, 33 (1), 55–66.

Reuss-Ianni, E. (1983), *Two Cultures of Policing: Street Cops and Management Cops* (London: Transaction Books).

Reuss-Ianni, E. and Ianni, F. A. (1983), 'Street Cops and Management Cops: The Two Cultures of Policing', in M. Punch (ed.), *Control in the Police Organization* (Cambridge, Mass.: MIT Press) 251–74.

Reynolds, K. M., Semukhina, O. B., and Demidov, N. N. (2008), 'A Longitudinal Analysis of Public Satisfaction with the Police in the Volgograd Region of Russia: 1998–2005', *International Criminal Justice Review*, 18 (2), 158–89.

Roberts, J. V. and Hough, M. (2011), 'Custody or Community? Exploring the Boundaries of Public Punitiveness in England and Wales', *Criminology and Criminal Justice*, 11 (2), 181–97.

Roberts, K. and Herrington, V. (2013), 'Organisational and Procedural Justice: A Review of the Literature and Its Implications for Policing', *Journal of Policing, Intelligence and Counter Terrorism*, 8 (2), 115–30.

Rock, P. (1993), *The Social World of an English Crown Court: Witness and Professionals in the Crown Court Centre at Wood Green* (Oxford: Clarendon) 390.

Rosenbaum, D. P., Graziano, L. M., Stephens, C. D., and Schuck, A. M. (2011), 'Understanding Community Policing and Legitimacy-Seeking Behavior in Virtual Reality: A National Study of Municipal Police Websites', *Police Quarterly*, 14 (1), 25–47.

Rosenbaum, D. P., Schuck, A. M., Costello, S. K., Hawkins, D. F., and Ring, M. K. (2005), 'Attitudes Toward the Police: The Effects of Direct and Vicarious Experience', *Police Quarterly*, 8 (3), 343–65.

Russell, K. (1976), *Complaints Against the Police: A Sociological View* (Leicester: Milltak) 130.

Russell, K. (1978), 'Complaints Against the Police—An International Perspective', *Police Journal*, 51 (1), 34–44.

Russell, K. (1986), *Complaints Against the Police Which are Withdrawn* (Leicester: Leicester Polytechnic).

Salvatore, C., Markowitz, M., and Kelly, C. E. (2013), 'Assessing Public Confidence in the Criminal Justice System', *International Social Science Review*, 88 (1 & 2), 3–16.

Sampson, R. and Jeglum-Bartusch, D. (1998), 'Legal Cynicism and (Subcultural?) Tolerance of Deviance: The Neighbourhood Context of Racial Differences', *Law and Society Review*, 32, 777–804.

Sampson, R. and Raudenbush, S. W. (1999), 'Systematic Social Observation of Public Spaces: A New Look at Disorder in Urban Neighborhoods', *American Journal of Sociology*, 105 (3), 603–51.

Sargeant, E., Murphy, K., and Cherney, A. (2013), 'Ethnicity, Trust and Cooperation with Police: Testing the Dominance of the Process-Based Model', *European Journal of Criminology*, 11 (4), 500–24.

Sasson, T. (1995), *Crime Talk: How Citizens Construct a Social Problem*, ed. J. Best (Social Problems and Social Issues; New York: Aldine de Gruyter).

Scaglion, R. and Condon, R. G. (1980), 'Determinants of Attitudes Toward City Police', *Criminology*, 17 (4), 485–94.

Schafer, J. A., Huebner, B. M., and Bynum, T. S. (2003), 'Citizen Perceptions of Police Services: Race, Neighborhood Context, and Community Policing', *Police Quarterly*, 6, 440–68.

Schuck, A. M., Rosenbaum, D. P., and Hawkings, D. F. (2008), 'The Influence of Race/Ethnicity, Social Class, and Neighborhood Context on Residents' Attitudes Toward the Police', *Police Quarterly*, 11 (4), 496–519.

Scribbins, M., Flatley, J., Parfrement–Hopkins, J., and Hall, P. (2010), 'Public Perceptions of Policing, Engagement with the Police and Victimisation: Findings from the 2009/10 British Crime Survey', *Home Office Statistical Bulletin* (London: Home Office).

Sculthorp, T. (dir.), *The Secret Policeman* (BBC 1, 2003).

Sedley, S. (1985), 'The Uniformed Mind', in J. Baxter and L. Koffman (eds.), *Police: The Constitution and the Community* (Abingdon, Oxon: Professional Books) 5–10.

Sela-Shayovitz, R. (2015), 'Police Legitimacy Under the Spotlight: Media Coverage of Police Performance in the Face of a High Terrorism Threat', *Journal of Experimental Criminology*, 11, 117–39.

Semukhina, O. and Reynolds, K. M. (2014), 'Russian Citizens' Perceptions of Corruption and Trust of the Police', *Policing and Society*, 24 (2), 158–88.

Shapland, J. and Vagg, J. (1987), 'Policing by the Public and Policing by the Police', in P. Willmott (ed.), *Policing and the Community* (London: Policy Studies Institute) 21–8.

Shapland, J. and Vagg, J. (1988), *Policing by the Public* (London: Routledge).

Shaw, C. R. and McKay, H. D. (1942), *Juvenile Delinquency in Urban Areas* (Chicago: University of Chicago).

Shaw, M. and Williamson, W. (1972), 'Public Attitudes to the Police', *The Criminologist*, 7 (26), 18–33.

Sherman, L. W. (1993), 'Defiance, Deterrence and Irrelevance: A Theory of the Criminal Sanction', *Journal of Research in Crime and Delinquency*, 30, 445–73.

Shute, S., Hood, R., and Seemungal, F. (2005), *A Fair Hearing? Ethnic Minorities in the Criminal Courts* (Cullompton: Willan) 160.

Sims, L. (2003), 'Policing and the Public', in C. Flood-Page and J. Taylor (eds.), *Crime in England and Wales 2001/2002: Supplementary Volume* (Home Office Statistical Bulletin; London: Research, Development and Statistics Directorate, Home Office), 105–18.

Sindall, K., Sturgis, P., and Jennings, W. (2012), 'Public Confidence in the Police: A Time–Series Analysis', *British Journal of Criminology*, 52 (4), 744–64.

Sivasubramaniam, D. and Goodman-Delahunty, J. (2008), 'Ethnicity and Trust: Perceptions of Police Bias', *International Journal of Police Science and Management*, 10 (4), 388–401.

Skogan, W. G. (1990a), *The Police and the Public in England and Wales: A British Crime Survey Report* (Home Office Research Study No 117; London: Home Office).

Skogan, W. G. (1990b), *Disorder and Decline* (New York: Free Press).

Skogan, W. G. (1994), *Contacts Between Police and Public: Findings from the 1992 British Crime Survey* (Home Office Research Study; London: HMSO) 78.

Skogan, W. G. (2005), 'Citizen Satisfaction with Police Encounters', *Police Quarterly*, 8, 298–321.

Skogan, W. G. (2006), 'Asymmetry in the Impact of Encounters with Police', *Policing and Society*, 16, 99–126.

Skogan, W. G. (2012), 'Assessing Asymmetry: The Life Course of a Research Project', *Policing and Society*, 22 (3), 270–9.

Skolnick, J. H. and Fyfe, J. J. (1993), *Above the Law: Police and the Excessive Use of Force* (New York: Free Press) 313.

Smith, D. (2010), *Public Confidence in the Criminal Justice System: Findings from the British Crime Survey 2002/03 to 2007/08* (Ministry of Justice Research Series; London: Ministry of Justice).

Smith, D. J. (1983), *A Survey of Londoners* (Police and People in London; London: Policy Studies Institute).

Smith, D. J. and Gray, J. (eds.) (1983), *Police and People in London*, vol 14 (London: Policy Studies Institute).

Snow, D. A. and Benford, R. D. (1992), 'Master Frames and Cycles of Protest', in A. D. Morris and C. M. Mueller (eds.), *Frontiers in Social Movement Theory* (New Haven, Conn.: Yale University Press) 133–55.

Southgate, P. and with the assistance of Paul Ekblom (1984), 'Contacts Between Police and Public: Findings from the British Crime Survey', *Home Office Research Study* (London: HMSO).

Southgate, P. and Ekblom, P. (1985), 'Contacts Between Police and Public: Findings from the British Crime Survey', in K. Heal, R. Tarling, and J. Burrows (eds.), *Policing Today* (London: HMSO) 131–41.

Southgate, P. and Ekblom, P. (1986), *Police–Public Encounters* (Home Office Research Study; London: HMSO).

Stanko, B., Jackson, J., Bradford, B., and Hohl, K. (2012), 'A Golden Thread, a Presence Amongst Uniforms, and a Good Deal of Data: Studying Public Confidence in the London Metropolitan Police', *Policing and Society*, 22 (3), 317–31.

Stewart, D. M., Morris, R. G., and Weir, H. (2014), 'Youth Perceptions of the Police: Identifying Trajectories', *Youth Violence and Juvenile Justice*, 12 (1), 22–39.

Stoddard, E. R. (1968), 'The Informal "Code" of Police Deviancy: A Group Approach to "Blue-Coat Crime"', *Journal of Criminal Law, Criminology and Police Science*, 58 (2), 201–13.

Stott, C., Hoggett, J., and Pearson, G. (2012), '"Keeping the Peace"', *British Journal of Criminology*, 52 (2), 381–99.

Stoutland, S. E. (2001), 'The Multiple Dimensions of Trust in Resident/Police Relations in Boston', *Journal of Research in Crime and Delinquency*, 38 (3), 226–56.

Sunshine, J. and Tyler, T. (2003), 'The Role of Procedural Justice and Legitimacy in Public Support for Policing', *Law and Society Review*, 37 (3), 513–48.

Surette, R. (1998), *Media, Crime and Criminal Justice: Image and Realities* (2nd edn.; Belmont, CA: Wadsworth).

Sykes, R. and Clark, J. (1975), 'A Theory of Deference Exchange in Police–Civilian Encounters', *American Journal of Sociology*, 81 (3), 584–600.

Sykes, R. E. and Brent, E. E. (1983), *Policing: A Social Behaviourist Perspective* (New Brunswick, N.J.: Rutgers University Press).

Tankebe, J. (2008), 'Police Effectiveness and Police Trustworthiness in Ghana: An Empirical Appraisal', *Criminology and Criminal Justice*, 8, 185–202.

Tankebe, J. (2009), 'Self–help, Policing, and Procedural Justice: Ghanaian Vigilantism and the Rule of Law', *Law & Society Review*, 43, 245–68.

Tankebe, J. (2010), 'Public Confidence in the Police: Testing the Effects of Public Experience of Police Corruption in Ghana', *British Journal of Criminology*, 50 (2), 296–319.

Tankebe, J. (2011), 'Explaining Police Support for the Use of Force and Vigilante Violence in Ghana', *Policing And Society*, 21 (2), 129–49.

Tankebe, J. (2013), 'Viewing Things Differently: The Dimensions of Public Perceptions of Police Legitimacy', *Criminology and Criminal Justice*, 51 (1), 103–35.

Taylor, N. (2003), 'Under-reporting of Crime Against Small Businesses: Attitudes Toward Police and Reporting Practices', *Policing and Society*, 13 (1), 79–91.

Taylor, R., Kelly, C., and Salvatore, C. (2010), 'Where Concerned Citizens Perceive Police as More Responsive to Troublesome Teen Groups: Theoretical Implications for Political Economy, Incivilities and Policing', *Policing and Society*, 20 (2), 143–71.

Taylor, R. B. and Lawton, B. A. (2012), 'An Integrated Contextual Model of Confidence in Local Police', *Police Quarterly*, 15 (4), 414–45.

Terrill, W. and Paoline, E. A., III (2007), 'Nonarrest Decision Making in Police–Citizen Encounters', *Police Quarterly*, 10 (3), 308–31.

Thomassen, G. (2014), 'Trust No Matter What? Citizens' Perception of the Police One Year after the Terror Attacks in Norway', *Policing: A Journal of Policy and Practice*, 8 (1), 79–87.

Thompson, B. L. and Lee, J. D. (2004), 'Who Cares if Police Become Violent? Explaining Approval of Police Use of Force Using a National Sample', *Sociological Enquiry*, 74 (3), 381–410.

Tuch, S. A. and Weitzer, R. (1997), 'The Poll Trends: Racial Differences in Attitudes Toward the Police', *Public Opinion Quarterly*, 61, 642–63.

Tuffin, R., Morris, J., and Poole, A. (2006), *An Evaluation of the Impact of the National Reassurance Policing Programme* (London: Home Office Research, Development and Statistics Directorate).

Turner, L. (dir.), *Ready for a Riot* (Channel Four, 2009).

Tyler, T. R. (1990), *Why People Obey the Law* (New Haven, CT: Yale University Press).

Tyler, T. R. (2004), 'Enhancing Police Legitimacy', in W. G. Skogan (ed.), *To Better Serve and Protect: Improving Police Practices* (Annals of the American Academy of Political and Social Science, 593: Sage Publications Ltd) 84–99.

Tyler, T. R. (2005), 'Policing in Black and White: Ethnic Group Differences in Trust and Confidence in the Police', *Police Quarterly*, 8, 322–42.

Tyler, T. R. (2009), 'Procedural Justice, Identity and Deference to the Law: What Shapes Rule-Following in a Period of Transition?', *Australian Journal of Psychology*, 61 (1), 32–9.

Tyler, T. R. (2011a), 'Trust and Legitimacy: Policing in the USA and Europe', *European Journal of Criminology*, 8 (4), 254–66.

Tyler, T. R. (2011b), *Why People Cooperate: The Role of Social Motivations* (Princeton: Princeton University Press).

Tyler, T. R. and Fagan, J. (2006), 'Legitimacy and Cooperation: Why Do People Help the Police Fight Crime in Their Communities', *Ohio State Journal of Criminal Law*, 6, 231–75.

Tyler, T. R. and Hollander-Blumoff, R. (2011), 'Procedural Justice and the Rule of Law: Fostering Legitimacy in Alternative Dispute Resolution', *Journal of Dispute Resolution*, 2011 (1), 1–20.

Tyler, T. R. and Huo, Y. J. (2002), *Trust in the Law: Building Public Cooperation with the Police and Courts* (New York: Russell Sage).

Tyler, T. R. and Mitchell, G. (1994), 'Legitimacy and the Empowerment of Discretionary Legal Authority: The United States Supreme Court and Abortion Rights', *Duke Law Journal*, 43 (4), 703–815.

Tyler, T. R., Schulhofer, S., and Huq, A. (2010), 'Policing against Terrorism: Legitimacy and Deterrence Strategies for Motivating Cooperation among Islamic Americans', *Paper presented at the annual meeting of the The Law and Society Association* (Chicago).

Tyler, T. R., Sherman, L., Strang, H., Barnes, G. C., and Woods, D. (2007), 'Reintegrative Shaming, Procedural Justice, and Recidivism: The Engagement of

Offenders' Psychological Mechanisms in the Canberra RISE Drinking-and-Driving Experiment', *Law & Society Review*, 41, 553.

Tyler, T. R. and Wakslak, C. J. (2004), 'Profiling and Police Legitimacy: Procedural Justice, Attributions of Motive, and Acceptance of Police Authority', *Criminology*, 42 (2), 253–82.

Uniform Crime Reports Section, FBI, United States Department of Justice (1993), *Killed in the Line of Duty: A Study of Selected Felonious Killings of Law Enforcement Officers* (Washington, DC: United States Department of Justice) 61.

Van de Walle, S. (2009), 'Confidence in the Criminal Justice System: Does Experience Count?', *British Journal of Criminology*, 49 (3), 384–98.

van Dijk, J. J. M., Mayhew, P., and Killias, M. (1990), *Experiences of Crime Across the World: Key Findings from the 1989 International Crime Survey* (Deventer and Boston: Kluwer Law and Taxation Publishers).

Viki, G. T., Culmer, M. J., Eller, A., and Abrams, D. (2006), 'Race and Willingness to Cooperate with the Police: The Roles of Quality of Contact, Attitudes Towards the Behaviour and Subjective Norms', *British Journal of Social Psychology*, 45, 285–302.

Vogel, B. L. (2011), 'Perceptions of the Police: The Influence of Individual and Contextual Factors in a Racially Diverse Urban Sample', *Journal of Ethnicity in Criminal Justice*, 9 (4), 267–90.

Waddington, P. A. J. (1991), *The Strong Arm of the Law* (Oxford: Clarendon).

Waddington, P. A. J. (1993), *Calling the Police* (Aldershot, Hants.: Avebury) 225.

Waddington, P. A. J. (1999), 'Police (Canteen) Sub-Culture: An Appreciation', *British Journal of Criminology*, 39 (2), 286–308.

Waddington, P. A. J. (2008), 'Police Culture', in T. Newburn and P. Neyroud (eds.), *Dictionary of Policing* (Cullompton: Willan) 203–5.

Waddington, P. A. J. (2012), 'Cop Culture', in T. Newburn and J. Peay (eds.), *Policing: Politics, Culture and Control* (Oxford: Hart) 89–110.

Waddington, P. A. J. and Braddock, Q. (1991), ' "Guardians" or "Bullies'?: Perceptions of the Police Amongst Adolescent Black, White and Asian Boys', *Policing and Society*, 2, 31–45.

Waddington, P. A. J. and Hamilton, M. (1997), 'The Impotence of the Powerful: Recent British Police Weapons Policy', *Sociology*, 31 (1), 91–109.

Waddington, P. A. J., Stenson, K., and Don, D. (2004), 'In Proportion: Race, and Police Stop and Search', *British Journal of Criminology*, 44 (6), 889–914.

Waddington, P. A. J., Badger, D., and Bull, R. (2006), *The Violent Workplace* (Cullompton: Willan) 204.

Waddington, P. A. J., Adang, O., Baker, D., Birkbeck, C., Feltes, T., Gabaldón, L. G., Paes Machado, E., and Stenning, P. (2009), 'Singing the Same Tune? International Continuities and Discontinuities in How Police Talk About Using Force', *Crime, Law and Social Change*, 52 (Special Issue on Policing Talk About the Use of Force: A Comparative International Perspective), 111–38.

Waddington, P. A. J., Kleinig, J., and Wright, M. (eds.) (2013), *Professional Police Practice: Scenarios and Dilemmas* (Oxford: Oxford University Press).

Walker, A., Flatley, J., Kershaw, C., and Moon, D. (2009), 'Crime in England and Wales 2008/09. Volume 1: Findings from the British Crime Survey and Police Recorded Crime', *Home Office Statistical Bulletin* (London: Home Office).

Walker, D., Richardson, R. J., Williams, O., Denver, T., and McGaughey, S. (1972), 'Contacts and Support: an Empirical Assessment of Public Attitudes Toward the Police and the Courts', *North Carolina Law Review*, 51, 43–79.

Webb, V. J. and Marshall, C. E. (1995), 'The Relative Importance of Race and Ethnicity on Citizen Attitudes Toward the Police', *American Journal of Police*, 14, 45–66.

Webster, W. H. and Williams, H. (1992), *The City in Crisis: A Report by the Special Advisor to the Board of Police Commissioners on the Civil Disorder in Los Angeles* (Los Angeles, Ca: Office of the Special Advisor to the Board of Police Commissioners City of Los Angeles) 222.

Weinberger, B. (1995), *The Best Police in the World: An Oral History of English Policing From the 1930s to the 1960s* (Aldershot: Scolar) 244.

Weisburd, D., Hinkle, J. C., Famega, C., and Ready, J. (2011), 'The Possible "Backfire" Effects of Hot Spots Policing: An Experimental Assessment of Impacts on Legitimacy, Fear and Collective Efficacy', *Journal of Experimental Criminology*, 7, 297–320.

Weitzer, R. (1999), 'Citizens' Perceptions of Police Misconduct: Race and Neighborhood Context', *Justice Quarterly*, 16, 819–46.

Weitzer, R. and Tuch, S. A. (1999), 'Race, Class, and Perceptions of Discrimination by the Police', *Crime & Delinquency*, 45, 404–507.

Weitzer, R. and Tuch, S. A. (2002), 'Perceptions of Racial Profiling: Race, Class, and Personal Experience', *Criminology*, 40, 435–56.

Weitzer, R. and Tuch, S. A. (2004a), 'Race and Perceptions of Police Misconduct', *Social Problems*, 51, 305–19.

Weitzer, R. and Tuch, S. A. (2004b), 'Reforming the Police: Racial Differences in Public Support for Change', *Criminology*, 42 (2), 391–416.

Weitzer, R. and Tuch, S. A. (2005a), 'Determinants of Public Satisfaction with the Police', *Police Quarterly*, 8, 279–97.

Weitzer, R. and Tuch, S. A. (2005b), 'Racially Biased Policing: Determinants of Citizen Perceptions', *Social Forces*, 83, 1009–30.

Weitzer, R., Tuch, S. A., and Skogan, W. G. (2008), 'Police-Community Relations in a Majority-Black City', *Journal of Research in Crime and Delinquency*, 45, 398–428.

Westley, W. A. (1953), 'Violence and the Police', *American Journal of Sociology*, 59, 34–41.

Westley, W. A. (1956), 'Secrecy and the Police', *Social Forces*, 34 (3), 254–7.

Westley, W. A. (1970), *Violence and the Police* (Cambridge, Mass.: MIT Press).

Wheatcroft, J. M., Alison, L., and McGrory, D. (2012), 'The Influence of Trust on Senior Investigating Officers' Decision Making in High-Profile Critical Incidents', *Police Quarterly*, 15, 386–413.

Wheeler, S. (1968), 'Socialization in Correctional Institutions', in D. A. Goslin (ed.), *Handbook of Socialization Theory and Research*, 1006–19.

White, M. F. and Menke, B. A. (1982), 'On Assessing the Mood of the Public Toward the Police: Some Conceptual Issues', *Journal of Criminal Justice*, 10 (3), 211–30.

Whitehead, E. (2001), *Witness Satisfaction: Findings from the Witness Satisfaction Survey 2000*, ed. D. Moxon (Home Office Research Study 230; London: Home Office Research, Development and Statistics Directorate).

Wilson, J. Q. and Kelling, G. (1982), 'Broken Windows', *The Atlantic Monthly*, 29–38.

Wolff Olins Corporate Identity (1988), *A Force for Change: A Report on the Corporate Identity of the Metropolitan Police* (London: Metropolitan Police).

Wortley, S. and Hagan, J. (1997), 'Just Des(s)erts? The Racial Polarization of Perceptions of Criminal Injustice', *Law & Society Review*, 31, 637–76.

Wu, Y., Sun, I. Y., and Triplett, R. A. (2009), 'Race, Class or Neighborhood Context: Which Matters More in Measuring Satisfaction with Police?', *Justice Quarterly*, 26 (1), 125–56.

Yim, Y. and Schafer, B. (2009), 'Police and Their Perceived Image: How the Community Influences Officers' Job Satisfaction', *Police Practice And Research*, 10 (1), 17–29.

Young, J. (1994), *Policing the Streets: Stops and Search in North London* (London: Centre for Criminology, Middlesex University).

Index